For my husband
RICHARD JAMES PIOLI

BODY
AND SOUL

BODY
AND SOUL

*Essays on Medieval Women
and Mysticism*

Elizabeth Alvilda Petroff

New York   Oxford
OXFORD UNIVERSITY PRESS
1994

Oxford University Press

Oxford   New York   Toronto
Delhi   Bombay   Calcutta   Madras   Karachi
Kuala Lumpur   Singapore   Hong Kong   Tokyo
Nairobi   Dar es Salaam   Cape Town
Melbourne   Auckland   Madrid

and associated companies in
Berlin   Ibadan

Library of Congress Cataloging-in-Publication Data
Petroff, Elizabeth.
Body and soul : essays on medieval women and mysticism / Elizabeth Alvilda Petroff.
p. cm.   ISBN 0–19–508454–3
ISBN 0–19–508455–1 (pbk.)
1. Women mystics—Europe.
2. Mysticism—History—Middle Ages, 600–1500.
3. Mysticism and literature.
4. Christian literature—History and criticism.
I. Title.
BV5077.E85P48   1994
248.2′2′082—dc20   93–37581

Chapter 4 first appeared in *Feminism, Utopia, and Narrative*,
ed. Libby Falk Jones and Sarah Webster Goodwin.
Copyright © 1990.
Used with permission of the University of Tennessee Press.

Chapter 5 first appeared in *Hrotsvit of Gandersheim: Rara Avis in Saxonia?*
ed. Katharina Wilson. Copyright © 1987.
Used with permission of The Edward Mellen Press.

2 4 6 8 9 7 5 3 1

Printed in the United States of America
on acid-free paper

Preface

Body and Soul: Essays on Medieval Women and Mysticism is a collection of
essays intended to fulfill two goals: to introduce readers to medieval
women mystics and their world, and to offer specialists close readings of a
number of important texts from the point of view of various theorists. The
general reader will, I hope, come away from reading this volume with a
greater appreciation of medieval women and their writings, and a desire to
learn more about and from them. Medievalists will have the opportunity to
see how literary theory can enrich our reading of these remarkable texts. I
have included essays on women writers in England, France, the Low
Countries, and Italy; the original texts were composed in Latin and in the
vernacular languages, and whenever possible, I have quoted from the original language and provided an English translation. Many biographical and
autobiographical texts by women are examined, as well as sermons, meditations, and lyric poems. I have also looked at writings about women;
several essays explore styles of hagiographic writing about women and
offer varying interpretations of how medieval holy women appeared to
their contempories. Eleven essays are included; together they discuss in
depth the lives and writings of sixteen women, and refer to many others.
Some of the essays have been published previously and revised; others have
been written specifically for this collection.

I have arranged the essays in three groups. Part I is introductory. The
opening essay, "Women and Mysticism in the Medieval World," describes
female mysticism and sketches out women's contributions in this area.
"Unmasking Women: Medieval Responses to the Unknowability of the

Medieval Lady," the second chapter, shows us what medieval women were up against in their world, by examining a common trope in the portrayal of women, the trope of unmasking. By acknowledging the pervasiveness of medieval misogny, we value more highly the literary gifts necessary for the emergence of the woman writer in this period, and we can better understand the great risks an individual woman took in becoming visible as a spiritual leader. The two chapters concluding Part I, "A New Feminine Spirituality: The Beguines and Their Writings in Medieval Europe," and "A Medieval Woman's Utopian Vision: The Rule of St. Clare of Assisi," look at specific women mystics and their remarkable contributions in literature and community life.

In the three chapters in Part II, I am concerned with the relationships between medieval women and tradition, as I trace elements of continuity as well as change in monastic and hagiographic contexts. "Eloquence and Heroic Virginity in Hrotsvit's Verse Legends" demonstrates the new model of female heroine created by Hrotsvit in the verse legends that the famous Saxon canoness wrote for her community. Here Hrotsvit departs from the earlier tradition of the Church in depicting virginity as an active vocation and as an emblem of spiritual leadership, both for the past women whose lives she tells and for the women of her own time. Unlike later writers, Hrotsvit emphasizes eloquence as a virtue for women as well as men; her saints persuade others by their speech as much as by their actions. A different model of female heroism is exemplified in the fourteenth-century biographies of Italian women saints discussed in "Transforming the World: The Serpent-Dragon and the Virgin Saint." In these texts, written by male followers of female saints, women speak more through gesture than through words, and their heroism is viewed through their relationship to a demonized natural world, as they deal with monsters allegedly sent by Satan. In the final chapter of this section, I again utilize evidence from the lives of Italian women saints to suggest a common hagiographic program that assimilated contemporary women saints into the Desert Fathers movement in early Christianity. I argue that the male writers of the *Lives* of Italian saints saw these women as living lives comparable to those led by the early Desert Fathers and that consequently their biographies of these women constitute a satellite cycle around the *Vitae Patrum*, the collection of the lives and sayings of the Desert Fathers in the fourth and fifth centuries.

Part III brings together chapters that explore the issue of female spiritual authority from various angles. The first chapter in this section, "Male Confessors and Female Penitents: Possibilities for Dialogue," looks at the portrayal of the relationships between these saintly women—Marie d'Oignies, Christina of Markyate, and Margery Kempe—and their confessors. All three relationships exhibit two outstanding traits: deep love and trust between the two parties, and obvious role reversals, in which the woman is accorded more power and authority than the male ecclesiastic. The knowledge in spiritual matters possessed by the woman is exchanged for the protection offered by the confessor. The next chapter, "The Rhetoric of Transgression in the *Lives* of Italian Women Saints," looks at some difficulties this power and authority presented to the biographers of Italian women saints contemporary with Marie, Christina, and Margery, and examines the rhetorical stategies that biographers employ to underplay the women's assumption of authority.

The last two chapters in this section, and the final chapters in the book, explore the issue of female authority as it is presented by women mystical writers. "Gender, Knowledge, and Power in Hadewijch's *Strophische Gedichten*" introduces this beguine writer of the early thirteenth century who created a prodigious collection of lyric poems dedicated to *Minne,* Lady Love. Utilizing the complex stanzaic forms and rhyme schemes of the French and Provençal love lyric in her vernacular, Dutch, Hadewijch capitalized on the conventions of courtly love finally to explode the boundaries of those conventions in her treatment of the relationship between a female divinity, *Minne,* and the individual loving soul. The concluding essay, "Writing the Body: Male and Female in the Writings of Marguerite d'Oingt, Angela of Foligno, and Umiltà of Faenza," utilizes the literary theories of Bakhtin, Certeau, Irigaray, and Cixous to explore the role of the body in the representation of women's mystical experience and in the assumption of a voice of authority.

As I reread these chapters, I am struck by two things: the radical difference between the way male biographers view saintly women and women's view of themselves, and the radically nontraditional nature of the texts by mystics. It is no surprise that male writers saw these women differently than they saw themselves, but it is very surprising (to me at least) to see one hagiographer, for instance, characterize a female saint by her silence, when she was a successful preacher and writer of sermons. Even if she claimed to be divinely inspired in all her speech, that speech existed and was heard by an audience, an audience that included her biographer. What mental gymnastics were invloved in supressing depiction of her speech? Or were the strictures on female speech so powerful that the best protection her biographer felt he could offer her was couched in a rhetoric of silence?

It seems obvious to me now, at this point in my study, that many of these female-authored texts are radically noncanonical. Many scholars are currently attempting to place women's writings within the canon of medieval literature, and I agree that women's writings must be included in courses on medieval literature and history. Nevertheless, I would suggest that medieval mystical texts by women will not fit into a traditional Western notion of literature, because they derive from a different experience of the body, a different epistemology, and a different relationship to language. I see these texts as a window onto a lost world of experience of thousands of women from late antiquity until just before the Renaissance, an experience that is recuperable by us only if we radically challenge prevailing ideas of what constitutes literature and what is the nature of reality.

In canonizing these texts, we risk losing some of their most valuable aspects. No matter how elastic we make our notion of the medieval canon, the canon cannot be stretched to include some of the most vivid of medieval women's writings, for the experiential and philosophical base of those writings is profoundly other. Women mystics were a vital force in medieval culture, but they were rarely mainstream figures, and their ideas were not a part of the intellectual debate of their time. Sometimes their ideas gained currency later, as the ideas of Hadewijch reappear in the writings of Meister Eckhart, for instance, and became widely discussed, but the reality shared by Hadewijch and Eckhart, the possibility for the divinization of the human, remained deeply threatening to traditional thinking.

I am grateful for the help of many editors at Oxford University Press for encouraging my writing and for facilitating the production of this book: Cynthia Read, first of all, and Peter Ohlin, Ellen B. Fuchs, Irene Pavitt, and the copy editor, Jerilyn Famighetti. I am especially grateful to my husband, Richard James Pioli, for his support and energy throughout the writing of these essays and the creation of this book.

Amherst, Mass.   E.A.P.
September 1993

Contents

BODY
AND SOUL

1

Women and Mysticism in the Medieval World

If one is not already a mystic, one can best understand mysticism by reading mystical texts, for mysticism is an experience, not an idea. This is especially true for medieval women mystics, whose works explore the manifold dimensions of this experience, as far as is possible in words. A few passages from the writings of women mystics can illustrate this.

> At last in the time that followed I saw a mystic and wondrous vision, such that all my womb was convulsed and my body's sensory powers were extinguished, because my knowledge was transmuted into another mode, as if I no longer knew myself. And from God's inspiration as it were drops of gentle rain splashed into the knowledge of my soul.[1]
>
> Hildegard of Bingen

> When the poor soul comes to court, she is wise and courtly, and so she looks upon her God with joy. . . . She is silent, intensely longing that He should praise her. Then with great desire He shows her His divine heart: it is like reddish gold, burning in a large charcoal fire. Then he places her in His ardent heart so that the Noble Prince and the little servant girl embrace and are united, as water and wine. Then she is brought to nought and abandons herself, as if she had no strength left, while He is sick with love for her, as He has always been, for (in this desire) there can be neither growth or lessening. Thus she speaks: "Lord, you are my consolation, my desire, my flowing fountain, my sun, and I am your mirror." Such is the journey to court of the loving soul, who cannot be without God.[2]
>
> Mechthild of Magdeburg

> In that same experience of vision I understood the writings of the prophets, the Gospels, the works of other holy men, and those of certain philosophers,

3

without any human instruction, and I expounded certain things based on these, though I scarcely had literary understanding, inasmuch as a woman who was not learned had been my teacher. But I also brought forth songs with their melody, in praise of God and the saints, without being taught by anyone, and I sang them too, even though I had never learnt either musical notation or any kind of singing.[3]

Hildegard of Bingen

O immeasurably tender love! Who would not be set afire with such love? What heart could keep from breaking? You, deep well of charity, it seems you are so madly in love with your creatures that you could not live without us! Yet you are our God, and have no need of us. Your greatness is no greater for our well-being, nor are you harmed by any harm that comes to us, for you are supreme eternal Goodness. What could move you to such mercy? Neither duty nor any need you have of us . . . but only love! . . . My heart is breaking and yet cannot break for the hungry longing it has conceived for you![4]

St. Catherine of Siena

Mysticism is the direct experience of the real, an unmediated experience of God. Mystical literature is an oxymoronic proposition, for how can we put into words what is beyond language, and how can we understand the language in which mystical experiences were often expressed? Susan Clark, in introducing Mechthild of Magdeburg's *The Flowing Light of the Divinity,* observes that "the individual mystic's world is, paradoxically, circumscribed and infinite in its possibilities, and access to it comes about only through the verbal medium that endures, a medium that is fundamentally at odds with the transcendent, non-verbal nature of the mystic's revelations."[5] The women writers of mystical literature often saw themselves at an additional disadvantage—not only was mystical experience difficult to communicate, but as women they lacked the authority, and the authoritative language, to communicate spiritual truths. "They wrote," says Fiona Bowie, "out of an inner urge to communicate a personal event of great importance."[6] This event was a mystical vision, "through which the mystic came to see herself as someone in direct relationship with God."[7] The authority to write came directly from God: "The claim that they were compelled to write by God, and not through any presumption on their part, recurs frequently in women's writing. Lacking the authority of formal theological education, clerical orders or male gender, the only justification for writing was that of being an instrument of the Creator."[8]

In her study of mysticism, written more than half a century ago, Evelyn Underhill anticipated current interest in the nature of the mystical experience; in *The Mystics of the Church* she recalls that the word *mysticism* comes from Greek religion, where "the *mystae* were those initiates of the 'mysteries' who were believed to have received the vision of the god, and with it a new and higher life."[9] This calling to a revealed higher life is what motivates mystics on their path, for mysticism is not just one event but a succession of insights and revelations about God that gradually transforms the recipient. This developing mystical path is typically described as having three stages—purgative, illuminative, and unitive—that at times blend into one another and overlap. Mysticism has also been called "the science of the love of God" and "the life which aims at union with God";[10] these definitions underscore the double nature of mysticism as knowing and as doing. The mystic knows God firsthand, and also knows herself in that same light of illumination; this double consciousness of self and God later becomes the content of her teaching. What Underhill says of one mystic is true for all: "He pointed to a rigorous self-knowledge as an important part of purification; meaning by this knowledge not only of our sins, but of our possibilities."[11]

Christianity has no monopoly on mysticism. Sufis, Tantrikas, Mongolian or Native American shamans—all are far more familiar with the mystical side of the experience of Hildegard of Bingen or Catherine of Siena than I am as I write this. Mira Bai and Mahādēvi in medieval India, like the women of medieval Europe, shattered the stereotypes of good feminine behavior to sing their love of God, because of their mystical experiences.[12] Mystics may be found in every religious tradition, sometimes as central participants but often on the periphery of accepted practice, for it is they who are found mapping out new experiences of the divine. There is no identifiable mystical type, although scholars at times have tried to identify one; mystics may be women or men, they may be educated or uneducated, they may come from wealthy or deprived backgrounds. Mystical experiences may be primarily visual or auditory, or they may be so abstract as to elude any verbal formulation; the mystical path toward enlightenment may be based either on developing love or on the growth of the intellect; its focus may be what theologians term Christocentric or theocentric. Since mysticism is a natural human capacity, mystical experiences can occur spontaneously, unexpectedly, at any time and any place; many religions endorse ascetic practices and modes of prayer that encourage the development of mystical experience in some people, although all religions seem to agree that mysticism is a special gift not under the control of the recipient. There also seem to be historical periods during which mysticism becomes uncharacteristically prevalent and authoritative and during which mystics are more needed by their communities. Valerie Lagorio agrees with Underhill that mysticism not only seems to intensify in certain periods, but is in itself a richly creative activity: "The great periods of mystical activity tend to correspond with the great periods of artistic, material, and intellectual civilization. . . . It is always as if [the mystic] were humanity's finest flower; the product at which each great creative period of the race had aimed."[13]

One such richly creative period was the high Middle Ages in Europe (1100–1450), a time of great art and great social change, as the feudal system gave way to capitalism, cities, and a new middle class. We think of the Middle Ages as the age of faith, and so it was, but it was also an age of crisis. In such a context, mysticism was not a retreat from the negative aspects of reality but a creative marshaling of energy in order to transform

reality and the perception of it. Scholars sought to define the nature and
variety of the mystical experience. Richard of St. Victor, a mystic from
Scotland who became prior of the Chapter of St. Victor, a school just
outside Paris that was famous as a theological and a spiritual center,[14]
distinguished four kinds of vision: two physical types and two spiritual.[15]
His first kind of seeing is normal physical sight, containing no hidden
significance; the second kind, still a bodily seeing, contains "a force of
hidden meaning." Richard says it was in this mode that Moses "saw" the
burning bush. The two modes of spiritual vision are more important for
the story of mysticism:

> Of the two modes of spiritual vision, one is that of the eyes of the heart, when
> the human spirit, illuminated by the Holy Ghost, is led through the likenesses
> of visible things, and through images presented as figures and signs, to the
> knowledge of invisible ones. This is what Dionysius had called symbolic vi-
> sion. The second, which Dionysius had called anagogic vision, occurs when
> the human spirit, through inner aspiration, is raised to the contemplation of
> the celestial without the mediation of any visible figures.[16]

Mystics were the teachers of this age; they were the inspired leaders
who synthesized Christian tradition and proposed new models for the
Christian community. We know some of the male mystics—St. Bernard of
Clairvaux, St. Francis of Assisi, St. Thomas Aquinas in his final years,
Meister Eckhart—but we are less familiar with female mystics, although
they were actually more numerous in this period. Women mystics, such as
Hildegarde of Bingen, Clare of Assisi, Mechthild of Magdeburg, Angela of
Foligno, Julian of Norwich, to name a few of the more famous ones, drew
on their personal experience of the divine to provide spiritual guidance for
others. Such women became highly respected leaders of the faithful; their
role as prophets and healers was the one exception to women's presumed
inferiority in medieval society. Although any generalization about female
mysticism is bound to leave out someone important, we can say that
medieval women's mysticism was primarily visual and affective; that is, the
mystic *saw* and felt truth, saw God or Christ or the saints, and was flooded
with love for what she saw. So powerful was this love that she felt compelled to share it with others, and so effective was the transformation
created in her by her mystical experiences that she discovered and invented
new ways to communicate her insights. We should not think of medieval
women mystics only or primarily as hermits withdrawn into a private
world of prayer and meditation, although most of them passed some part
of their lives as hermits or recluses. They were very active women who had
completed a lengthy apprenticeship in the spiritual life and were capable of
being spiritually responsible for large numbers of people.

No one knows exactly why medieval European mysticism was largely
female, in contrast to mystical revivals in other periods, but we can speculate on some of the factors involved. The only approved form of religious
life available to women was contemplative and enclosed, partly because

medieval society believed that women had to be protected from the violence of others and from their own sexuality and partly because women were thought to be "naturally" passive, meditative, and receptive.[17] Men with religious vocations and leadership ability had a number of choices—they could be active or contemplative, priests, friars, monks, or hermits. But according to long-established custom in the medieval Church, women who felt themselves called to the religious life were severely restricted in the ways they could act on their vocation. They could not participate in the public sacramental life of the Church: they were forbidden to administer the sacraments, to hear confessions, or to grant absolution, and they were not allowed to preach. They could (if they had the price of a dowry) join convents, where they were expected to live a contemplative life of prayer, fasting, and vigils. They were not supposed to have commerce with the secular world once they entered a convent; their role was to pray for the salvation of their own souls and for the souls of the Christian community.

Nevertheless, women did emerge as leaders in medieval society, and it is useful to speculate on how mysticism, spiritual practices, and leadership came together in some women's lives. Some aspects of convent life probably encouraged the development of mystical and leadership abilities. Until the fourteenth century, a religious community was the only place a woman could find the opportunity to read and write, along with a library of books and other scholars to talk to; it was also the only place a woman had any privacy, where she could be expected to be alone with her thoughts.[18] The vow of celibacy exempted women from pregnancy and childbearing, and accorded them much longer lives than were common for married women. Convents also provided opportunities for leadership and teaching, whether in keeping accounts, tending the sick, or instructing children. But if convent life was the only approved mode of life, it was not the only lifestyle chosen by women. Many women mystics preferred, and managed to live in, more fluid structures for their spirituality; they were beguines or tertiaries or recluses in cities. Nevertheless, they shared with their convent-enclosed sisters celibacy, common spiritual practices, access to books and ideas, and opportunities for leadership.

During the Middle Ages, for the first time in European history, women outnumbered men.[19] This meant that not all women could expect either to marry or to become nuns. Women developed very creative responses to this situation, which allowed them to develop new life-styles more in accordance with their needs, and, beginning in the twelfth century, some came together to form new religious communities. These women—called beguines in northern Europe,[20] Franciscan or Dominican tertiaries in southern Europe[21]—lived together in groups, supporting themselves by manual labor and devoting their lives to serving others and growing spiritually. Many famous medieval mystical writers, among them Hadewijch of Antwerp, Mechthild of Magdeburg, Angela of Foligno, and Catherine of Siena, belonged to these informal communities.

Finally, we can see that the spiritual practices recommended to medieval women (and possibly invented by them) encouraged the kind of growth and mental concentration that often lead to visions and mystical experiences. By the thirteenth century, these practices were quite similar for all ranks of women, whether rich or poor, married or unmarried. They were shared by the laity but not usually by the men in religious communities, who had a more intellectual education. In addition to the seven canonical hours of daily prayer (the rule in convents), women (and men) were expected to perform two sorts of penitential acts: acts of contrition, such as self-flagellation, fasting, and vigils; and acts of mercy toward others, such as tending the sick and assisting the poor. Understanding the meaning of these spiritual practices has been the focus of two recent studies on medieval women.[22] We know that women's practice of asceticism and self-denial was more austere than men's and, in some cases, perhaps self-destructive. Mantric or repetitive prayer, consisting of countless recitations of the Hail Mary and the Our Father, was practiced daily, even by the totally illiterate. The kind of meditation taught to women was visual and creative, not intellectual or abstract: the devout woman was to imagine herself as an observer and a participant in the life of Mary and of Christ. Most of the visual imagery for these mental pilgrimages was available to everyone in the pictorial cycles in parish churches and in convents.

The conditions of women's lives led to visions, and visions gave an individual woman a voice, a belief in herself as chosen to speak. They also gave her the experience of inner transformation, which she felt compelled to communicate to others. Perhaps the only voice women heard that told them to *do* something was God's voice in visions. But God's voice was the only one that was really necessary, for with divine permission and guidance, anything was possible. As Julian of Norwich said in her *Showings,*

> God forbid that you should say or assume that I am a teacher, . . . for I am a woman, ignorant, weak and frail. But I know very well that what I am saying I have received by the revelation of him who is the sovereign teacher. . . . [B]ecause I am a woman, ought I therefore to believe that I should not tell you of the goodness of God, when I saw at that same time that it is his will that it be known?[23]

The lives of the great women mystics are highly individualized, although some common themes emerge in their writings. Here I would like to introduce eight women from four different geographical areas and three different time periods. All these holy women—Hildegard of Bingen and Mechthild of Magdeburg (Germany), Marguerite Porete of Brabant and Hadewijch of Antwerp (the Netherlands), Angela of Foligno and Catherine of Siena (Italy), and Christina of Markyate and Julian of Norwich (England)—were mystics, and all left autobiographical and didactic writings. The lives and life-styles of these eight women illustrate the various possibilities open to women with spiritual vocations; their styles of mysticism are illustrative as well of the variety of paths to the divine that may be termed mystical and visionary. Two of the women—Hildegard and

Christina—became leaders in Benedictine houses after having spent a number of years enclosed as recluses; one, Julian of Norwich, became a recluse in response to her visions, which she continued to study and write down in solitude.[24] Two were tertiaries in the mendicant orders: Catherine of Siena was a Dominican tertiary, and Angela of Foligno was Franciscan. Both lived in the world and had public preaching careers. Three of the eight women belonged to that fluid classification known as beguines—women who were committed to a spiritual life, but did not live enclosed lives and did not take permanent vows.[25] One of these three—Marguerite Porete— was burned at the stake as a heretic. Only three of the eight women were well educated, which at this time meant knowing Latin and having access to a sizable library of spiritual classics. Yet seven of the eight were writers, and some were the earliest and best writers of the vernacular languages in their own countries. All were bilingual and bicultural.

I begin with two women—Christina of Markyate and St. Hildegard of Bingen—who were born just as the First Crusade was launched, at the beginning of a period of great change and cultural contact.

Christina of Markyate

Christina of Markyate (1096/1098–ca.1160) was born into an influential Anglo-Saxon family in Norman England. Two documents connected with her provide many clues to her spiritual life—her biography and her prayer book. Her anonymous biography, *The Life of Christina of Markyate*,[26] is incomplete and breaks off around 1142, when Christina is in her forties and has become a professed nun in the Benedictine community of St. Albans. Her life story is an adventurous one, told with great energy and with a novelist's sense of suspense. Her biography begins with her childhood and the awakening of her desire for a spiritual life. The reader is soon introduced to her influential parents and their rage when she tries to refuse the marriage they have arranged for her. We see the Anglo-Saxon social world that Christina wishes to repudiate, when, similar to Wealtheow in *Beowulf,* she is commanded to carry the mead cup to all the guests at a feast. But this story is told from a female viewpoint, and whereas Wealtheow's private thoughts are not recorded, Christina's are. The narrator tells us that in this instance Christina's mother has pushed her into offering mead in the hope that Christina will get drunk and that her betrothed, Burthred, will be able to seduce her and thus consecrate the marriage. The holy girl, knowing that her future depends on her ability to stay sober and clearheaded, only pretends to drink and to participate in the merriment. She fights off the advances of Burthred (this is just one instance out of many attempts), as well as those of a corrupt churchman, takes her case against marrying to court, wins, and then sees the decision reversed as a result of her parents' well-placed bribes. Helped by the Virgin Mary in visions, she is able to think out an escape, and she runs away to live as a hermit, first with a famous female recluse and then with a local holy man. Her determination is tested by the need to live and to perform her spiritual practices secretly, locked into a kind of closet during the day in the hermit Roger's dwelling, until Burthred publicly releases her from their betrothal and she can safely appear in public.

Her biographer recognizes that her visionary life and her psychic intuitions help her to grow spiritually and to defend herself against the many threats to her integrity, and he gives the reader full accounts of these experiences. We do not know who the writer was, but it is clear that he knew Christina (or Theodora, as she was called before her profession) well and that in composing this *Life* he often transcribed her first-person accounts of her adventures and visions. Christina's visions were primarily personal, intended to provide guidance to her individually without commenting on a larger community. But her visions often foretold future events, and this fact seems to have conferred personal power on her. Other visions concerned local matters, such as how the abbot of St. Albans should behave. (We delve further into these visions and into Christina's relationship with her spiritual friend Geoffrey, the Norman abbot of St. Alban's, in Chapters 2 and 8.)

The contents of the *St. Albans Psalter* (which is believed to be Christina's prayer book, although her name is nowhere inscribed in it) tell us much about her daily life and spiritual exercises.[27] The calendar at the beginning gives the death dates of many of Christina's family members and makes a special reference to the death of Roger, the hermit with whom she lived for so many years and whose cell she inherited. The calendar is followed by thirty-nine scenes of the life of Christ, devotional images for meditation and contemplation. The next major section is the text, in French, of the *Chançon d'Alexis,* a story clearly related to her own life experience, since it depicts a "bridegroom who leaves his bride on his wedding night to wander the world":[28]

> The St Albans psalter can be seen to be in every part a book "made" for Christina, it reflected her own experience, and provided for her a means of reflecting on it. It is worth emphasizing what rich material it gave her: the great corpus of the psalms enriched with drawings to stimulate meditation, pictures of Christ's life which combined features of Anglo-Saxon and Byzantine iconography in a new form, a newly translated poem from the Byzantine world, and the Emmaus series, taking up the pilgrim theme dear to Christina, besides having other meanings in her world.[29]

Although we have no mystical texts written by Christina herself, we have precious evidence in the psalter of a spiritual program that helped shape the powerful and fascinating woman we read of in her *Life.*

Hildegard of Bingen

The seer Hildegard of Bingen (1098–1179) was Christina's contemporary. Unlike Christina, who evidently dictated her experiences to someone within the same community and who probably never expected her biography to be circulated, Hildegard composed her works for the world outside the walls of her convent. Emilie Zum Brunn and Georgette Epiney-Burgard say of her: "Hildegard offers us the finest example of what a woman could achieve in the twelfth century, as regards active life, as well as spiritual and artistic life. She is outstanding for the quality of her natural gifts, her prophetic charisma, and her dynamic reforming attitude."[30]

Hildegard's writings—letters, visions, prophecies, song sequences, a morality play, even a handbook on medicine—fill an entire volume of the *Patrologia Latina*.[31] Her religious life began at age seven or eight, when she joined her aunt Jutta, who was a recluse; their retreat was later opened and turned into a convent, where Hildegard made her profession as a nun at age fourteen. Although she was unable to write German and was unsure of the correctness of her Latin, her dictated writings exhibit wide learning. Although she claimed that all her knowledge came from a mystical source, it is obvious that she was familiar with the Scriptures, natural science, classical Latin literature, and neo-Platonic philosophy. She was taken seriously as a prophet by everyone—from St. Bernard of Clairvaux and the pope down to the humblest laborers. Hildegard's self-identification as prophet was the key to having a public voice, for as a woman lacking a systematic education in Latin, she had no individual voice, as Sabina Flanagan points out in her biography of Hildegard:

> To the people of the Middle Ages, as to the ancients, prophecy implied the revelation of divine secrets concerning the past, the present, and the future. Hildegard's belief that she possessed such priviliged knowledge would not have been enough to insure her success, if her superiors had not seen it the same way. . . . There were both biblical and early Christian precedents for the role of female prophet. Moreover, a woman could be a prophet without upsetting the perceived natural order, since no particular attributes of her own were required, except, possibly, humility. Indeed, there was some suggestion that God might specifically choose the weak and despised to confound the strong. Thus to be a female prophet was to confirm women's authority, rather than to deny it.[32]

Throughout her period of prolific writing, Hildegard was a forceful administrator of her convent. She began the *Scivias,* her first visionary and autobiographical work, when she was forty-two, but she had been having visions since she was five. Although she struggled with illness throughout her life, she insists that she saw her visions in spiritual and psychological wholeness, when she was fully conscious and aware of her surroundings. She distinguished between two grades of spiritual vision: her ecstatic awareness of "the Living Light" in which she could see nothing and a "more diffused radiance which she calls the Shade of the Living Light, and within which her great allegorical visions were seen."[33] Although she is perhaps more famous now for her visionary trilogy, she was also a writer of lyrical and dramatic poetry. Peter Dronke believes that "these songs contain some of the most unusual, subtle, and exciting poetry of the twelfth century."[34]

Of Hildegard's theology, Barbara Newman believes that "[w]e may boldly claim Hildegard as the first Christian thinker to deal seriously and positively with the feminine as such, not merely with the challenges posed by and for women in a male-dominated world."[35] Around four traditional female figures—Eve, Mary, Ecclesia, and Sapientia, or Caritas—"Hildegard developed a richly nuanced theology of the feminine that belongs wholly to the realm of the symbolic."[36] Using these four female figures allowed Hildegard "to see the feminine as a species of incapacity and frailty, yet also as a numinous and salvific dimension of the divine nature."[37] Hildegard's mission, as Newman sees it, was the mission of all the female mystics studied here: "to unlock the mysteries of Scripture, to proclaim the way of salvation, to admonish priests and prelates, to instruct the people of God."[38]

Two Beguine Mystics: Hadewijch of Antwerp and Mechthild of Magdeburg

The thirteenth century produced a number of visionary women writers, but I focus on just two here: Hadewijch of Antwerp and Mechthild of Magdeburg. Both were beguines; both wrote not in Latin, as had Hildegard, but in their vernacular languages; and both contributed to a new style of spirituality that came to be known as Rheno-Flemish mysticism. Dom Porion, in his introduction to his French translation of Hadewijch's "Letters to a Young Beguine" and Beatrijs's *Seven Degrees of Love*,[39] finds the most telling characteristic of the beguine mystics to be

> the inner orientation, the impetus which urges the soul to overpass herself in order to be lost in the simplicity of the Divine Being. This is what distinguishes those among our holy women whose picture is most clearly drawn by documents and testimonies. Marie d'Oignies, Lutgard de Tongres, Yvette d'Huy, as well as Beatrice and Hadewijch, plunge their gaze into the Divine Essence, showing that It is visible to the inner eye if it manages to recover its original nakedness. It is on account of this testimony that their names must be preserved and their voices transmitted: bold women who remind us why we were born.[40]

There is also a theological difference between the beguine mystics and the mystics, like Hildegard, who preceded them. According to Zum Brunn and Epiney-Burgard, in Hildegard's writings "the soul, at the summit of the vision, becomes similar to God," while for the beguines "the soul is annihilated to become 'what God is'":[41]

> Their mysticism of abandonment is expressed, in fact, in an ontological dilemma: the creature must shed his particular, created, separated being, in order to find once again his true, "uncreated," "non-separated" being in God. Thus it is that the "non-willing," which consists of willing nothing apart from God Himself, leads to a real annihilation of the soul considered in her particular and egoistic being. But she loses herself thus only to find herself at an

incomparably higher stage or "being," having become, as Hadewijch says, "God with God," or, as Meister Eckhart will say, "God in God."[42]

Hadewijch of Antwerp

Hadewijch of Antwerp was a Flemish beguine who lived in the second quarter of the thirteenth century. Although she and her writings were known in the fourteenth century, she achieved no particular fame in her own lifetime as far as we know. What little is known of her is the result of inference. Her familiarity with the vocabulary of chivalry and courtly love suggests that she was from the higher classes and that she probably attended good convent schools. She knew about higher education, the universities, and the curriculum of the seven liberal arts, for she used the metaphors of the curriculum and the school masters in her "school of love" poems. We know almost nothing of her external life, but we have three books by her: a collection of poems, "Poems in Stanzas" and "Poems in Couplets,"[43] in Mother Columba Hart's translation; a set of letters, known as "Letters to a Young Beguine," on the spiritual life, and a book of Visions. Hart believes that Hadewijch either founded or joined a beguine group and became its mistress, supervising the spiritual development of a number of young beguines whom she believed were specially called to mysticism, when she ran into opposition.[44] Her authority was called into question by members of her group and by outsiders, and her closest companions were sent away from her: "The general opinion of scholars at present seems to be that Hadewijch actually was evicted from her beguine community and exiled; that she was made the talk of the town because of her doctrine that one must live Love."[45] According to Hart, we do not know where she went or how she died, but, considering how often she urged her sisters to care for the sick, it may be conjectured that she joined a leprosarium or a hospital for the poor, where she would have been able to serve others and to sleep and pray in the chapel that was always attached to such institutions.

She wrote in Dutch and is thought to have lived and participated in the rich culture of Antwerp. A brilliant poet herself, she obviously knew the latest poetry in Latin, Old French, and Provençal, as well as in Dutch. Each of her three works exhibits its own particular way of viewing her experience of love, which for her is a female being: *Minne,* or Lady Love. As a mystic she believed that the soul, created by God in his own image, longs to be one with divine love again, "to become God with God," as she puts it.[46] As I point out in Chapter 10, in her *Strophische Gedichten,* she never apologizes for herself as a woman, and she never underrates her education and her intelligence; the formulae of modesty employed by most female mystics are not for her. Reason and intelligence are important to her—"to her friends she recommends attention to their intellectual progress as a source of spiritual progress. They must seek information, pose questions, and study!"[47] In the end, however, reason cannot go far enough: "In Vision VIII she is led by a guide who is a scholastic theologian; he cannot accompany her to the summit of union because he has put intellect before love."[48]

> Love and reason go hand in hand: the latter teaches the former which, in turn, enlightens reason. But reason can touch God only in what He is not (that is, reason sees by means of images, arguments, and symbols, all of which can express His Being only in an imperfect manner). Love, on the other hand, touches the very Being of God, insofar as it abandons itself to Him, plunging into the abyss hidden from each creature, where fruition is reached.[49]

Mechthild of Magdeburg

Mechthild of Magdeburg (ca. 1212–1282?),[50] the most famous of the German beguines, author of *The Flowing Light of the Divinity*,[51] decided at twenty-two to devote her life to God and went to Magdeburg, where she knew no one, to become a beguine. In 1270 she came to the convent of Helfta, perhaps advised to make such a retreat because of her outspoken criticism of corruption in the Church. Her autobiographical *Flowing Light* comprises seven books, written at different stages of her life and utilizing all the poetic and narrative resources of her time—lyric poetry, dialogue, courtly allegory, even homely folk wisdom. (Her work was collected by a Dominican friar, Henry of Halle; we do not know to what extent she was involved in the ordering and arranging of each chapter.) The Benedictine convent at Helfta was a center of learned feminine spirituality under the direction of the abbess Gertrude of Hackeborn, and when the aged Mechthild of Magdeburg arrived there, two other famous mystics were already in residence: Mechthild of Hackeborn and St. Gertrude the Great. The first page of *The Flowing Light* announces the danger to which Mechthild is exposed because she is a mystic: "I have been put on my guard about this book, and certain people have warned me that, unless I have it buried, it will be burnt. . . . Yet," she continues, "I in my weakness have written it, because I dared not hide the gift that is in it." She discovers, along with Hadewijch, a new subjective mode, according to Peter Dronke:

> Hadewijch's and Mechthild's poetry is a poetry of meditation; it is their inner colloquy with divine Love. . . . Love (*die Minne*) is a womanly figure, divinely beautiful and seductive; she is both relentless tyrant and sweet enchantress. Under her spell, these women know and recreate in themselves all the heights and all the abysses, the raptures and the torments of the beloved in the Song of Songs.[52]

Hadewijch and Mechthild are profoundly different in the poetic "I" they present, however. Mechthild, who dictated her skillful poems, seems much more vulnerable, sure of herself only when she feels that God is speaking through her, but when inspired she can be fiercely critical of her supposed superiors. She has many voices, as does Lady *Minne,* and we should not presume to see Mechthild's historical figure in just one of them. Hadewijch, too, has many voices, personae distinguished from one another by their experience of *Minne,* some male and a few female, and her visionary experience must include all these personae. Mysticism involves the total self, and in these two women of great poetic gifts, the mystic vision takes shape in sophisticated poems of love. Hadewijch utilized the complex stanzaic forms of troubadour poetry to explore her unique vision of the soul's path to God. (The poetic forms she used are discussed in Chapter 10.) Mechthild, perhaps because she composed orally, utilized many poetic forms:

> Mechthild's poetry . . . consists of numerous lyrical interludes, in a rhyming free verse, in her book of meditations. Sometimes they are long, passionate dialogues of the soul with *Minne,* with God, or with the senses; or again they can be as short as two lines, spoken by the divine *Minne:*

> > I come to my loved one
> > like a dew upon the flowers.[53]

Marguerite Porete

Marguerite Porete, a French beguine from Hainault, shared the beguine culture that had inspired Hadewijch and Mechthild fifty years earlier, and, like them, she writes of the return of the soul to its true nature, becoming God in God. The only source for our knowledge of her, apart from the records of her trials, is her book, *The Mirror of Simple Souls,* which she wrote in French. Identification of the Marguerite who was burned at the stake in 1310 with the writer of *The Mirror of Simple Souls* was made only in 1946, by Romana Guarnieri, and an edition was published in 1965. Like Mechthild, Marquerite was very critical of the lapses of the Church and its leaders. Sometime between 1296 and 1306, she wrote her book, which was condemned as heretical. Since she refused to give any testimony during the year and a half she spent in prison in Paris, the Dominican Inquisitor extracted a list of articles from her book and submitted them, out of context, to the theological regents of the University of Paris. They declared the articles heretical, and Marguerite was swiftly judged a "relapsed" heretic (she had been arrested several times before) and, in 1310, executed in the Place de Grève in Paris.

While she was being pursued by the Inquisition, Marguerite sent her book to three noted scholars, all of whom approved of it. The book, despite being condemned, circulated widely, and by the latter half of the fourteenth century had been translated into Latin, Italian, and Middle English.

> Far from ceasing with Marguerite's death, the persecutions by the Inquisition continued and may be said to bear witness to the success of the *Mirror* in the fourteenth and fifteenth centuries. It overcame linguistic barriers as did no other contemporary mystical writing in the vernacular. Proof of this fact is furnished by the six versions which have been preserved, in Old French, Old

Italian, Middle English and in Latin. . . . At present they are accessible in about fifteen manuscripts, while others have been reported to exist in various places but have then mysteriously disappeared.[54]

Marguerite's crime was that she insisted on speaking publicly and teaching her ideas publicly and that she did so in her own voice and those of others like her. She may have been heretical in her views—although even experts in theology cannot agree about this—but the very evolved spirituality she presents seems no more or less dangerous than the spiritual teachings of Hadewijch and Mechthild. She was, however, much more visible than they, for she refused to hide behind God's voice or to submit to the hierarchical Church. As a poet, she is exquisitely expressive.

Formally, her long and beautiful book is a dialogue between Love and Reason and concerns the conduct of a Soul. The dialogue is often interrupted by various allegorical figures with a commentary in verse and exempla. There is still no complete translation into English; we have to be content for now with brief sections that have been published in various anthologies. Lerner has written of the politics of her role, and Dronke has written of her poetry.[55] Here is a passage in illustration:

> LOVE: This soul swims in the sea of Joy, that is to say, in the sea of delights which issues and flows from the Divinity; and so she feels no joy, for she herself *is* joy, and thus she swims and floats in joy without feeling any joy, for she dwells in Joy and Joy dwells in her; she is joy herself by the force of joy that has transformed her into Itself.
>
> There is now a common will, the will of the lover and that of the beloved; they are like fire and flame, for Love has transformed this soul into Herself.
>
> SOUL: Ah, most sweet, pure, and divine Love, what a suave transformation it is to be transformed into what I love more than myself. And I am so transformed that I have lost my name in order to love, I who can love so little; it is into Love that I have been transformed; for I love nothing but Love.[56]

Angela of Foligno

A rather different mystic was the Franciscan Blessed Angela of Foligno, Marguerite's older contemporary, who was born in 1248 and who died in 1309, the year before Marguerite's death. Foligno, only a few miles from Assisi, was a center of Franciscan spirituality, and it was not unusual for pious married women living there to become tertiaries. Angela confessed that she had joined the Third Order for the prestige it would give her, for she wanted the reputation of being a virtuous married woman. But when her mother, her husband, and all her children died suddenly, her attachment to St. Francis and his order became more profound. She underwent a powerful conversion experience in 1285, and in 1291, when she was forty-three, she had a vision of God's love for her as she was walking on a pilgrimage to the shrine of St. Francis in Assisi. Since she was illiterate, she dictated her experiences to Brother A. (probably her uncle and confessor,

Fra Arnaldo, a Franciscan priest); the book, *Liber de vere fidelium experientia* (*The Book of the Experience of the Truly Faithful*), was read immediately and was widely copied and circulated. The first of the three treatises that compose Angela's book details her inner life from the time she becomes a tertiary. Angela identifies nineteen steps in her penitential period. At the eleventh, she desires to commit herself fully to poverty, although she has doubts that she will be able to withstand the temptations that will come to her if she is compelled to beg for sustenance. It is only when she has decided on full renunciation of property that she begins to experience the joys, as well as the difficulties, of the spiritual life. Profoundly aware of her own limitations, she is comforted by a deep and unceasing awareness of the goodness of God.

The second part of Angela's book tells of her visions during the next seven stages of her illumination, including the one best known to students of mysticism—her wooing by the Holy Spirit as she was on a pilgrimage to Assisi. The third part of the book, dictated to various unidentified scribes and known as "the treatise on evangelical doctrine," is composed of letters and discourses based on additional visions and addressed to her spiritual sons and daughters. Believing that the beginning and the end of true wisdom is to know God and ourselves, Angela traces in moving language and images the pace of her movement toward God and his toward her. She uses anecdotes from her own experience to show how she came to resolve conflicts and doubts, and she manages to avoid both false humility and inflated self-satisfaction. (In Chapter 11, I examine Angela's use of the language of the body.) Her mysticism is violent, gestural, performative: she does not sing of her love; she acts it out publicly.

> Angela of Foligno, revered by Franciscan advisers in her lifetime, became the object of a cult. However extravagant her emotional utterances, Angela did not lay claim to any new belief, any idea that challenged the prevailing world-picture of theologians of her time. Her innovations were startling; yet they were confined, we might say, to the form in which she experienced and retold accepted spiritual realities; she did not impinge upon their content. Thus one can begin to understand why her memorial, her book, was unfailingly treasured, whilst the far greater book of her contemporary, Marguerite Porete, led to Marguerite's being atrociously put to death.[57]

St. Catherine of Siena

Caterina Benincasa, the future St. Catherine of Siena, was born in 1347, the year before the Black Death began its sweep over all Europe. By the time she was a year old, the population of Siena was one-fifth what it had been before the plague. Her mission was to see God in the horror and disorientation and loss of faith in the aftermath of the disaster. Like Angela of Foligno, Catherine was a woman of great strength and personal magnetism who attracted many followers. She discovered her visionary path when she was still a child; her first recorded vision occurred as she was walking along a lonely road just outside the city wall with one of her brothers. Sometime after this event and before she was fifteen, she had a vision of a mystical marriage with Christ in which she vowed her virginity to him. Her visions led to the performance of ascetic practices that indicate her tremendous strength of will. In spite of the limitations of her sex and her class—her father was a dyer; her mother, a washerwoman—she did not allow herself to be deterred from her goals. She resisted her family's pressure to marry, and when as a punishment she was reduced to a kind of servitude in her parents' home, she transformed the situation by visualizing family members as the holy apostles and her parents as the divine family. At about seventeen, she was stricken with smallpox, and she used this opportunity to force her mother to arrange an interview with the Dominican Sisters of the Third Order, called the Mantellate. Although the Dominicans were unwilling to admit any woman who was not a mature widow— they were not cloistered and could not protect a virgin—Catherine was so disfigured by the smallpox and so sober in speech that she became the first virgin tertiary in the Dominican order. Her new status as a tertiary was very congenial to her, because she wanted to live outside a detailed fixed Rule. During her years of silence in her parents' home, she had learned to build an internal cell that she could enter in order to meditate; the value of such an imagined retreat was one of the teachings she passed on to her followers.

Catherine had only a little more than ten years—from 1367 to 1380— of active ministry. She joined the Dominican tertiaries in 1363 or 1364 and lived in isolation in her parents' home until 1367, when she was twenty. On the last day of Carnival in that year, she experienced her mystical marriage to Christ, and this event marked the beginning of a more public ministry. From then until 1370, she gradually widened her circle of contacts and worked to help the sick and the needy. In 1370 she suffered a mystical death during which she received a command to go abroad into the world to save souls.

> It is precisely in 1370, when Pope Urban V leaves Rome for Avignon, that Catherine's life changes radically. Catherine has a vision: Jesus, the beloved that by now she knew intimately, because he had been appearing to her and speaking with her for years now, this time opens her breast, draws out her heart, and substitutes his own. This is the sign of a complete mystical transformation: now Catherine possesses the heart and spirit of Jesus, while he has that of Catherine.[58]

She was only twenty-three years old, yet, impelled by her vision, the unlearned young woman took on the greatest problems of her country: a papacy under foreign domination, continual war between the pope and the city-states of the northern Italy, all taken within the context of the Hundred Years' War between France and England, and a corrupt and distrusted Church that failed to help or heal its members.

Claudio Leonardi stresses Catherine's role as prophet from 1370 to

1380 and demonstrates that she envisioned a three-stage plan with which to reestablish a moral and peaceable Christendom: the return of the papacy to Italy, where she believed it once again could be a spiritual institution for all of Christendom, rather than a political agency under the control of the political agenda of France; the establishment of peace among the warring factions in Italy and in Europe; and the undertaking of a Crusade to bring Christianity to the Islamic world.[59] Leonardi insists that she did not conceive of this Crusade in the bloody model of the earlier attempts to gain control of the Holy Land. Instead, she was following in the tradition of St. Francis, "who sought out the Sultan without arms, seeking with words alone to bring him to belief in Christ."[60]

She besieged Pope Gregory XI with letters, begging him to have the courage and faith to return to Rome. By 1374, she had attracted enough attention to be called to Florence to be examined on her beliefs and activities by the General Chapter of her order. On April 1, 1375, she had a vision in which she received the stigmata and prophesied the Great Schism, which took place four years later. In 1376 she undertook to try to make peace between Florence and Pope Gregory XI and finally convinced the pope to return to Rome from Avignon; two years later, after peace was established by Gregory's successor, Pope Urban, she turned to composing the *Dialogue,* her major visionary work. At the end of 1378, she was again living in Rome, serving as Urban's trusted adviser. During these last years of her life, she offered herself as an expiatory victim for the sins of the Church. Shortly before her death, she had a vision of the weight of the ship of the Church descending on her shoulders and her physical sufferings increased. She died in Rome on April 3, 1380, at thirty-three years of age.

Julian of Norwich

Julian of Norwich (1343–1413) was a recluse attached to the church of St. Julian in Norwich, England. In 1373, at the age of thirty, she experienced a series of visions, or "showings," on the Passion of Christ. These visions became the basis for meditation over the rest of her life and may have determined her choice of the anchoress's life. Although she makes the usual apologies for her lack of formal education—usual, especially among women—her work indicates that she was quite well read. Her book of revelations exists in two different redactions. The short text must have been written soon after her experience. Each vision is described in careful sensual detail and is followed by brief comments concerning its spiritual meaning. We learn from reading the long text that certain visions or narrative scenes were not included in the first text because Julian had not yet understood them. It was only in 1388 that she finally reached an understanding of some of her early experiences, an understanding that developed further as she wrote them down in 1393. In her commentaries on the meaning of each vision, she reveals much about her own questions about Christianity and about the process by which she worked through to an understanding of theological questions. She "reads" each vision as a kind of allegorical drama in which every detail of the imagery and the dialogue is significant— the color of clothing, the movements and gestures of the characters, the similes that occur to her as she reviews her experiences. Her powers of observation are acute, and she draws on a wide variety of experience to illustrate her perceptions—for instance, her teachings on the Motherhood of Christ.

If we look over the life histories and writings of these women as a group, we can see more clearly how their mystical experiences enabled them to overcome the restrictions facing them. We have already noted how re-spected visionary experience was in the medieval world. To have the repu-tation of a mystic was useful for both men and women who wanted to be spiritual leaders, and such a reputation granted essential status especially to women, who, because of their gender, had no other way to achieve this status. Second, the conditions of female monastic life and the training of women in meditation encouraged the emergence of visionary experience. Visions themselves initiated further learning and growth, granting the visionary both greater wisdom in dealing with others and greater ability to help those in need. Skill in meditation improved the ability to envision conflict situations creatively and to find solutions to them. Mystical women seem to have become more valuable to their communities as they grew older and gained wisdom and experience.

Female mysticism is connected to the female life cycle. Although medi-eval women mystics came from different class backgrounds in different parts of Europe and experienced their spiritual awakenings at different ages, many of them (e.g., Hildegard, Angela, Umiltà of Faenza, and, later, St. Teresa of Avila) did not become great teachers until they reached middle age. Although, of course, there were great mystics, such as St. Catherine of Siena, whose ministries were relatively brief and who died young, the more common pattern for medieval women mystics called for a peak in activity fairly late in life. As children, they were marked by preco-cious piety, and their rebellion often took the form of asceticism. From adolescence through their thirties, they often lived withdrawn or secluded lives. If they were married, they were silently absorbed in family respon-sibilities and childbearing; if they were in convents, they withdrew in prayer as much as possible. All this changed, however, around their forti-eth year. As older women, they could be visible as active leaders and effectively offer spiritual advice to others. The meditation techniques they practiced and their innate gifts gradually led them to visions, and during this growth process they learned about where they were needed. Em-powered by the divine voices of their visions, they were able to bring about change.

Finally, women's mysticism is connected to freedom. Most of the women mentioned in this discussion were extraregular in some way. Al-though convent life offered a structure in which piety might develop into mysticism, that structure could often seem too rigid. The freer approach of the beguines, with the possibility for alternating times in community and times of reclusion, seems to be much more congenial for discovering an individual voice as a writer. But to be outside convents was dangerous because of the Church's mistrust of women's leadership; Mechthild had to flee to the convent of Helfta in her old age, and Marguerite Porete was burned at the stake. The succeeding chapters in this volume explore the problems that women faced in their spiritual paths, showing both women's successes and their failures. In all the works by medieval women studied here, we see what is missing in the literature of the rest of the medieval world—a female subject, living autonomously in a world she defines, speaking a language she invents and controls.

Notes

1. Quoted in Peter Dronke, *Women Writers of the Middle Ages: A Critical Study of Texts from Perpetua to Marguerite Porete* (Cambridge: Cambridge University Press, 1984), p. 62.

2. Quoted in Emilie Zum Brunn and Georgette Epiney-Burgard, *Women Mystics in Medieval Europe* (New York: Paragon, 1989), p. 57.

3. Quoted in Dronke, *Women Writers of the Middle Ages,* p. 145.

4. Quoted in Valerie Lagorio, "The Medieval Continental Women Mystics: An Introduction," in *An Introduction to the Medieval Mystics of Europe,* ed. Paul Szarmach (Albany: State University of New York Press, 1984), p. 191.

5. Susan Clark, Introduction to *Mechthild von Magdeburg: Flowing Light of the Divinity,* ed. Susan Clark, trans. Christiane Mesch Galvani (New York: Garland, 1991).

6. Fiona Bowie, ed., and Oliver Davies, trans., *Beguine Spirituality: Mystical Writings of Mechthild of Magdeburg, Beatrijs of Nazareth, and Hadewijch of Brabant,* Crossroad Spiritual Classics Series (New York: Crossroad Books, 1989), p. 41.

7. Ibid.

8. Ibid.

9. Evelyn Underhill, *The Mystics of the Church* (London: James Clark, 1925), p. 10.

10. Ibid., p. 20.

11. Ibid., p. 82.

12. For the poems of Mahādēvi, a twelfth-century Indian mystic, see A. K. Ramanujan, ed. and trans., *Speaking of Siva* (Baltimore: Penguin, 1973), pp. 111–142. For selections from the works of other Indian women poets, see Aliki Barnstone and Willis Barnstone, eds., *A Book of Women Poets from Antiquity to Now* (New York: Schocken, 1981), pp. 64–79.

13. Lagorio, "Medieval Continental Women Mystics," p. 161.

14. On the school of St. Victor and teachers associated with it, see Jean Leclercq, François Vandenbroucke, and Louis Bouyer, *The Spirituality of the Middle Ages,* History of Christian Spirituality Series, vol. 2 (New York: Seabury Press, 1982), pp. 229–242. St. Victor was founded in 1108 by William of Champeaux, as he retired from teaching at Notre Dame in Paris; in 1113, William adopted the Augustinian Rule and resumed his teaching. Hugh of St. Victor entered the community "about 1115 or 1118, taught there from 1125, and about 1133 succeeded

William of Champeaux as Master of the school. He remained in that office until his death in 1140 or 1141" (pp. 229–230). Richard became "Prior in 1162 and died in 1173" (p. 235). For connections between the Victorine school, William of St. Thierry, and the beguines, see Zum Brunn and Epiney-Burgard, *Women Mystics,* pp. xvii–xxxiv, 74, 98, 107.

15. Here I am relying on Dronke, *Women Writers of the Middle Ages,* p. 146.

16. Ibid., pp. 146–147.

17. For the history of enclosure, see Jane Tibbitts Schulenburg, "Strict Active Enclosure and Its Effects on the Female Monastic Experience (ca. 500–1100)," in *Medieval Religious Women,* vol. 1, *Distant Echoes,* ed. John A. Nichols and Lillian Thomas Shank (Kalamazoo, Mich.: Cistercian Publications, 1984), pp. 51–86.

18. See Lina Eckenstein, *Woman Under Monasticism* (Cambridge: Cambridge University Press, 1896). This remains the best, and most readable, history of women in the monastic tradition.

19. This was probably the result of the Crusades, but the issue is debated by historians.

20. The standard works on the beguines are Ernest W. McDonnell, *The Beguines and Beghards in Medieval Culture* (New Brunswick, N.J.: Rutgers University Press, 1953; New York: Octagon, 1969); Herbert Grundmann, *Religiöse Bewegungen im Mittelalter,* 2nd ed. (Hildesheim: Olms, 1961); Dayton Phillips, *The Beguines in Medieval Strasbourg: A Study of the Social Aspect of Beguine Life* (Ann Arbor: University of Michigan Press, 1941); and Simone Roisin, *L'Hagiographie cistercienne dans la diocèse de Liège au xiiie siècle* (Louvain: Bibliothèque de l'université, 1947), and "L'Efflorescence cistercienne et le courant féminin de piété au xiiie siècle," *Revue d'histoire ecclésiastique* 39 (1945): 458–486.

21. Benjamin de Trouyer, "Beguines et Tertiares en Belgique et aux Pays-Bas aux XII–XIVe siècles," in *I Frati Penitenti de S. Francesco . . . ,* ed. Mariano d'Alatri (Rome: Istituto Storico dei Cappuccini, 1977), pp. 133–138; Pierre Peanò, "Les Béguines du Languedoc ou la crise du T.O.F. dans la France méridionale . . . ," in *I Frati Penitenti,* ed. d'Alatri, pp. 139–158.

22. Rudolph Bell, *Holy Anorexia* (Chicago: University of Chicago Press, 1985); Caroline Walker Bynum, *Holy Feast and Holy Fast: The Religious Significance of Food to Medieval Women* (Berkeley: University of California Press, 1987).

23. *Julian of Norwich Showings,* trans. and ed. Eric Colledge and James Walsh (New York: Paulist Press, 1978), p. 135.

24. Recent scholarship suggests that she may not have been enclosed when she received her first visions, since she speaks of her mother standing next to her as she believes she is dying.

25. McDonnell, *Beguines and Beghards;* R. W. Southern, *Western Society and the Church in the Middle Ages* (Baltimore: Penguin, 1970), pp. 318–331.

26. *The Life of Christina of Markyate* [*De S. Theodora Virgine, Quae et dicitur Christina*], ed. and trans. C. H. Talbot (Oxford: Clarendon Press, 1959). See also Christopher J. Holdsworth, "Christina of Markyate," in *Medieval Women,* ed. Derek Baker (Oxford: Basil Blackwell, 1978), pp. 185–204.

27. I am following Holdsworth's description of the psalter. For illustrations, see *The St. Alban's Psalter,* ed. Otto Pächt, C. R. Dodwell, and Francis Wormald (London: Warburg Institute, 1960).

28. Holdsworth, "Christina of Markyate," p. 191.

29. Ibid., p. 193.

30. Zum Brunn and Epiney-Burgard, *Women Mystics,* p. 3.

31. *Opera Omnia,* in *Patrologiae cursus completus, series latina,* vol. 197, ed. Jacques-Paul Migne (Paris, 1882).

32. Sabina Flanagan, *Hildegard of Bingen: A Visionary Life* (London: Routledge, 1989), pp. 14–15.

33. Underhill, *Mystics of the Church,* p. 76.

34. Peter Dronke, *Poetic Individuality in the Middle Ages: New Departures in Poetry, 1000–1150* (Oxford: Clarendon Press, 1970), p. 151. More study of Hildegard's song sequences is found in Flanagan, *Hildegard of Bingen,* pp. 106–140, and in Barbara Newman, *Sister of Wisdom: St. Hildegard's Theology of the Feminine* (Berkeley: University of California Press, 1987), and *Saint Hildegard of Bingen Symphonia (A Critical Edition of the Symphonia armonie celestium revelationum [Symphony of the Harmony of Celestial Revelations])* (Ithaca, N.Y.: Cornell University Press, 1988).

35. Newman, *Sister of Wisdom,* p. xvii.

36. Ibid., p. xviii.

37. Ibid., p. 36.

38. Ibid., p. 4.

39. Beatrijs of Nazareth (1200–1268) was a contemporary Netherlands mystic. Educated in beguine and convent schools, she became the prioress of the Cistercean convent of Nazareth in 1236. Her life and work are discussed in Chapter 3.

40. Quoted in Zum Brunn and Epiney-Burgard, *Women Mystics,* p. xix*n.*

41. Ibid., p. xxiv.

42. Ibid.

43. These are the *Mengeldichten* attributed to Hadewijch II or Pseudo-Hadewijch, a later poet (ibid., pp. 129–131).

44. *Hadewijch: The Complete Works,* trans. Mother Columba Hart (New York: Paulist Press, 1980), p. 4.

45. Ibid.

46. See the sections on Hadewijch in Zum Brunn and Epiney-Burgard, *Women Mystics,* pp. 97–139, and in Bowie, *Beguine Spirituality,* pp. 96–125.

47. Zum Brunn and Epiney-Burgard, *Women Mystics,* p. 98.

48. Ibid.

49. Ibid., p. 107.

50. Her dates are problematical. Zum Brunn and Epiney-Burgard say she was born between 1207 and 1210, went to Magdeburg about 1230, and began writing about 1250 (ibid., p. 39); Clark says, "Born in the late first or early second decade of the thirteenth century, Mechthild began to compose her mystical revelations in 1250" (Introduction to *Mechthild von Magdeburg,* p. xii).

51. The most recent translation is Galvani, *Mechthild von Magdeburg.* The other English translation, only a partial one and often inaccurate as well, is *The Revelations of Mechthild of Magdeburg, or The Flowing Light of the Godhead,* trans. Lucy Menzies (London: Longmans Green, 1953). Another complete translation, under the general direction of Gertrud Jaron Lewis, will be published by Cistercian Publications within the next few years.

52. Peter Dronke, *The Medieval Lyric* (New York: Harper & Row, 1969), p. 81.

53. Ibid., p. 83.

54. Zum Brunn and Epiney-Burgard, *Women Mystics,* p. 147.

55. Robert E. Lerner, *The Heresy of the Free Spirit in the Later Middle Ages*

(Berkeley: University of California Press, 1972); Dronke, *Women Writers of the Middle Ages,* pp. 202–228.

56. Quoted in Zum Brunn and Epiney-Burgard, *Women Mystics,* p. 154.

57. Dronke, *Women Writers of the Middle Ages,* p. 217.

58. "[P]roprio nel 1370, quando Urbano V lascia Roma per Avignone, che la vita di Caterina muta radicalmente. Caterina ha una visione: Gesù, l'amato che ormai ben conosceva, perché da anni le appariva e le parlava, questa volta le apre il petto, ne estrae il cuore e lo sostituisce con il suo. È il segno della piena transfor-mazione mistica: Caterina ha il cuore e lo spirito di Gesù, Gesù ha quello di Caterina" (Claudio Leonardi, "Caterina la mistica," in *Medioevo al femminile,* ed. Ferruccio Bertini [Rome: Laterza, 1989], p. 178).

59. Ibid., pp. 171–195.

60. Ibid., p. 187.

2

Unmasking Women: Medieval Responses to the Unknowability of the Lady

On his first evening as the guest of Lord Bercilak, Sir Gawain meets two ladies. Of the first he says:

> Ho watȝ þe fayrest in felle, of flesche & of lyre
> & of compas & colour & costes of alle oþer,
> & wener þen Wenore, as þe wyȝe þoȝt.[1]

> [She was the fairest of skin, in flesh and complexion
> fairest of all in form and coloring and manners,
> fairer than Guinevere, as the man thought.]

This lady leads by the hand a woman who is older and held in high respect by the men gathered about them. Gawain feels obliged to compare the two:

> For if þe ȝonge watȝ ȝep, ȝolȝe watȝ þat oþer;
> Riche red on þat on rayled ay-quere,
> Rugh ronkled chekeȝ þat oþer on rolled.[2]

> [For if the one was fresh, the other was faded;
> A rich red color bedecked the one,
> And rough wrinkled cheeks hung in folds on the other.]

The short lines of the bob and wheel that conclude this section of the poem place emphasis on Sir Gawain's conclusion:

> Hir body watȝ schort & þik,
> Hir buttokeȝ bay & brode;

More lykker-wys on to lyk
Watȝ þat scho hade on lode.[3]

[Her body was short and thick,
Her buttocks round and wide;
More toothsome to his taste
Was the one she had with her.]

Readers of *Sir Gawain and the Green Knight* will recall that there are
some surprises in the identities of these two women, and one of the surprises is that the older woman, whom Gawain dismisses so unchivalrously
on the basis of her appearance, is actually his aunt, the powerful Morgan le
Fay. Gawain is not to be blamed for his inability to read these two women
properly, however. Most male observers of the medieval scene probably
would have agreed that medieval woman was not what she seemed to be.
In fact, it may be that the only consensus about woman in the Middle Ages
concerned her unknowability. In the theoretical writings about women—
patristic or scientific—women did not fare very well, for women, unlike
men, were not made in God's image.[4] But contradictory doctrines
abounded in both the secular and ecclesiastical worlds. Recent scholarship
on the position of women in the Middle Ages has upheld what Eileen
Power observed in 1926: views on the true nature of woman "oscillated
between a pit and a pedestal."[5] The result of this confusion was that, as the
lines from *Sir Gawain* indicate, attitudes toward women were stereotyped
and polarized; each woman was seen as embodying half of a pair of
opposites—beautiful or ugly, good or evil, Mary or Eve. In literature, the
dominant assumption was likely to be that woman was rarely what she
seemed. Her very ambiguity was threatening, as was her beauty or her
power.

I believe that this set of doubts about the nature of woman in the
Middle Ages points to a real fear that perhaps woman was fundamentally
unknowable. Medieval writing—chronicles, poems, saints' lives—preserved numerous anecdotes about attempts to unmask women, to subject
them to tests, and to expose them for what they really were. In these
anecdotes, some of which I discuss in this chapter, women appear to be
either good or bad, and the reality beneath the appearance may confirm the
appearance or contradict it. Sometimes good women are unmasked as
good women; they may also turn out to be evil. Evil women may turn out
to be truly evil, or the appearance of evil may be accounted for so that true
goodness may be seen. I am not simply repeating here what we have all
learned: that the medieval world was deeply ambivalent about the nature of
the feminine, as it was about the nature of sexuality. I am concerned with a
particular kind of response to ambivalence—the desire to unmask—that
implies a fear that the truth of a woman may not be knowable to the
unmasker. The need to unmask may be especially poignant when the
woman is loved, but the fear that a beautiful woman may be evil and thus
lead the lover to damnation can also bring out much cruelty in the attempt

to unmask. It may be objected here that women in medieval literature also try to unmask men. The witty women in Boccaccio's *Decameron* delight in exposing hypocrisy as much as the men do, and Guinevere, if not actually trying to unmask Lancelot, is certainly trying to determine the limits of his devotion to her. But these examples do not quite cover what interests me. I use the term *unmasking* to refer to a certain social and psychological pattern in which a male figure attempts to expose the true nature of a particular woman by stripping off her mask and eliminating her usual appearance, with the end of getting her to admit her true nature.

The woman who needs unmasking is obviously someone important to the would-be unmasker. He must be vulnerable to her in some way, he must need her or love her or be otherwise visibly related to her, and because of that vulnerability he must need to know her true identity. There is no intrinsic reason why the gender distinctions might not be reversed, and they may be in other historical periods. But for the medieval period, the need to unmask is at base a reassertion of male power, power that seems to be in the hands of a female (whether she is a prostitute or a poet's beloved or a politically active saint does not matter as much as the question of relative power in the relationship) in a world that knows that women ought not to wield power. "Unmasking" is one manifestation of the almost institutionalized antifeminism of the Middle Ages. It is likely that the idealization of women in aristocratic literature, given that role reversals in love relationships are often tolerated in that context, might have exacerbated the need.

In courtly literature in the vernacular, the lover often seems compelled to unmask his beloved, and in courtly romance the attempt to unmask may be shifted to the court or to the public. In the story of Tristan and Iseult, the would-be unmaskers of Iseult are termed felons; they fail in their attempt to expose Iseult's adultery publicly. Yet the moral ambiguity of Iseult remains to haunt Tristan, and he masks himself in order to test her, to learn if her love for him is a mask.[6] Patient Griselda submits to Count Walter's vicious attempts to unmask her, to trap her into exposing a less than perfect submission to the pain he causes her.[7] Perhaps one reason for the popularity of the Griselda story—told by Boccaccio, Petrarch, and Chaucer, among others—is that the audience can have it both ways: it can participate in Walter's need to know, his compulsion to unmask, at the same time that it recognizes that Griselda is fully as good as she appears to be.[8] In order to explore this motif of unmasking, I would like to present passages from a number of texts, some literary and some documentary, in which this motif is illustrated. Examples could be found all over Europe, but my selection is based on texts from Italy, England, and France.

My first example comes from the literary biography of Jacopone da Todi, a lawyer, poet, and mystic who lived in Italy in the thirteenth century.[9] A gifted young man from an old and noble family, Jacopone was educated to be a notary. It was probably in 1267, when he was thirty, that he married

Vanna di Bernardino di Guidone, of the family of the counts of Col-
lemedio. The young couple lived a fashionable life in Todi; Jacopo, we are
told, "lived with much vanity and took great pleasure and delight in his
wife's going about well adorned."[10] Within a year she was dead:

> One time at the wish of her husband, Ser Jacopo, she went to a party, a usual
> one in that town, adorned as always to honor those who had invited her and
> her husband. . . . While they were dancing and having a good time, the
> balcony on which they were dancing suddenly fell, and everyone fell down
> with it.[11]

Everyone on the balcony was injured, but Vanna was the only one killed.
Jacopo, who had missed the party because of business, arrived quickly and
had her carried home:

> [H]e had those vain vestments taken off her to prepare her for burial. Finally
> he found on her bare flesh a harsh hair-shirt; seeing which the husband . . .
> was most astounded and stupefied. He considered the vain life which she had
> shown in appearance and how he had never known such a thing by the least
> act. So . . . Jacopo was struck in his mind and stricken in his heart and
> deprived of his senses.[12]

To Jacopo, Vanna's death, and his failure to see who she really was,
constituted a divine warning to convert, and he did so immediately, with a
violence and a suddenness that equalled those of his wife's death. The point
of the narrative of his conversion is that he never knew her—and the shock
of realizing that she had not been what she had seemed (that, in fact, she
had been much better than she had seemed) was enough to bring him to a
new religious consciousness. The pious woman wearing the hair shirt
obviously had been his real wife, and in this respect Jacopone's conversion,
his abandonment of his former profession and social status to become a
mad beggar and then a powerful poet, was his attempt to be true to her
true nature.[13] Whether this incident really took place (recent scholarship
suggests that it is true) is unimportant; what is significant is that a climate
of belief existed that saw the divine unmasking of Jacopone's wife as necessary and sufficient motivation for his later prophetic voice.[14] One of the
crucial assumptions of this text is that Jacopo felt guilty at Vanna's death
and that he is to be blamed for not having known her true nature. The
discovery of the hair shirt is what is thought to be important for his
spiritual life, not the fact of Vanna's sudden death after less than a year of
marriage or the loss of someone he loved.

My second example of unmasking comes from the city archives of Florence.[15] In 1398, Angela, wife of Nofri di Francesco, was brought to trial
on charges of practicing prostitution without wearing the required garb,
"gloves on her hands and a bell on her head."[16] Her neighbor Bartolo
Gadino was one of the witnesses against her. He testified that he had
observed "many men coming openly to her house to copulate with her for
money."[17] The public knowledge of her activities is underscored by Bar-

tolo's statement that during the previous November and December, "on behalf of all his neighbors and conforming to their will, he asked Angela to abandon her prostitute's career and live honestly."[18] Apparently someone had realized that there might be more to Angela's life-style than pure lust, for Bartolo had promised, on behalf of the same neighbors,

> to furnish her with a basket of bread each week for her sustenance. But Angela replied that she did not wish to give up prostitution unless her neighbors first gave her two florins. Otherwise she intended to pursue the whore's life since she earned much more money than the amount which her neighbors wished to give her.[19]

Angela could not be allowed to get away with this, so she was convicted and sentenced to wear the bell and gloves. It is probably the ambivalence toward prostitution that accounts for the contradictions in this account of Angela's motivations. Implicit in the entire document is the medieval belief that women choose prostitution because all women are whores at heart; attempts to regulate prostitution are attempts to identify the women involved, lest they deceive unsuspecting men. But the Florentine government, like those of most medieval towns, regarded prostitution as a necessity—to protect married women. This document also reveals an awareness that women might choose prostitution for economic reasons; to survive, women may be forced to sell the only thing of value they possess. From this point of view, Angela's crime is that she thinks she is worth more than a basket of bread each week; her reply indicates that she is not properly ashamed of her prostitution and not properly content with her social position and her poverty. Legal means have been necessary to unmask her, to force her to take her appropriate place in the scheme of things by wearing the garb that signals her whorelike nature.

My third example comes from a hagiographical text of an earlier period in England.[20] Christina of Markyate, whom we discussed in Chapter 1, was born into an influential Anglo-Saxon family in Norman England, probably between 1096 and 1098.[21] First a hermit, then an anchoress, and later an abbess, she gathered around her many disciples, both male and female. To reach this status, she had to fight her family, the husband to whom her family had betrothed her against her will, several bishops, and other members of the lesser and greater nobility. All along the way, the genuineness of her vocation and of her psychic powers was tested, as much by those hostile to her as by difficult circumstances.[22]

One of Christina's most influential followers was the Norman abbot Geoffrey. Their relationship was clearly an intimate one, and Christina, in public, had called him her beloved (*dilectum*), an action that was misinterpreted to suggest a physical relationship. For this reason, Christina's biographer explicitly points to the chastity of the Christina–Geoffrey relationship. Still, Christina did not try to disguise the fact that it had been difficult for her to remain chaste with Geoffrey, and a part of her biography is devoted to describing her struggle with her own sexual desires. At any rate, it seems to have been characteristic of Geoffrey to want to make sure that Christina really was what she claimed to be. She had claimed that she received a divine forewarning whenever Geoffrey was about to visit her, so he determined to surprise her. As he prepared for the lengthy journey to see her, he took care that no word of his plans should reach her. She at the same time was taking care to provide witnesses to her foreknowledge:

In crastino vero Pentecosts convocatis tribus de secum morantibus puellis. Iam enim crescente fama Christine crescebat numerous puellarum. Predixit eis precordialem suum ipso die affuturum. Monuit honeste cuncta componere, religiose se habere, ne religionis amicus quicquam quod sibi displiceret offenderet. Credule ille, spem enim sumebant de preteritis, mandatis parent domine. Moratur abbas. Proposuerat enim nullum adventus sui cuiquam fieri indicium, nisi forte virginem latere potuisset. Celebratur missa, nuncius abbatis nullus precedit. Respectant se invicem virgines facti moram admodum admirantes. Hoc solum sibi certum erat: Christinam nec falli posse nec fallere. Cum ecce preveniens nuncius, omnes de adventu letificat abbatis. Advenit vir venerandus, colloquium dulce et salutare tractat cum virgine. Interumque loquendo, nunc scio ait subitum nostrum vos adventum latuisse. Advocat illa cum quibus de hiis prius contulerat. M. scilicet sororem et secretorum suorum consciam et jubet ut edicant quid de ejus audierint adventu. Fatentur verum, veritatis obtemperantes amice. Laus Dei in commune resonat, spiritus sancti gracia diffusius eo die sentitur.

[On the morrow of Whitsunday, having called together three of the maidens who were living with her (for with her growing reputation the number of maidens grew) she foretold that her beloved would come on that day. She ordered them to put everything in good order and to behave devoutly lest the friend of devotion should find anything that displeased him. Believing what she said (for past events gave them confidence), they obeyed their mistress. The abbot was long in coming. For he had decided to tell no one of his visit, so that, if possible, the maiden might not know. Mass was said: no messenger came from the abbot. The maidens looked at one another, very surprised at the delay. Only one thing was certain: Christina could not have misled them or made a mistake. Suddenly the arrival of a messenger gladdened their hearts at the abbot's coming. The venerable man arrived, and had an edifying talk with the maiden. Whilst they were speaking, he said, "This time I know my sudden coming took you by surprise." She called to her sister Margaret who knew her secrets, and the others to whom she had spoken on this matter and ordered them to say openly that they had heard about his visit. They admitted it was true, obeying the friend of truth. Praise to God rose from all; and the grace of the Holy Spirit was felt more abundantly that day.][23]

The tone of this entire episode is playfully competitive, yet the details reveal that the participants had much at stake. Since prophetic ability—the ability to read minds and to foretell the future—was one of the necessary characteristics of the future saint, hagiography abounds in anecdotes describing tests of this ability. Usually the testing is done by an enemy of the saint, who thinks he knows that she is false and who wants to unmask her publicly; often the tables are turned quite decisively when the saint, before the skeptic has an opportunity to open his mouth, announces to all that the would-be unmasker has come with that purpose in mind.[24] In Christina's case, the saint and her tester are friends, and it is the resolution of ambiguity that is important. What texts like this emphasize is that the issue of unmasking women is so crucial, and so accepted by both men and women, that the failure to unmask, the proof that the woman was not wearing a mask, is extraordinarily reassuring for all involved.

In courtly literature, too, there is a search for a similar kind of reassurance, a reassurance that can be gained only as a result of attempting to unmask a beloved. The unmasking motif in lyric is developed more indirectly, for the relevation of the true nature of the beloved, the lady behind all masks, is sought through the exploration of the impact of the beloved on the lover's psyche. In general, lyric poetry makes little attempt to explore the woman's mind; it is her power over the man that must be investigated, must be traced back to her true nature. It is this exploration of female power, of the effect (often chaos-producing) on an articulate man of an apparently passive and powerless beloved object, that creates the supposedly inverted hierarchy in courtly poetry.

In the poetry of the *Vita Nuova,* Dante employs this tradition. We may take as fairly representative his treatment of the figure of Beatrice in sonnet XI.

> Ne li occhi porta la mia donna Amore
> per che si fa gentil ciò ch'ella mira;
> ov'ella passa, ogn'uom ver lei si gira,
> e cui saluta fa tremar lo core,
>
> sì che, bassando il viso, tutto smore,
> e d'ogni suo difetto allor sospira:
> fugge dinanzi a lei superbia ed ira.
> Aiutatemi, donne, farle onore.
>
> Ogne dolcezza, ogne pensero umile
> nasce nel core a chi parlar la sente,
> ond'è laudato chi prima la vide.
>
> Quel ch'ella par quando un poco sorride,
> non si pò dicer ne tenere a mente,
> sì è novo miracol e gentile.
>
> [The power of Love borne in my lady's eyes
> imparts its grace to all she looks upon.
> All turn to gaze at her when she walks by,
> and when she greets a man his heart beats fast,
>
> the color leaves his face, he bows his head
> and sighs to think of all his imperfections.
> Anger and pride are forced to flee from her.
> Help me to honor her, most gracious ladies.

> Humility and every sweet conception
> bloom in the heart of those who hear her speak.
> (Praise to the one who first saw what she was!)
>
> The image of her when she starts to smile
> dissolves within the mind and melts away
> a miracle too rich and strange to hold.][25]

As the woman herself is unknowable, so, ultimately, is the effect she has on the poet unknowable and unexplorable—at least at the time of the composition of the poems in the *Vita Nuova*.[26] In recognizing this fact, Dante is, I think, simply making explicit something that was inherent in the courtly lyric tradition from the beginning. What Dante is presenting here, particularly in the final lines of the sonnet, in which even the mental image of Beatrice is self-consuming, is not the ineffable experience of the visionary.[27] In accounts of the visionary's encounter with divine love, there is usually an attempt to make that experience reachable by the hearer or reader, to provide through words or images the ladder that leads up to the final unspeakable glimpse, which the mystic-poet can neither describe nor circumscribe but which he may nevertheless make accessible to his audience. (This is, of course, consistent with the fact that most accounts of mystical experience are found in guides to contemplation and the spiritual life, guides intended to be followed by the properly prepared contemplative.) In fact, it is just this kind of preparation that Dante later provides for the attentive reader of the *Commedia*. In the *Commedia*, one might say, consciousness expands almost to infinity through meditative steps; in the *Vita Nuova*, consciousness folds in on itself, collapsing at the moment of potential transcendence. The young poet forgets his experience; the experience is self-consuming, for the love expressed in this poem is self-consuming, rather than self-illuminating.[28]

There is no doubt that the *donna* of the poem dominates. It is she who determines the scene, assigns the proper values, manifests the power of love—in fact, as Dante says in his prose commentary, it is she who creates love where it did not exist in potentiality before.[29] In her eyes, the lady carries the love that ennobles all it looks on. Where she passes, "every man turns himself toward her." This ambiguous power of attraction is not necessarily spiritual, for all the line really says is that heads turn as she goes by. The first unambiguous clue to her spiritual power is found in the next line ("She makes tremble the heart of him whom she greets"), but the full effect of the lady's salutation is not described until the next tercet. Here we find the moral effect of her greeting: the man whose heart is trembling must lower his glance, so overcome and pale is he, and he begins to sigh at his suddenly recognized defects. The result of this new self-examination is that certain sins—pride and wrath—leave him. He no longer feels that he alone can praise his lady, so he asks other ladies for help.

The first tercet shows the new thoughts that are born in this purged or humbled heart—every sweetness, every humble thought—born at the sound of her voice, her greeting of line four. For this reason, the poet assures us, he who first sees her should be praised, is praiseworthy, not blessed, not transformed. Conventional as this idea may be, the expression "è laudato chi . . . la vide" turns the poem back toward that self-centeredness it seemed to have lost for an instant. The newly acquired humility of thought has vanished, and the process of deconstruction of the poem and of the experience has begun. We are told of the impact of her smile, which erases the very mental image it creates: "sì è novo miracol e gentil."

We need not believe all the poet's assertions concerning the novelty of his love experience, for assertions of novelty are themselves an essential part of the literary tradition:

> The images suggest at one and the same time the ennobling effect of the love as present in Andreas' *De Amore,* the sighs of the "courtly" lover, and also a more spiritual love in the use of the phrase "fa gentil," indicating the bestowal of a spiritual grace as well . . . although this too is consonant with the courtly love discussed in Andreas' treatise.[30]

What is newer than the depiction of the lover dazzled by his lady's power is the spiritual identification of the lady. The result of the poet's description of Beatrice in this sonnet is to establish her as a miracle rather than as a woman. Joan Ferrante sees this as a characteristic of the *dolce stil novisti* and cites the use of such angelic and miraculous imagery in the works of Guido Cavalcanti, Guido Guinizelli, Lapo Gianni, and others.[31] She observes:

> Of course there is a good deal of hyperbole in these comparisons, but it is nonetheless significant that, if he would attribute beneficial effects to the woman, the poet must make her a supernatural being. . . . It is almost as if, to counter the idea of woman as the tool of the devil . . . and to save the object of their love and poetry, the *stilnovisti* had to make women the tools of God.[32]

What is unusual in Dante is that he uses Beatrice's death "to build a system by which the woman can, literally as well as figuratively, draw the lover to God, but he is the only poet of this school to do so."[33]

Sonnet XI of the *Vita Nuova,* then, has unmasked Beatrice by describing her powers—and, along with the mask, her humanness and her womanness have been removed. At the close of the poem, even her smile, like that of the Cheshire cat, disappears. But something has been accomplished from the audience's point of view; the lady's unknowability is no longer disturbing, has been explained and made acceptable, for she is a miracle. Not only does this account for her ability to create love in persons in whom love had not previously existed, even in potential, but the language of miracles suggests a divine context in which the unexplainable is the norm, rather than the exception. The figure of the beloved is still ambiguous, but that ambiguity has been raised to the spiritual level—the heavenly only seems ambiguous to human sight. To me, this indicates that Dante does not yet see Beatrice as a God-bearing image. Through his poetic language, he has created the conditions that will make such a reading of her possible, but at this point, in this poem, her presence limits rather than expands his consciousness.

The medieval audience, whether secular or clerical, was undoubtedly far more familiar than we are with the nature of the beatific vision, and its members would have recognized that the beatific vision did not cause consciousness to collapse in on itself, although conceptual thinking and the image-making faculty had no place in the highest reaches of mystical experience. As Angela of Foligno's spiritual autobiography and mystical guide, *The Book of the Experience of the Truly Faithful,* demonstrates repeatedly,[34] the truly beatific vision is expansive, not contractive. Only after Beatrice's death will it be possible for Dante to remain conscious of what is heavenly in Beatrice, and only then will she be able to lead his mind upward. In this case, it seems that, like Jacopone da Todi, Dante sees his lady as herself only at her death; while she is still alive, her presence is too powerful to remain unmasked to him.

One of the most influential *dolce stil nuovo* poems was Guido Guinizelli's "Al cor gentil rempaira sempre amore" ["Love always repairs to the gentle heart"]. In this poem, Guinizelli treats love philosophically as well as sensually, thus creating a context for speaking of *gentilezza* apart from noble birth, as something intimately related to the capacity for love. But for our purposes, it is the sixth stanza that is important, for it provides the background to Dante's and Petrarch's sonnets. Here the poet, in his imagination, has died and stands before the judgment seat of God, prepared to defend his love for a mortal lady. And what is his response to God's accusation that he has profaned divine love by giving to a mortal what ought to be offered only to God or the Virgin Mary? The poet places the responsibility squarely on God: "She had the semblance of an angel, as if she were of your realm. I am not to blame for loving her" [Dir Li porò "Tenne d'angel sembianza / Che fosse del Tuo regno; / Non me fu fallo, s'in lei posi amanza"].[35]

The irony of this response to the lady's ambiguity must have seemed both amusing and profound to a medieval audience. Guinizelli knows that his lady only appears to be an angel, and so does Petrarch. What is at stake is the deeper, truer meaning of this appearance, this seeming. Does the lady's angelic appearance provide a clue to her spiritual nature, or is it misleading, a hint that apparent virtue is real vice? Throughout the *Canzoniere,* Petrarch perceives a tension between Laura and some higher good. He is drawn to Laura as if she were some kind of absolute, as if she could fulfill his yearning for completion, yet he knows that she is not that absolute, that he can never be fulfilled by her or by loving her. He cannot abandon his yearning for her, nor can he trust that yearning enough to surrender to it. This is the conflict that underlies the two representative poems presented here: sonnet XC, written while Laura was still alive, and sonnet CCLXXIX, written after her death.

Sonnet XC

Erano i capei d'oro a l'aura sparsi
Che 'n mille dolci nodi gli avolgea,
E 'l vago lume oltra misura ardea
Di quei begli occhi, ch'or ne son sì scarsi;

E'l viso di pietosi color farsi
(Non so se vero o falso) mi parea:
I' che l'esca amorosa al petto avea,
Qual meraviglia se di subito arsi?

Non era l'andar suo cosa mortale,
Ma d'angelica forma; e le parole
Sonavan altro che pur voce umana:

Uno spirto celeste, un vivo sole
Fu quel ch'i'vidi; et se non fosse or tale,
Piaga per allentar d'arco non sana.[36]

[The golden hair was loosened in the breeze
that twined it in a thousand charming knots;
and beyond measure burned the lovely light
in those pretty eyes, that now are lacking light,

giving her face a pitying cast—
I don't know if real or false—it seemed to me:
I who had in my breast the loving tinder,
what marvel if I all at once caught fire?

Her gait was not a mortal thing,
but of angelic form, and her words
sounded unlike a merely human voice.

A celestial spirit, a living sun
was what I saw; if now it was not such,
the wound heals not by loosening the bow.]

Sonnet CCLXXIX

Se lamentar augelli, o verdi fronde
Mover soavemente a l'aura estiva,
O roco mormorar di lucide onde
S'ode d'una fiorita e fresca riva,

Là 'v 'io seggia d'amor pensoso et scriva,
Lei che'l Ciel ne mostrò, terra n'asconde,
Veggio et odo et intendo, ch'ancor viva,
Di sì lontano a' sospir miei risponde.

—Deh, perché inanzi 'l tempo ti consume?
—Mi dice con pietate—a che pur versi
Degli occhi tristi un doloroso fiume?

Di me non pianger tu; ch'e' miei dì fersi
Morendo, eterni; et ne l'interno lume,
Quando mostrai de chiuder, gli occhi apersi.[37]

[If birds' moaning, or green leaves
Moving gently in the summer air
Or a hoarse murmur of shining waves
is heard from a flowering fresh bank,

There where I sit thoughtful about love, and write,
her, whom heaven shows us and earth hides
I see, and I hear, and I understand that still alive,
from far away, she responds to my sighs:

"Ah, why do you consume yourself before your time?"
she says to me in pity, "for what do you still pour
forth a grievous river from your saddened eyes?

Don't weep for me; for my day by dying became
eternal, and in the internal light,
when I seemed to close my eyes, I opened them."]

In a poet like Petrarch, so concerned with expressing the delicate ambiguities of his beloved Laura, we should expect a special subtlety in the treatment of unmasking. Yet the opening five lines of sonnet XC provide a relatively straightforward description of the lady's golden hair and shining eyes—only those "dolci nodi" and the "lume oltra misura" could give us pause. The problem of appearances emerges with the "mi parea" [it seemed to me] of line six, which governs syntactically the preceding clauses and which is reinforced by the qualifier "Non so se vero o falso" [I don't know if real or false]. The doubt applies directly to the pity manifested in Laura's face but carries an element of unreality into the entire sensually described scene. The rest of the sonnet is devoted to justifying the poet's enamoured response to the image he has just re-created for us. The lady's voice was more than human, her way of walking was "not a mortal thing" but of angelic form. The poet stresses that what he perceived was a "celestial spirit" and a "living sun." If none of this were true (and here, of course, he employs the subjunctive mood: "se non fosse or tale"), it no longer matters, for the wound he bears, a wound that does not heal, is real enough. The implication is that the entire scene, except for the metaphor of the wound, is not real, but the poet never says so; he is content to use the ambiguous "it seemed to me" and "I don't know if real or false," underscoring that ambiguity by use of the subjunctive, which in itself suggests a category of experience neither real nor unreal.

The problem of appearances, and the desire to unmask the lady, take a far more hallucinatory tone in sonnet CCLXXIX. The opening quatrain has a wistful, self-indulgent quality, and, as in sonnet XC, the scene depicted is governed syntactically by a phrase that calls into question its reality. Here it is the use of "se" [if] that governs the perception of an animated, sweetly melancholy natural world. *If* I hear birds lament and waves murmur, *and* I sit thinking about love and writing, *then* these conditions produce a vision of Laura, in which I see and hear and understand that she is still alive, although very distant, and that she responds to my sighs. But this syllogistically constructed comfort soon dissipates when she speaks, for Laura chides the poet for his fixation on her bodily existence and bodily death. The reality of that death, she reminds him, was rebirth into immortality, and her then-closed eyes are now open wide. But the poet seems unable to open his own eyes, and, as an object of meditation, the image of Laura is self-consuming; the poet is left alone with his awareness of his poem's hallucinatory, deceptive power. The greater reality of Laura's spiritual existence erases the hallucinatory unreality of her first appearance, but leaves the poet with nothing to see.

After Petrarch, this awareness of the absolute unknowability of the lady often is treated with irony; a tendency toward detached, urbane skepticism is particularly apparent in those elements of courtly lyric that found their way into the romance tradition. One of the most amusing examples of what may become of the need to unmask the unknowable lady is found in Ariosto's treatment of Orlando and Angelica in the *Orlando Furioso*. For this angelic-appearing lady has in real life been enjoying herself sexually with the soldier Medoro. Orlando tries very hard not to believe this, although it is written on every tree in the forest. The author puts Orlando's musings in the subjunctive: "Pensa come possa esser che non sia la cosa vera" [He thinks how it might be that the thing were not true].[38] Unable to maintain the self-deception, he goes mad. Giamatti observes:

> Now Orlando is not simply a victim of the fact that things are not what they seem; he embodies that fact. . . . This is an assault on the convention of Petrarchan love on two levels. First Orlando's (ultimately) *fin amors* and Petrarchan ideas about the aspiring lover and the disdaining lady are shattered, because . . . Angelica has succumbed. . . . But Ariosto also attacks the love that is consummated, showing it to be not a tender, if realistic, romance between the princess and the soldier, but rather, beneath the elegant language of love, a crude transaction in physical needs. . . . Aristo is attacking the social myths and their conventional language because they lie.[39]

To accept Angelica unmasked is intolerable, but the conventions of courtly love are equally unacceptable. The only answer, as Orlando learns from Astolpho's journey to the moon[40] and as Rinaldo recognizes when the drinking horn is passed around, is to not drink, to not accept the challenge to unmask, but to live with the illusion, knowing it to be illusion.[41] Otherwise, one becomes a Medoro, writing sonnets to Angelica in return for the *commodità* of her body.[42]

It may be objected that the Orlando episode just cited is better interpreted as Ariosto's remarkable and subtle presentation of the nature of self-deception, that the real difficulty is not that Angelica is unknowable and can be unmasked only by herself, but that Orlando prefers her to be unknowable because what he really loves is her angelic image, not her reality. However, Angelica is not presented through the eyes of Orlando alone, and thanks to her knowledge of magic, her part-time possession of the ring of invisibility, and her skill at disguising herself, she is only partly visible to the men in the poem and graspable by none of them except Medoro. Her resistance to being known carnally by her pursuers is understandable and comic for the audience and confusing to her would-be lovers. Although she cannot be taken as representative of womanhood in the poem (for in Ariosto's poem no one character is representative of the work's fluid and complex system of representation), she forcefully exhibits what Caretti terms "la particolare natura della narrative ariostesca," founded essentially on the "fluidità dinamica dell'azione, e quindi sulla velocità dei trapassi e sui mutamenti improvvisi di situazione."[43]

In Tasso's *Gerusalemme Liberata* (completed in 1577, forty-five years after the publication of the definitive third edition of the *Orlando Furioso* in 1532), we find the attempt to unmask another type of the unknowable woman, the female warrior. Clorinda, an Amazonian champion on the Saracen side, is modeled in some respects on the figure of Camilla in Vergil's *Aeneid,* as well as on the woman warriors of the *Orlando Furioso,* Bradamante and Marfisa. To Tancredi, the Christian knight who has fallen in love with her, Clorinda is closer in appearance to the figure of Petrarch's Laura. Although she always appears to him in armor, he can recognize her only when she removes her helmet, for it is her lovely face and long golden hair that have enamoured him. Although her particular skill is as an archer (a fact that unites her iconographically with images of Diana and of Camilla), she resents the fact that as an archer she is removed from actual hand-to-hand combat; in her encounters with Tancredi, she has usually made her way into the thick of battle in spite of the Saracen policy of keeping her on the ramparts. The conflict between love and war is acted out each time Tancredi encounters her, for he attempts to attack, but then recognizes her and is unable to continue.[44] In the sixth canto, Tancredi has been selected as the Christian champion who is to meet the Saracen Argantes in single combat, but he has ridden only part-way across the field when he suddenly sees Clorinda and is paralyzed, forgetful of his very purpose:

> Ed a quel largo pian fatto vicino,
> ov'Argante l'attende, anco non era,
> quando in leggiadro aspetto e pellegrino
> s'offerse a gli occhi suoi l'alta guerriera.
> Bianche via piú che neve in giogo alpino
> avea le sopraveste, e la visiera
> alta tenea dal volta; e sovra un'erta,
> tutta, quanto ella è grande, era scoperta.[45]

> [To that wide plain he had not yet drawn near
> There where Argantes now awaited him,
> When the tall warrior maid her aspect

Fair and strange presented to his eyes.
Whiter than snows on highest alpine ridge
The surcoat was she wore, open her visor
to display her face. Sublime she was revealed,
Above a steep ascent.]

He stands like a stone, "gelido tutto fuor, ma dentro bolle" [all ice without, but inside raging heat] and "sol di mirar s'appaga" [satisfied only by admiring her].[46] Masked by her armor, Clorinda is dangerous as a warrior; unmasked, she is even more dangerous, because she incapacitates one of the best warriors in the Crusaders' army. But there is more to her unmasking than this, for she does not recognize herself as the lovely woman beloved of Tancredi, and, in fact, she does not know who she is. Her white skin and her silvery-white armor are the signs, as yet unacknowledged, of her true identity. She has internalized a masculine idea of heroism, and, wishing to save the Saracen city from attack singlehandedly, she insists on making a midnight raid with Argantes to burn the battering rams built by the Christian army. Ismeno, her guardian, who has taken care of her since infancy, has a premonition of her death and must finally tell her of her true identity.

She is not a Saracen; her parents were both Ethiopian Christians, both black of skin. Clorinda herself was a miraculous birth: her father, Senapo, jealously guarded his beautiful wife in one room, on the walls of which was painted the story of St. George rescuing a fair white virgin from a dragon. When his wife gave birth to a white-skinned child, she was terrified that her husband would suspect her of adultery, and she had Ismeno sneak the infant Clorinda away after promising that he would raise her as a Christian. Haunted by guilty dreams, he has realized that she must be baptized; although she admits to similar dreams, she is loyal to the faith in which she has been raised and shrugs off the idea of conversion. Instead, she dresses herself in black armor so she will be invisible and sets off to fire the battering rams. But she is unable to return to the city walls and so is locked outside. It is then that Tancredi sees her and challenges her to battle. The scene is suffused with a tragic and almost perverse eroticism, for the lovers do not recognize each other:

Tre volte il cavalier la donna stringe
con le robuste braccia, ed altrettante
da que' nodi tenaci ella si scinge,
nodi di fer nemico e non d'amante.
Tornano al ferro, e l'uno e l'altro il tinge
con molte piaghe; e stanco e anelante
e questi e quegli al fin pur si ritira,
e dopo lungo faticar respira.[47]

[Three times the knight his lady clasps
With his strong arms, and thrice in turn
She frees herself from those tenacious bonds,
Of enemy steel and not for lovers made.

> They take their swords again, and each the other's
> Body dyes with many wounds until
> Exhausted and deprived of wind
> Both he and she at length declare an end
> And after long labor stop to breathe.]

As dawn begins to lighten, Tancredi can see the wounds he has made and rejoices. When he asks her to reveal her name, she refuses, and, enraged, they battle again. Finally, he inflicts the final blow:

> Spinge egli il ferro nel bel sen di punta
> che vi s'immerge e 'l sangue avido beve;
> e la veste, che d'or vago trapunta
> le mammelle stringea tenera e leve,
> l'empie d'un caldo fiume. Ella già sente
> morirsi, e 'l pie le manca egro e languente.[48]

> [In her fair bosom now he drives his sword
> Till point is bathed and thirsty drinks her blood;
> The shirt she wears, quilted rare with gold,
> That had embraced her soft and tender breasts,
> Is filled now with a torrent warm of blood.
> She knows she's dying, and
> Her weakened languid feet give way.]

Dying, Clorinda forgives him and asks to be baptized. He runs to a nearby brook to fill his helmet with water and returns to undo her helmet. Only then is she truly unmasked, truly revealed, to Tancredi and to herself. He manages to speak the words of baptism, and then collapses in a parody of union with her in death: "Già simile a l'estinto il vivo langue / al colore, al silenzio, a gli atti, al sangue" [The living man resembles now his lady dead, / in color, silence, wounds, and blood].[49] Both bodies must be carried to the Christian camp, where Tancredi, too weak to rage at his loss, slides toward despair. He is prevented from suicide by the firm words of Peter the Hermit: God is punishing Tancredi for having made himself "a heathen damsel's thrall" [drudo d'una fanciulla a Dio rubella].[50] As if in compensation for the holy man's severity, Clorinda appears to him in a dream, dressed in celestial glory, and declares her love for him.

These passages, all devoted to ladies who have died (the wife of Jacopone da Todi, Beatrice, Laura, Clorinda), come closest to successfully unmasking women and to finding a positive image that reveals the true nature of the beloved while reconciling the opposition between the earthly and the heavenly. Death, for the medieval audience and for that of the Counter-Reformation, invariably directed the gaze toward absolute and unchanging truths; after some natural indulgence in grief and the expression of loss, the poet-lover would inevitably imagine his lady among the blessed in heaven. With the perspective of five centuries, it is obvious how a dead and risen Beatrice was a more effective God-bearing image for Dante than the living woman, with her troubling physicality and blinding glance. But this does not explain why Laura cannot be a comparable God-bearing image for Petrarch, why Laura's image, instead, keeps alive for Petrarch (and for numerous poets after him) all the unresolved contradictions of the medieval view of women and of sense experience. If Laura's image bears anything for Petrarch that is analogous to what Beatrice's image carried for Dante, it is that Laura is a poetry-bearing image. In fact, it was suggested by contemporaries that Laura had never been a real woman, but had always been a fiction representing the power of poetry. In 1336 (twelve years before Laura died), Petrarch responded to this accusation in a letter to his friend Giacomo Colonna:

> [Y]ou say . . . that I invented the beautiful name of Laura to give myself something to talk about and to engage many minds to talk about me! And that in fact there is no Laura in my mind except that poetic Laurel for which evidently I have aspired with long-continued, unwearying zeal; and that concerning the living Laura, by whose person I seem to be captured, everything is manufactured; that my poems are fictitious, my sighs pretended. Well, on this head I wish it were all a joke, that it were a pretense and not a madness! But believe me, no one can simulate long without great effort; to labor to appear mad, to no purpose, is the height of madness. Add that we can in health imitate the behavior of the sick, but we cannot simulate real pallor. My pallor and my pains are well known to you.[51]

This is the same ingenuous argument made by sonnet XC: Laura is and is not real. If the reality that the ambiguous Beatrice points toward symbolically is Christ, the reality behind Laura's ambiguous image is the correspondingly ambiguous image of poetry. And later, in Ariosto, the reality behind Angelica is the human problem of illusion—that one cannot live without convention and illusion, but one must not be taken in by them, either. Love is a kind of madness, for the lady is not what she seems, and to love her unknowableness, her mystery, as one ought to love God, and stay sane is not possible. One must accept the masks of the courtly tradition or come to terms with the fact that, finally, the ladies of these poems do not exist (or, like Clorinda, must be killed): they are simply representative of a larger and more comfortably abstract philosophical problem. The troubling existence of real flesh-and-blood ladies is ignored, while the argument is transferred to a higher plane.

The courtly solution to the unknowability of women was the creation of self-consuming image of loveliness, often distant and unattainable.[52] But, in addition to the courtly context, there were other contexts that remind us of the grotesque and obsessive aspects of the drive to unmask women. I spoke earlier of the reassurance that came from the failure to unmask the saintly Christina of Markyate. But there are other unmaskings in saints' lives. Raymond of Capua, the confessor and biographer of St. Catherine of Siena, tells of being confounded and embarrassed by her teaching. She was ill and bedridden, but had to speak with him about some revelations she had experienced that day.

Qui cum ad eam venissem, astiti lectulo: et ipsa, quamvis febricitans, coepit more suo de Deo sermocinari, et recitare quae illa die fuerant sibi revelata. Ego autem audiens tam ingentia similiter et aliis insueta, immemor et ingratus primae gratiae tam receptae, intra me cogitavi in quibusdam: Putasne sint omnia vera quae dicit? Dumque sic cogitarem, et in faciem viri barbari, qui me fixis oculis intuendo, nimium terruit eratque facies oblonga, aetatis mediae, non prolixam habens barbam coloris triticei, majestatemque praeferens in aspectu, ex qua se manifeste Dominum ostendebat: nec aliam pro tunc ibi faciem discernere poteram, praeter illam.

[When I arrived I stood beside the bed and she, though feverish, began as usual to speak about God, and to tell me what he had revealed to her that day. As I listened to her speaking of things of such vast import and so far out of this world, oblivious of the former favour granted me, I ungratefully gave way to self-questionings once more. I said to myself: "Can I really take as true all that she is saying?" As she was speaking, and as these doubts were running through my mind, I kept my eyes fastened on her face. Suddenly it became the fact of a bearded man, gazing fixedly at me and filling my soul with awe. It was an oval face, that of a man of middle age, with a beard of medium length and of wheaten colour. The whole countenance bore a stamp of majesty which unmistakably marked out its owner as a lord amongst men. And whilst I gazed on it, no other face was visible but it alone.]53

Once Raymond realized that Christ was the true face and voice of Catherine, he was able to see her face again. He had no more doubts.

Blessed Villana dei Botti, a holy woman of fourteenth-century Florence, was unmasked by her mirror; she saw, as in a glass darkly, a horrifying vision of the inner deformity of her soul. Villana, born in 1332 into a rich merchant family, was precocious in piety. Imitating the life of St. Clare of Assisi, she attempted to run away from home to join a convent, but was caught by her father and immediately married. She discovered that she enjoyed the embraces of her husband, becoming, according to her biographer, a veritable Magdalen, and she abandoned herself to the joys of expensive dresses and jewels. One day, elaborately dressed and coiffed to attend a festivity at church with her husband, she paused in front of a mirror to admire her image:

[A]enigmatice prospexit, quantum apud Deum interioris animae plenitudo iam fuisset deformata: nempe, cum iterum atque iterum lumina studiosius infigeret, teterrimi spiritus imaginem se gestare, non hominis, in ipsis vestibus manifeste deprehendit.54

([S]he perceived as in a glass darkly how deformed her interior fullness of soul was in relation to God; and indeed, when she anxiously fixed her eyes again and again, she grasped very clearly, in those very clothes, an image of a most loathsome spirit, not a human being, presenting itself.)

Struck by the truth of this representation of herself, she tore off her fine clothing, rushed to the nearby church of Santa Maria Novella to confess, and embarked on a new life.[55] The unmasking has not been engineered by any human agency as far as she and her biographer are concerned, although we may suspect that sermons to women about the sins of expensive clothing and the sumptuary laws in effect in Florence may have helped bring the self-revelation to consciousness. The message is very clear in human terms—this pretty lady in the beautiful clothes is really a loathsome evil spirit.

The cruelest reminder that the drive to unmask derives from medieval misogyny is found in a French fabliau, also from the fourteenth century and known as "La Dame escolliée," translated as "The Lady Who Was Castrated."[56] The main plot—and its message—may easily be reconstructed from the title. There is a very contrary and domineering lady who has a weak husband and a beautiful daughter. A visiting count is smitten by the daughter's beauty and wishes to marry her, but he is appalled by the father's lack of authority and the consequent disordered situation in which his future bride is being taught by her mother how to treat men. The count cannot tolerate the appearance of role reversal in public. We overhear the mother tell her daughter:

> "Bele fille, levez la chiere,
> vers vostre seignor soiez fiere;
> Prenez essample a vostre mere
> Qui toz jors desdit vostre pere;
> Ainc ne dist riens ne desdeist
> Ne ne commanda c'on feist.
> Se vos volez avoir henor,
> Si desdites vostre seignor;
> Metez le arriere et vos avant,
> Petit faites de son coumant.
> S'ainsi faites, ma fille estres;
> Se nel faites, vos comparrez."

["Dear daughter, keep your head up. Be proud toward your lord. Follow your mother's example, always contradicting your father. He has never said anything that I haven't denied, and I've never done anything he commanded. If you want to have honor, contradict your lord. Thrust him back and push yourself forward, and seldom obey his commands. If you do this, you will be my daughter; if you don't, you will pay for it."][57]

The father, as we might expect in this context, is the voice of proper tradition:

> "Se vos honor avoir volez,
> Cremez vostre seignor le conte,
> Si que nun ne vos die honte;
> Soiez toz jors a son acort.
> Se nel fetez, vos avrez tort,
> Et s'en serez par tot blamee."

["If you want to have honor, fear your lord, the count, so that no one can speak shamefully of him. Always agree with him. If you don't, you will be wrong and criticized by everyone."]⁵⁸

As soon as the advice giving is completed, the worried count leaves with his new bride. His first didactic device is to present her with lessons along the way, killing her palfrey and greyhounds for disobeying his commands. Nevertheless, she still has an independent spirit, and when they arrive at court she contradicts his orders for the preparation of the meal. She is so severely beaten for this that she is bedridden for several months and repents. But then her mother comes to visit. The count, "qui dolenz ert / De son seignor, qui feme a male" [sorrowful because the lord had a bad wife]⁵⁹ and fearful that he still has not conquered his own wife, sends his father-in-law hunting to get him out of the way. Meanwhile, he prepares a stronger remedy for the problem—a mock castration—to remove the source of his mother-in-law's pride. As he observes to her:

> "[V]os avez de nostre orgueil,
> Vos avez coilles comme nos,
> S'en est vostre cuers orgueillous . . .
> ses ferai oster."

["You have our sort of pride. . . . You have balls like ours, and that's why your heart is so proud. . . . I'll have them removed."]⁶⁰

We can spare ourselves the details; what is important is that the lady herself comes to believe in the reality of her unmasking, as she is hacked up and a bull's balls are pulled out from under her skirt. The final outcome is exactly what is wanted:

> Dit la dame: "Sire, merci,
> Certes lealment vos affi,
> Et sor sainz le vos jurerai,
> Que mon seignor ne desdirai:
> Servirai le si com ge doi;
> Tenez, gel vos affi par foi."

[The lady said, "Sire, mercy! I swear to you truly, I'll swear on the saints that I won't contradict my lord. I will serve him as I ought to. I swear to you, on my honor."]⁶¹

Her husband also believes in the reality of the castration:

> Cil quide quo trestot voir soit
> Por les coillons que iluec voit;
> Por la dame qu'il voit navree
> Cuide qu'ele soit amendee.
> Le soirement e la fiance
> Fist la dame sanz demorance.
> Ses plaies li font reloier
> Et la letiere apareillier;
> Si l'enportent sor deus chevaus.

Ses plaies ne sont pas mortaus;
Bon mire ot qui bien l'a gari,
Son seignor ama et servi:
Onques puis nel desdit de rien.

. . .

Teus est de cest flabel la some;
Dahet feme qui despit home!

[The other thought that this was all true, since he saw balls there; and he thought that the wounded lady was improved. The lady swore her oath and promised, without delay. They had her wounds bound up, a litter prepared, and the two horses carried her off. Her wounds were not mortal. She had a good doctor who healed her completely. She loved and served her lord and never again contradicted him in anything. . . . This is the end of this fabliau: "Damn the woman who despises a man!"][62]

The translator's comment at the close of this tale is a masterpiece of understatement: "This tale is a vigorous, infuriated reassertion of the traditional male dominance of women in the face of the growing cult of courtly love."[63]

We can now see a number of patterns in the use of the motif of unmasking in both literary and documentary sources. Perhaps the most obvious pattern is that unmasking occurs when women either act independently of male authority or present themselves as authority figures. If a saint or a beloved lady tells her admirers what to do, the source for her authority must be revealed, for only if she is proved to be more spiritual, closer to heaven than they are, can she be allowed a dominant role. As Sir Gawain learns to his chagrin, appearances of women are deceiving, and control (such as the authority wielded by Morgan le Fay) may be manifested almost invisibly. A beautiful woman, one who creates desire, must also be unmasked; her beauty must be spiritualized, as in the *stilnovisti,* or her sexuality must be identified and repressed. This does not mean that Dante or Petrarch or Ariosto or Tasso was consciously misogynistic; rather, the presence of unmasking patterns in their poems indicates a deep structure of mistrust of female ambiguity in medieval and Renaissance culture. The unmasking of Blessed Villana indicates that women, too, had internalized a mistrust of physical beauty that might at times verge on self-hatred.[64] In the last analysis, the motif of unmasking fails to address the problems of the unknowability of women in medieval literature, for the women, unmasked, turn out to be angels or whores or castrated males or demons—but not female human beings.

Notes

1. *Sir Gawain and the Green Knight,* ed. L. Gollancz, Early English Text Society 210 (London: Oxford University Press, 1940), lines 943–945. [My translation]

2. Ibid., lines 951–953.

3. Ibid., lines 966–969.

4. For texts of the most influential writings, see Julia O'Faolain and Lauro Martines, eds., *Not in God's Image: Women from the Greeks to the Victorians* (New York: Harper & Row, 1973), and Susan Groag Bell, ed., *Women from the Greeks to the French Revolution* (Belmont, Calif.: Wadsworth, 1973). For an analysis of the impact of scientific and patristic teaching about women, a good starting point is Bernard P. Prusack, "Woman: Seductive Siren and Source of Sin?" in *Religion and Sexism,* ed. Rosemary Radford Reuther (New York: Simon and Schuster, 1974), pp. 89–116.

5. Eileen Power, "The Position of Women," in *The Legacy of the Middle Ages,* ed. C. G. Crump and E. F. Jacob (Oxford: Oxford University Press, 1938), p. 401.

6. I am thinking of the episode in the *Tristan* of Thomas in *Les Fragments du Roman du Tristan,* ed. Bartina Wind (Leiden: Brill, 1950). For an English translation, see *Gottfried von Strassburg Tristan with the Tristran of Thomas,* ed. and trans. A. T. Hatto (New York: Penguin, 1960).

7. The story of Patient Griselda is "The Clerk's Tale" in Chaucer's *Canterbury Tales* (*The Works of Geoffrey Chaucer,* ed. F. N. Robinson [Boston: Houghton Mifflin, 1957], pp. 101–112).

8. Chaucer's Clerk says that he learned the tale from a learned clerk named Fraunceys Petrak in Padua. The tale was first written down by Boccaccio as the closing tale in the *Decameron*. Petrarch was attracted to the story and translated it into Latin. For details on the transmission of the story, see J. Burke Severs, "The Clerk's Tale," in *Sources and Analogues of Chaucer's Canterbury Tales,* ed. W. F. Bryan and Germaine Dempster (New York: Humanities Press, 1958), p. 288.

9. For the poetry, see Jacopone da Todi, *Laude,* ed. Franco Mancini, Scrittori d'Italia 257 (Bari: Laterza, 1974). For a biographical and critical study, see George T. Peck, *Fool of God Jacopone da Todi* (University: University of Alabama Press, 1980).

10. Peck, *Fool of God,* p. 7. Peck is quoting from an early Franciscan biography.

11. Ibid., pp. 7–8. This is the *La Franceschina* text.

12. Ibid., p. 8.

13. For a full discussion, see ibid., pp. 225–233.

14. In treating this episode as an example of unmasking, I am deliberately ignoring certain political events within the Franciscan order that may have to do with the emphasis on asceticism and poverty in Jacopone's biography. Jacopone became a Franciscan, on the side of the Spirituals, at a time when St. Francis's ascetic ideals seemed impossibly harsh to many. Peck is quoting from an "official" biography in which the ascetic bias is immediately apparent. For more on this division within the order, and on Jacopone, see John Moorman, *A History of the Franciscan Order from Its Origins to the Year 1517* (Oxford: Clarendon Press, 1968), pp. 265–272 passim.

15. For a collection of Florentine documents, see Gene Brucker, ed., *The Society of Renaissance Florence: A Documentary Study* (New York: Harper & Row, 1971).

16. The documents concerning Angela are found in ibid., pp. 191–192.

17. Ibid., p. 191.

18. Ibid.

19. Ibid., p. 192. The clothes required of prostitutes were the same as those required of lepers; leprosy was generally thought of as a venereal disease (Saul N. Brody, *The Disease of the Soul: Leprosy in Medieval Literature* [Ithaca, N.Y.: Cornell University Press, 1974]).

20. *The Life of Christina of Markyate* [*De S. Theodora Virgine, Quae et dicitur Christina*], ed. and trans. C. H. Talbot (Oxford: Clarendon Press, 1959).

21. Christopher J. Holdsworth, "Christina of Markyate," in *Medieval Women,* ed. Derek Baker (Oxford: Basil Blackwell, 1978), pp. 185–204.

22. Eleanor McLaughlin, "Women, Power, and the Pursuit of Holiness in Medieval Christianity," in *Women of Spirit: Female Leadership in the Jewish and Christian Traditions,* ed. Rosemary Reuther and Eleanor McLaughlin (New York: Simon and Schuster, 1979), pp. 99–129, esp. pp. 108–115.

23. *Life of Christina of Markyate,* pp. 144–145.

24. On psychic (prophetic) power as essential to a reputation for sanctity, see Elizabeth A. Petroff, *Consolation of the Blessed: Women Saints in Medieval Tuscany* (Millerton, N.Y.: Alta Gaia, 1979); for statistics and commentary on the incidence of prophetic power in women saints' lives, see Donald Weinstein and Rudolph M. Bell, *Saints and Society: The Two Worlds of Western Christendom, 1000–1700* (Chicago: University of Chicago Press, 1982), esp. pp. 282–285.

25. Dante Alighieri, "La Vita Nuova," in *Tutte le Opere de Dante,* ed. Fredi Chiapelli (Milan: Mursia, 1969), pp. 387–388; Mark Musa, *Dante's Vita Nuova: A Translation and an Essay* (Bloomington: Indiana University Press, 1973), p. 39. The standard edition of the *Vita Nuova* is that by Michele Barbi (Florence: Bemporad, 1965).

26. Musa, *Dante's Vita Nuova,* pp. 89–174; Robert Hollander, "Vita Nuova: Dante's Perceptions of Beatrice," *Dante Studies* 102 (1974): 1–18. For English-speaking readers, the starting point for any study of the *Vita Nuova* is Charles S. Singleton, *An Essay on the Vita Nuova* (Baltimore: Johns Hopkins University Press, 1949). For works in Italian, see the entries on the *Vita Nuova* by Mario Pazzaglia in the *Enciclopedia Dantesca* and the bibliography cited there.

27. The groundwork on the mystical antecedents of the *Vita Nuova* in the Victorine school and St. Bonaventure is provided in A. Marigo, *Mistica e scienza nella "Vita Nuova" di Dante. L'unità del pensiero e le fonti mistiche, filosofiche e bibliche,* (Padua, 1914). Recent scholarship in English sees this aspect of Dante's work, and of earlier courtly poetry, as a deliberate parallel to the mystical experience. See Barbara Nolan, *The Gothic Visionary Perspective* (Princeton, N.J.: Princeton University Press, 1977); Bernard S. Levy, "Beatrice's Greeting and Dante's 'Sigh' in the *Vita Nuova,*" *Dante Studies* 92 (1974): 53–62; and Mario Pazzaglia, "La *Vita Nuova* fra agiografia e letteratura," in *Letture Classensi* (Ravenna: Longo Editore, 1978), vol. 6, pp. 189–210.

28. Here it is very important to distinguish between the *libro de la mia memoria,* in which the sonnets and poems to Beatrice are first written, and the *libello* of the *Vita Nuova,* the later commentary on those poems and on the experience they presented to the young poet. See Marziano Guglielminetti, "La *Vita Nuova* come autobiografia," in *Letture Classensi,* vol. 6, pp. 79–96. Forgetfulness, whether concerning a spiritual insight such as the perception of Beatrice's smile or involving the recollection of a more sustained vision, is a sign of undeveloped spiritual faculties; it would seem that the more mature Dante, writing the commentaries on the poems of his younger self recognized that the young Dante was not seeing and not remembering all that was being shown to him by the figure of Beatrice.

29. "Poscia che trattai d'Amore ne la soprascritta rima, vennemi volontade di volere dire anche in loda di questa gentilissima parole, per le quali io mostrasse come per lei si sveglia questo Amore, e come non solamente si sveglia la ove dorme, ma la ove non e in potenzia ella, mirabilmente operando, lo fa venire" (Dante, "Vita Nuova," p. 387). Musa translates: "Having dealt with Love in the last sonnet, I felt a desire to write more, this time in praise of that most gracious lady, showing how, through her, this Love is awakened, and how she not only awakens him there where he sleeps, but also, how she, miraculously working, brings him into existence there where he does notpotentially exist" (*Dante's Vita Nuova*, p. 39).

30. Levy, "Beatrice's Greeting," pp. 56–57.

31. Joan Ferrante, *Woman as Image in Medieval Literature* (New York: Columbia University Press, 1974), p. 126.

32. Ibid., p. 127.

33. Ibid.

34. For an English translation of the first part of her book, see Blessed Angela of Foligno, "From the *Liber de Vere Fidelium Experientia (The Book of the Experience of the Truly Faithful,"* in *Medieval Women's Visionary Literature,* ed. Elizabeth A. Petroff (New York: Oxford University Press, 1986), pp. 254–263. For the Latin text, see *Le Livre de l'experience des vrais fideles par Sainte Angele de Foligno,* ed. M.-J. Ferre, trans. M.-J. Ferre and L. Baudry (Paris: Editions Droz, 1927). Paul Lachance has translated Angela of Foligno for the Classics of Western Spirituality Series. He is the author of *The Spiritual Journey of Blessed Angela of Foligno According to the Memorial of Frater A.* (Rome: Pontificium Athenaeum Antonianum, 1984).

35. Guido Guinizelli, "Al cor gentil rempaira sempre amore," in *Medieval Song,* ed. James J. Wilhelm (New York: Dutton, 1971), pp. 216–217, 393–394.

36. *Petrarch's Lyric Poems: The Rime Sparse and Other Lyrics,* ed. Robert M. Durling (Cambridge, Mass.: Harvard University Press, 1976), p. 193. [My translation]

37. Ibid., p. 459.

38. Ludovico Ariosto, *Orlando Furioso,* in *Opere,* ed. Adriano Seroni (Milan: Mursia, 1970), Canto XXIII, stanza cxiv, line 102. For English translations, see Ariosto, *Orlando Furioso,* ed. Stewart A. Baker and A. Bartlett Giamatti, trans. William Stewart Rose (Indianapolis: Bobbs-Merrill, 1968), and *Orlando Furioso,* trans. Guido Waldman (Oxford: Oxford University Press, 1983).

39. A. Bartlett Giamatti, "Headlong Horses, Headless Horsemen: An Essay on the Chivalric Epics of Pulci, Boiardo, and Ariosto," in *Italian Literature: Roots and Branches,* ed. Giose Rimanelli and Kenneth John Atchity (New Haven, Conn.: Yale University Press, 1976), p. 301.

40. Ariosto, *Orlando Furioso,* Canto XXXIV, stanzas lxx–xcii.

41. Ibid., Canto XLII, stanzas ci–civ.

42. Giamatti, "Headlong Horses," p. 299, speaking of Canto XXIII.

43. Lanfranco Caretti, *Ariosto e Tasso* (Turin: Einaudi, 1977), p. 31.

44. For a new reading of this theme, see Paolo Braghieri, *Il Testo come soluzione rituale: Gerusalemme Liberata* (Bologna: Patron Editore, 1978). For a general introduction, see Caretti, *Ariosto e Tasso,* pp. 81–175. The first encounters are Canto I, 47–48; Canto III, 23–28.

45. Torquato Tasso, *Gerusalemme Liberata,* ed. Anna Maria Carini (Milan: Feltrinelli, 1961), p. 126. [My translation]

46. Ibid.

47. Ibid., p. 283.
48. Ibid., p. 285.
49. Ibid., p. 286.
50. Ibid., p. 290.
51. *Letters from Petrarch,* comp. and trans. Morris Bishop (Bloomington: Indiana University Press, 1966), p. 31. For the Latin text, with Italian translation, see *Francisco Petrarca Le Familiari,* ed. Enrico Bianchi (Turin: Einaudi, 1977), pp. 16–17.
52. Aldo Scaglione suggests that we do find real flesh-and-blood ladies in the works of Boccaccio, especially in the *Decameron* (*Nature and Love in the Late Middle Ages* [Berkeley: University of California Press, 1963], pp. 55–56). In writings by women, we also find female characters or female narrators who are more "real," less polarized into demonic or spiritual figures. One thinks of the women in the *lays* of Marie de France, the voices of the women troubadours, and the figure of Heloise in the correspondence with Abelard. See Katharina M. Wilson, ed., *Medieval Women Writers* (Athens: University of Georgia Press, 1984). Courtly writing by women, as might be expected, does not seem to believe that people—men or women—are unknowable. Individuals may wear masks in society, but intimacy allows lovers to remove their disguises for a time, at least. Male writers seem to think the nature of women is grounded in ambiguity, but female writers do not seem to think the same of men. There are, of course, exceptions to such a generalization—Ovid's *Heroides,* for instance, or Boccaccio's *Elegia di Madonna Fiammetta.*
53. *Vita S. Catharinae Senensis,* part 1, chap. v, par. 90, in *Acta Sanctorum quotquot toto orbe coluntur vel a catholicis scriptoribus celebrantur . . . ,* ed. Johannes Carnandet, 65 vols. (Paris, 1863–1931), April 30; *The Life of S. Catherine of Siena by Raymond of Capua,* trans. Conleth Kearns (Wilmington, Del.: Michael Glazier, 1980), p. 82. The *Acta Sanctorum* is the collection, begun by the Belgian Bollandist Fathers in the seventeenth century, of the lives of all those who have been canonized or beatified by the Catholic Church. The lives are indexed according to the saints' (death) days. December and the last twenty days of November are not included. Since the pagination of each edition of the *Acta Sanctorum* differs slightly, it is best to look up the saints' lives by date, and then by chapter and paragraph number.
54. *Vita de B. Villanae Bottiae,* chap. i, par. 5, in *Acta Sanctorum,* August 26. [My translation]
55. Blessed Villana was born in 1332 and died in 1360. The Black Death is not mentioned in her story, but it is worth noting that she would have been sixteen in 1348; this vision evidently took place shortly after her marriage, and Florentine girls were usually married by sixteen. She ran to the church of Santa Maria Novella, where the storytellers of Boccacio's *Decameron* met and where Passavanti preached repentance after the plague. For more details on this pattern of conversion in women saints, see the evidence in Weinstein and Bell, *Saints and Society.*
56. "La Dame escolliée," in *Recueil general et complet des fabliaux des XIIIᵉ et XIVᵉ siècles,* ed. Anatole de Montaiglon and Gaston Raynaud (Paris: Librarie des Bibliophiles, 1890), vol. 6, pp. 95–116; "The Lady Who Was Castrated," in *Bawdy Tales from the Courts of Medieval France,* trans. and ed. Paul Brians (New York: Harper & Row, 1972), pp. 24–36.
57. "La Dame escolliée," p. 103; "Lady Who Was Castrated," p. 28.
58. "La Dame escolliée," p. 103; "Lady Who Was Castrated," p. 28.

59. "La Dame escolliée," p. 110; "Lady Who Was Castrated," p. 32.
60. "La Dame escolliée," p. 112; "Lady Who Was Castrated," p. 33.
61. "La Dame escolliée," p. 113; "Lady Who Was Castrated," p. 34.
62. "La Dame escolliée," p. 115; "Lady Who Was Castrated," p. 35.
63. "Lady Who Was Castrated," p. 36.
64. Weinstein and Bell, *Saints and Society,* pp. 98–99.

3

A New Feminine Spirituality: The Beguines and Their Writings in Medieval Europe

If we were to chart the history and the geography of women's spirituality in search of those times and places in which women were particularly empowered to develop spiritual gifts, we would have to return to the early thirteenth century and focus on the beguines in the parish of Liège (medieval Lotharingia, modern Belgium) and in nearby Antwerp. On the peripheries of urban centers, we would see self-supporting communities of women who lived by the work of their hands, cared for the sick and the poor, experimented with new devotional practices that increased their compassion and wisdom, and wrote devotional and mystical treatises, works that scholars are first beginning to appreciate and study as remarkable explorations of feminine psychology. Here,

> as nowhere else in Europe, the newly emancipated women religious were able to evolve a way of life hitherto unknown in the West, free from monastic enclosure, observing the rules which they themselves devised to meet the needs of individual communities, following lives of intense activity which might be devoted to prayer, to teaching and study, to charitable works, or to all three.[1]

The end of the twelfth century and the beginning of the thirteenth were unusual and creative times for women, unlike earlier centuries and far different from what was to come. At this time (ca. 1175–1250), and for reasons still not entirely understood, a movement developed all over western Europe of women with religious vocations who were unwilling—or simply too poor—to fit into the earlier models of female monasticism or of marriage and childbearing. In great numbers, women were seeking an unstructured, nonhierarchical spiritual life that was both active (in the sense of ministering to the needs of others) and contemplative (in the sense that meditation and visionary experience were highly valued and developed).[2] The communities that evolved were radical in medieval terms and would still be considered radical today.

In northern Europe, this women's movement was identified with the beguines; in southern Europe, the same kinds of impulses and social arrangements were to be found among the Umiliati and the early followers of St. Francis and St. Clare. Laymen were also involved in this movement, as beghards and as male tertiaries, as were a few churchmen, but the majority were women, women who could not, or who did not wish to, become either wives or nuns. The women's movement was a part of the new spirituality of this period, which emphasized a return to apostolic Christianity and focused on the humanity of Christ and his mother.[3] Women sought a life of evangelical poverty so that they could live as Christ and his mother had lived; they wanted the opportunity to work, wanted a self-sufficiency based not on income from property but on the work of their hands. They wanted a daily religious practice, the education to pursue that practice intelligently, and the opportunity to discuss spiritual ideas among themselves. They desired flexibility of commitment and of life-style so that there would be room for active charity in the world as well as for a solitary contemplative existence when the need arose. They were happy to live chaste lives in completely female communities, but they preferred not to take permanent vows of chastity, and they resisted strict enclosure.[4]

There is much we still have to learn about the beguines, but we have an invaluable introduction in the *Life of Marie d'Oignies,* written by her confessor and disciple, Cardinal Jacques de Vitry. Here we see the beliefs that guided a new generation of spiritually oriented women,[5] for this *Vita* was intended to publicize the activities of Marie and her followers in Liège and to protect this new group by establishing for it a pedigree that would be acceptable to ecclesiastical authorities suspicious both of women and of innovations in the spiritual life.

Marie d'Oignies is the first "beguine" whose biography we know. She was born around 1177 to a wealthy and respected family of Nivelles in the diocese of Liège. She was married when she was fourteen, in 1191. That same year, she and her husband, agreeing on a vow of chastity, went to work in the leper colony at Willambrouk.[6] In 1207, when she decided she wanted a more austere and more spiritual life, she moved to the Augustinian community of St. Nicholas of Oignies near Namur; four years later, in 1211, Jacques de Vitry would be a regular canon there. The community of St. Nicholas of Oignies was a coenobium founded by secular priests for those seeking apostolic perfection and a balance of contemplation and intensive pastoral care. It was not affiliated with any religious order, and it admitted lay sisters and brothers. A group of women, who seem to have been attracted to the community's life-style and to Marie's example, also joined, living next to the canons of St. Nicholas. But soon, perhaps by 1210 but certainly by the death of Marie in 1213, their residence had become overcrowded, and a new beguinage had to be built. This new beguinage in turn became the center of a cluster of beguine-occupied dwellings. Municipal records from the 1280s indicate that women had for some time been willing their houses to other single women so that they might live in the area of the new beguinage. Each sister occupied her own cottage, but the sisters spent most of their time in common and ate meals together.[7] Surely Marie moved to St. Nicholas because she saw something in the community that she wanted to share, but she also brought something new to it. This "something new" has been difficult to define; contemporary observers commented on the intensity of her rejection of her background and the depth of her devotion to Christ and her fellow Christians. Like many women in northern and southern Europe, she came from a well-to-do background, and yet she desired a mendicant life. As Jacques de Vitry tells it,

> She conceived such a great love for poverty through the spirit of fear that she barely even wanted to possess the necessities of life. Thus one day she made plans to flee so that, unknown and despised among strangers, she might beg from door to door, that naked she might follow the naked Christ. . . . Thus she wished to be fed with alms and she wanted to be received in strangers' houses. She burned with such a desire for poverty that she took with her a little bag in which to put alms and a little cup from which she might drink water or into which she might put food if it were given to her while she was begging.[8]

Her friends were so horrified at her intention that she was forced to heed their pleas, and she abandoned her plan. (St. Clare of Assisi evidently had the same impulse and, even when forced to accept an enclosed life, clung fiercely to what she called the "privilege of poverty," the right to live in community without owning property. Her commitment to evangelical poverty is discussed in Chapter 4.)

The term *beguine* probably originated as a derogatory label for a female heretic, perhaps associated with the Albigensians, perhaps referring to the color of the robes worn by beguines.[9] The movement as a whole—never codified by its members and never identified with individual leaders— lasted in northern Europe (especially in the area around Liège) until the French Revolution. Ernest McDonnell believes that the beguine movement was characterized by four stages. In the first stage, individual ecstatic women lived scattered about the city, leading strict religious lives while remaining in the world. Theirs was a spontaneous movement with no founder and no legislator, and the women were simply called "holy women" (*mulieres sanctae*). Only at the beginning of the thirteenth century did these holy women begin to organize themselves into congregations centered on spiritual discipline and common tasks:

> The women submitted to a grand mistress, aided by a council of other mistresses, each with a specific function. In organization and daily practices they

often emulated the nunnery. They held meetings, followed common exercises, performed acts of charity, and recommended compulsory prayers. But ordinary religious practices remained parochial as before. To foster piety, practical or contemplative, to hold aloof from the dangers of the world without stopping ordinary work, such was their aim.[10]

It was at this second stage of growth in McDonnell's schema that the Church intervened, believing that if the women were going to build communities, those communities ought to be under the control of one of the existing orders. But the existing orders were not interested in taking in more women, especially poor women without dowries, and they made no allowance for women who supported themselves by working. At this point, Jacques de Vitry became the beguines' spokesman, and the women received papal consent to form their own self-regulated communities.[11]

The third stage identified by McDonnell was that of enclosure: communities, at first quite small, grew around infirmaries and hospices in which the holy women worked. At the same time, other women who identified themselves as beguines continued to live at home or as solitaries, meeting occasionally with other like-minded women. Spiritual guidance for these communities was generally provided by Franciscan or Dominican friars or by the Cistercians, who were supposed to preach to them and to hear the women's confessions regularly. In terms of ecclesiastical organization, this was a new departure that required a break with parish life and the assignment of spiritual advisers specifically for these groups. The men who took on the role of spiritual adviser were quite enthusiastic about it, to judge by the words of Jacques de Vitry and Thomas de Cantimpré, biographers of the first beguines in Liege.

The fourth stage organized the beguine enclosure into a parish:

> The full-blown beguinage comprised a church, cemetery, hospital, public square, and streets and walks lined with convents for the younger sisters and pupils and individual houses for the older and well-to-do inhabitants. In the Great Beguinage at Ghent, with its walls and moats, there were at the beginning of the fourteenth century two churches, eighteen convents, over a hundred houses, a brewery, and an infirmary.[12]

Male writers defended the holy women on the ground of the exemplary simplicity and purity of their life-style, the importance of their economic self-sufficiency, and the profound emotionality of their spiritual life. The emotional fulfillment that may have been lacking in the medieval notion of marriage and motherhood was found by beguine women in their relationship with the divine and, no doubt, was reinforced by their living and working together to create a supportive environment. As R. W. Southern summarizes: "In many ways it is an idyllic picture—women escaping from the sordid frustrations of the world into the liberty of an unpretentious spiritual life: enjoying vivid experiences of a loving God, and occupied in useful services ranging from the care of the sick to the embroidery of ecclesiastical vestments."[13] Yet, he adds, "these women and their way of life raised up enemies, all in some degree afraid and not all unreasonably."[14]

Perhaps one of the reasons the new holy women elicited such varying responses was that their lives were so various—each woman or small cluster of women might take a different path to the same goal of spiritual enlightenment. Brenda Bolton, speaking of the first movement of holy women around Liège, emphasizes the multiplicity of life-styles:

> [T]heir lives bring us into contact with most of the possible forms of religious life available to women at the time in this area: a beguine, Mary of Oignies, a recluse Ivetta of Huy, a Dominican tertiary Margaret of Ypres, a Cistercian nun Lutgard of Aywieres and Christina of St. Trond, called *Mirabilis,* claimed by Benedictines, Cistercians and Premonstratensians alike but who in reality was not attached to any religious order nor to a beguine group.[15]

The earliest description we have of the behavior of these loosely affiliated groups of women was written by Jacques de Vitry, in his *Life of Marie d'Oignies.*[16] This biography is at once a defense of a whole community of women[17] and of their experiences of love:

> You . . . saw . . . some of these women dissolved with such a particular and marvelous love toward God that they languished with desire, and for years had rarely been able to rise from their cots. They had no other infirmity, save that their souls were melted with desire of Him, and sweetly resting with the Lord, as they were comforted in spirit they were weakened in body. . . . The cheeks of one were seen to waste away, while her soul was melted with the greatness of her love. Another's flow of tears had made visible furrows down her face. Others were drawn with such intoxication of spirit that in sacred silence they would remain quiet a whole day, with no sense of feeling for things about them, so that they could not be roused by clamour or feel a blow. . . . I saw another who sometimes was seized with ecstasy five-and-twenty times a day, in which state she was motionless, and on returning to herself she was so enraptured that she could not keep from displaying her inner joy with movements of the body, like David leaping before the ark.[18]

This is the language of the Song of Songs and of a certain kind of medieval love poetry, of *amour courtois* and *Minnemystik,* of the great beguine writers Hadewijch of Antwerp and Beatrijs of Nazareth (also known as Beatrijs van Tienen), whose works we discuss in this chapter. The behavior he is describing suggests that some of the women of Liège were practicing a very physical *imitatio Christi.*[19] But de Vitry is utilizing this rhetoric for specific ends. Carol Neel alerts us to de Vitry's interest in proposing the beguine life-style, and Marie's life in particular, as an orthodox alternative to Albigensian women's roles.[20] But there is more going on in this lengthy description of women's spiritual experiences. In this passage he does not speak of the contents of the visions these women were experiencing; he is describing them as creditable ecstatics, primarily on the basis of their physical behavior. He is, in fact, protecting them by making them seem harmless—that is, by making them seem traditional or by assimilating them into a medieval stereotype, the holy nun. You would not expect, reading this passage, that such women were experiencing visions of violence and dismemberment, as well as of erotic love. You would not think that such women could go out and change the world, yet that is exactly what they did. Perhaps the greatest contribution of the women associated with the beguine movement is to be found in their writings, for it is there that they explored the experience of both human and divine love in new and unforgettable ways. The experiences of love and desire that de Vitry describes from the outside are described as interior states by the beguine writers of the next generation.

Two Mystical Beguines: Beatrijs of Nazareth and Hadewijch of Antwerp

In their mystical writings, both poetry and prose, in Latin and in the vernacular languages, the beguine writers do what women have rarely done in literature: they describe, represent, praise, and worship their experience of love, desire, and *jouissance,* providing modern readers with an unparalleled map to the territory. Hadewijch of Antwerp[21] and Beatrijs of Nazareth[22] both recognize the complexity of desire and acknowledge its experience as disturbing, exhilirating, chaotically new, even maddening. Both women are concerned with mapping out this new experience, with writing topologies and typologies of it. For them, desire or love is *Minne,* a feminine noun; it is both a yearning for love and the nature of love itself. Although there is obviously a painful side to love, imaged as wounding, capture, transfixion, penetration (the metaphors come equally from the language of the hunt and from that of the crucifixion), and a dependence on love for satisfaction, it is the joys of love, desire both as pleasure in itself and as a process of transformation, that dominate in their writings.

In speaking their love, Hadewijch of Antwerp and Beatrijs van Tienen, like other medieval women mystics, show us a colloquy between a woman and her god that implies, as Julia Kristeva says of Plato, that "at the very base of philosophical discourse love and the soul cannot be separated."[23] The experience of love is founded less on what Lacan terms desire, which is masculine, born of separation and ever-deferring satisfaction, as it is on *jouissance,* a primal, contiguous sexuality, existing outside of linguistic norms in the realm of the poetic.[24] This feminine experience of love, which often purported to be an "out-of-the-body" trance state, actually describes the body in loving through the sensuality, the eroticism, and the description of ecstatic states, as well as by the attention to bodily functions, such as eating and not eating, and by the manifestation of bodily illness as a symptom of love. Love must be learned through relationship, and in the representation of such a relationship we see the discovery of the woman, the mother in god, and the god(dess) in the woman.

Much of the literature of the Middle Ages, beginning with the twelfth century, speaks of love, in personal lyrics as well as in popular romances.

While the vocabulary of secular love poetry clearly influenced women's language, more directly influential were Scripture (notably the Song of Songs) and scriptural commentaries (particularly the Bernardine and Cistercian commentaries on the Song of Songs, along with meditative texts on the life and crucifixion of Christ, such as the Pseudo-Bonaventure *Meditations on the Life of Christ*).[25] Investigation of what devotional books beguines owned, commissioned, composed, or illuminated is just beginning, and it may be that we will find that in the beguines' private devotions, female figures, such as St. Catherine of Alexandria[26] or the Virgin Mary, were just as significant as the male figure of Christ. Current philosophical ideas on the nature of love emanating from the School of Chartres may have had some influence on Hadewijch's language for love, but for the most part the women mystics were independent thinkers, using Scripture to validate their experience and the vocabulary of secular poetry to describe some aspects of desire and inventing their own terminology for experiential states not spoken of in secular love lyrics. The desire they speak of is the highest good, equated with God in some way, and in other respects larger than God.

Beatrijs of Nazareth

Beatrijs of Nazareth (named for the Cistercian convent where she was prioress) was a Netherlands mystic, born in 1200 at Tienen (Tirlemont) in the diocese of Liège into a family that was wealthy, pious, and well-educated.

> Gertrude, her mother, was renowned for her holiness and charity; her father, Barthélémy, after his wife's death, accompanied his daughters, Beatrice, Christine, and Sibylle, to their various convents which he helped to found. . . . Together with his son, who like him had become a lay brother, he followed the Cistercian Rule but still found time to look after the practical affairs of the convents of Florival (Bloemendael), Val des Vierges (Maagdendael), near Oplinter in Brabant, as well as Nazareth, near Lierre. Two other children of his had also entered religious orders.[27]

Beatrijs was taught to read by her mother and was said to have memorized the Psalms by the time she was five. Her mother died when Beatrijs was about seven, and Beatrijs was sent to the beguine school at Léau, where she began her study (in Latin) of the liberal arts. When she was ten, she entered the convent school at Florival, where she finished all seven liberal arts, the trivium and the quadrivium.[28] She was accepted as a novice at Florival when she was fifteen and took her vows a year later, when she was sent to the convent of La Ramée to study calligraphy and manuscript illumination. In 1221 she moved again, this time to the Val des Vierges convent at Oplinter; she took her final vows there in 1225. She moved to the convent of Nazareth in 1236; she was prioress there from 1237 until her death in 1268.

Beatrijs wrote a vernacular treatise in rhymed prose (perhaps originally a section of her autobiography in Dutch[29]) called *Seven manieren van Minne,* or *Seven Manners of Loving.*[30] *Minne,* or love, is an evolutionary process, a maturation, in which Beatrijs distinguishes seven phases or styles. Although typically these manners proceed in succession, it seems likely that one might "revert" to earlier phases from time to time. Distinguishing the stages in the growth of love was characteristic of the mystical writings of the Victorine school, with which Beatrijs was clearly familiar, but she surpasses her models to an astonishing degree and at the same time creates a new vocabulary in Dutch (rather than Latin) to communicate her mystical experiences.

The first sentence of the work suggests a Platonic orientation:

"Love takes seven forms which come from the apex (*uten hoegsten*) and return to the summit (*ten oversten*)." Love starts from what is highest and comes back to this height: it is the Neo-Platonic movement of exit and return. . . . But this happens within an exchange of her love with a transcending Love, an abyss of love drawing the soul so that she may reach her profound being in God Who is "High and supreme nobleness in His essence" (I, par. 7, line 61). This gift arouses desire which, in its turn, is nourished by the gift. "To render love to Love" surely presumes the encounter of two subjects.[31]

The first manner or stage of love, says Beatrijs, begins with a choice, a self-conscious "active longing" based on the desire for perfection and the awareness of a lack; it is a gaining of self, not a loss: "The soul striving with whole attention and great longing to preserve itself." Activity is stressed; the soul is seeking, entreating, learning, gaining Love, whose nature is purity, exaltation, supreme excellence. "It is this striving which love teaches to those who serve love."[32]

Beatrijs' second manner of loving is compared to a "maiden who serves her master only for her great love of him . . . to serve love with love, without measure, beyond measure, and beyond human sense and reason."[33] The key concepts are the boundlessness and unconditionality of love as the soul actively serves love, limitlessly offering herself without asking anything in return. Again, the soul *is* Love as she serves her.

The third manner combines the first two; "desire grows violent" in the soul, wanting to make all its works "perfect in love, withholding nothing and counting nothing." *Excess, violence,* and *torment* are repeated words here, for what the soul "longs to do is impossible and unnatural to created beings, but it cannot moderate or restrain or calm itself."[34] The lover finds she has made an absolute and active commitment of all her nature to desire and to the pain of being unable to live out that absolute.

The fourth manner of loving brings sweetness to desire; God or Love begins to work within the soul, and a new being comes into existence. The eroticism here is delicate, unlike the violence of the previous stage. As the soul is "powerfully assailed" and "altogether conquered by love," the heart is "tenderly touched," "wholly encompassed," "lovingly embraced." The subjective experience is of "great closeness to God," "spiritual brightness," "wonderful richness," a "noble freedom" in the "great compulsion of violent love" and "overflowing fullness of great delight." This detailed analysis speaks of what happens to the body, too. "The spirit sinks down into Love, the body seems to pass away, the heart to melt, every faculty to fail . . . the limbs and senses lose their powers."[35]

One might expect that the experience of desire could go no further, but we are only at the midpoint of Beatrijs's scheme. In the fifth manner, the soul is again very active; the eroticism and the violence are intensified, as Love is "powerfully strengthened" and "rises violently up," seeming to "break the heart with its assault." Simultaneously, the soul is characterized by a seemingly limitless energy, or potency, so that even when it is "resting in the sweet embrace of love," it feels "there is nothing it cannot do and perform." The soul suffers from dependence, impatience, deep dissatisfaction, but it can go no further, so the heart is wounded again and again; it seems the "veins are bursting, the marrow withering, the bones softening, the heart burning, the throat parching . . . in the fever of love." The soul is being transformed in the crucible of desire, and Love is a "devouring fire," relentless, uncontrollable, trying to force the soul beyond what it would have believed possible. Reason has no place here; the soul is "so conquered by the boundlessness of love that it cannot rule itself by reason," for it loves through a contradiction: "what most afflicts and torments the soul is that which most heals and assuages it."[36]

The sixth manner of loving is stable and confident; the soul's transformation is complete, and desire has become not the object of knowing but a way of knowing. Beatrijs uses three metaphors for this state of desire. The soul is like a housewife "who has put all her household in good order and prudently arranged it and well disposed it" and always "knows how everything should be." The soul is exploring a new world, "like the fish, swimming in the vast sea and resting in its deeps, and like the bird, boldly mounting high in the sky, so the soul feels its spirit freely moving through the vastness and the depths and the unutterable richnesses of Love."[37] The following of desire has brought the soul knowledge, order, and freedom.

What the soul does not yet know (for Love still keeps something hidden) is that it is "master of itself . . . living the life of the angels here in the flesh." This is the seventh and final stage, in which the soul is drawn "above humanity, into love, and above human sense and reason and above all the works of the heart . . . with love into eternity and incomprehensibility . . . and into the limitless abyss of Divinity," but it suffers at remaining in estrangement on earth and longs to go home, "where already it has established its dwelling."[38]

Hadewijch of Antwerp

Hadewijch of Antwerp was a Netherlands mystic whose life was contemporary with that of Beatrijs. She was a prolific writer, and, while she reveals

a great deal about her inner life in her poems, visions, and letters, hardly
anything is known of her outer life.[39] She seems to have edited her own
works, balancing the forty-five poems in stanzas in the troubadour tradition with a group of forty-five other compositions (thirty-one letters and
fourteen visions). Her theory of *Minne*, or Love, is too complex to try to
summarize here, and my intention in quoting from her works is to give the
flavor of her personal experience of desire, in its most difficult as well as in
its most fulfilling moments. (I discuss her stanzaic poems, the *Strophische
Gedichten*, in Chapter 10.)

Hadewijch's collection "Letters to a Young Beguine" is intended to
guide young women through *orewoet*, or "stormy longing," to fruition, and
she is very forthright about the frustration and suffering involved in the
pursuit of *Minne*. In the opening letter she says: "[T]hough I talk of an
unbearable sweetness I have never, never known it, except only in the wish
of my heart."[40] But she clearly has experienced and feels entitled to some
kind of fruition, or *jouissance*, for later in the same letter she says: "But it is
He who has taken himself away from me. What He is, that He consumes in
the sweetness of his joy, and leaves me to lament thus, deprived of that
delight . . . burdened down with my fruitless longings . . . joyless of
all the joys that should replenish me."[41]

Love is playing a game with her: "Now it is as if someone were making
sport of me, offering me something and then, as I stretch out my hand,
knocking it away and saying, 'Wouldn't you like it?' and taking it away
again."[42]

In Letter 8, she addresses the process of the transformation of the soul
into Love that Beatrijs described as the fifth manner of loving, but Hadewijch's representation of the experience is more brutal, more violent. She
begins with observing that there are two kinds of "dread" in love. The first
is that ennobling type her readers must have been familiar with from
secular love poetry. The lover, afraid he is not worthy of his love, improves
himself morally, grows in humility, and generally behaves himself more
wisely and charitably than he did earlier. It is the second type of dread that
interests Hadewijch—the fear that Love does not love one enough. "This
noble mistrust," this dread, she says,

> breaks the conscience wide open. Even if a man loves until he fears that he is
> going mad, till his heart grows sick, till the blood chills in his veins and his soul
> perishes, if it is true Love which he loves, this noble mistrust prevents him
> from feeling or trusting Love. . . . [M]istrust renews longing, for he can
> never be sure. . . . One fears that he does not love enough and that he is not
> loved enough.[43]

He must learn "to accept all sufferings, not justify himself with ready
answers," and he must make a place in his heart "for the peace of true love,
even if this meant loving the devil himself."[44] Desire leads one straight out
of society, Hadewijch seems to say, into a place in the mind where there are

no guidelines from past experience, no rules, just a continuing deep openness of longing.

In Letter 9, Hadewijch speaks of the mutual indwelling of Love in both lovers that unites them yet leaves them in possession of individual selves:

> Love so dwells in all the beloved that neither can perceive difference between them. But they possess one another in mutual possession, their mouths one mouth, their hearts one heart, their bodies one body, their souls one soul, and sometimes one sweet divine nature transfuses them both, and they are one, each wholly in the other, and yet each one remains and will always remain himself.[45]

This exalted love is like that between all lovers—literally consuming, "concealing little, giving much, finding most in their close communion with one another, each one as it were tasting all, eating all, drinking all, consuming all the other."[46]

Hadewijch sees Love as her highest good, an abstract principle that yet has physical, bisexual, attributes: "In this joy no one can have a part who is without Love . . . but only that soul which is suckled at the breast of the boundless joy of our great Love, which is chastised by Love's fatherly rod, which cleaves inseparably to him, which reads its sentence in His countenance, and then remains in peace."[47]

"True love," she says, "is no material thing; true Love is beyond matter, immeasurable in God's great freedom, giving always from its superabundance, working always in its ability, always growing in its nobility."[48] Endlessly giving, endlessly potent, endlessly noble—this is the nature of desire. Is Love more than God? In another letter she observes: "Love holds God's divinity captive within its nature."

In the writings of Beatrijs and Hadewijch, along with those of other beguine-associated writers, we find a number of shared beliefs. The view expressed of the nature of desire, especially the insistence on the fact that yearning is both painful and satisfying in itself and that "satisfaction," or "fulfillment" (whatever those terms mean), itself encloses and releases desire, suggests to me that beguine writers envisioned love as what contemporary theorists call *jouissance,* a kind of boundaryless sexuality in which desire and satisfaction cannot be distinguished, just as masculine and feminine cannot be distinguished. This indistinguishability of masculine and feminine, the inherent bisexuality of loving, seems to be another common element in the beguine writers' representations of desire. If we look at their writings as explorations of ways of knowing, we see that body is deeply implicated in their epistemology: knowing is performed not by the soul alone, but by the whole person—body, soul, and heart.

There are also common traits in the representation of the ideal object of desire, the ideal lover, who in turn cannot be separated from the ideal, the desired, relationship. The beloved depicted by medieval beguines emphasizes equality—in fact, male and female in the relationship are almost interchangeable. Hadewijch speaks of the two lovers merging, becoming indistinguishable. Since one of the lovers is God, such merging implies that desire is Godlike, that God's desire is human. It is the mutuality of desire, in fact, that creates the two lovers as equals. The ideal love relationship is based on communion, communication, support; God speaks with the women he loves, tells them how wonderful they are, rewards them publicly for their actions on his behalf. Ultimately, the most important characteristic of desire for these women is that it is empowering: without love, without feeling desire, the women are alone, isolated, abandoned; once they surrender to desire and follow its lead, they are empowered, capable of anything and all things.

Notes

1. Eric Colledge, ed. and trans., *Mediaeval Netherlands Religious Literature* (New York: London House and Maxwell, 1965), p. 8.

2. On beguines in general, see Ernest W. McDonnell, *The Beguines and Beghards in Medieval Culture* (New Brunswick, N.J.: Rutgers University Press, 1953; New York: Octagon, 1969), and R. W. Southern, *Western Society and the Church in the Middle Ages* (Baltimore: Penguin, 1970), esp. pp. 309–331. On the beguines as a women's movement and its economic goals, see Elise Boulding, *The Underside of History* (Boulder, Colo.: Westview Press, 1976), pp. 415–449; Carolly Erickson, *The Medieval Vision* (Oxford: Oxford University Press, 1976), pp. 210–217; and JoAnn McNamara and Suzanne Wemple, "Sanctity and Power," in *Becoming Visible: Women in European History,* ed. Renate Bridenthal and Claudia Koonz (Boston: Houghton Mifflin, 1977). On the problems caused by women's desires for a new spiritual life, see John B. Freed, "Urban Development and the 'Cura Monialium' in Thirteenth-Century Germany," *Viator* 3 (1972): 311–327; and Brenda Bolton, "Mulieres Sanctae," in *Women in Medieval Society,* ed. Susan M. Stuard (Philadelphia: University of Pennsylvania Press, 1976), and *"Vitae Matrum:* A Further Aspect of the *Frauenfrage,"* in *Medieval Women,* ed. Derek Baker (Oxford: Basil Blackwell, 1978), pp. 253–273. On feminine piety in the diocese of Liège in Belgium, see Simone Roisin, *L'Hagiographie cistercienne dans la diocèse de Liège au xiiie siècle* (Louvain: Bibliothèque de l'université, 1947), and "L'Efflorescence cistercienne et le courant féminin de piété au xiiie siècle," *Revue d'histoire ecclésiastique* 39 (1945): 458–486.

3. On the evangelical life, see M.-D. Chenu, *Nature, Man, and Society in the Twelfth Century: Essays on New Theological Perspectives in the Latin West,* ed. and trans. Jerome Taylor and Lester K. Little (Chicago: University of Chicago Press, 1968), pp. 202–269.

4. For information on specific communities, see Roisin, *L'Hagiographie cistercienne;* Benjamin de Trouyer, "Beguines et Tertiares en Belgique et aux Pays-Bas aux XII–XIVe siècles," in *I Frati Penitenti de S. Francesco . . . ,* ed. Mariano d'Alatri (Rome: Istituto Storico dei Cappuccini, 1977), pp. 133–138; Pierre Peanò, "Les Béguines du Languedoc ou la crise du T.O.F. dans la France méridionale . . . ," in *I Frati Penitente,* ed. d'Alatri, pp. 139–158; Joseph M. H. Albanes, *La Vie de Sainte Douceline, fondatrice des béguines de Marseille* (Marseille: E.

Camoin, 1879); Brenda Bolton, "Some Thirteenth-Century Women in the Low Countries: A Special Case?" *Nederlands Archief voor Kerkgeschiedenis* 61 (1981): 7–29; Charles McCurry, "Religious Careers and Religious Devotion in 13th Century Metz," *Viator* 9 (1978): 325–333; and Dayton Phillips, *The Beguines in Medieval Strasbourg: A Study of the Social Aspect of Beguine Life* (Ann Arbor: University of Michigan Press, 1941).

5. On the importance of this *Life*, see Bolton, *"Vitae Matrum,"* pp. 253–273.

6. Or did their home become a leper hospital? Carol Neel has questioned the view of Marie as the first beguine and suggests that there was more continuity between women's activities in Premonstratensian and Cistercian communities than Jacques de Vitry was willing to acknowledge. She asserts that Marie "quickly convinced her young husband John that the two should dedicate themselves to chastity and charity. Toward this end, the young couple converted their house at Willambrouk into a hospital and tended the sick and leprous with their own hands" ("Origins of the Beguines," *Signs* 14 [1989]: 321–341).

7. McDonnell, *Beguines and Beghards*, pp. 71–73.

8. Jacques de Vitry, *The Life of Marie d'Oignies*, 2nd ed., trans. and ed. Margot H. King (Toronto: Peregrina Press, 1989), pp. 61–62.

9. Herbert Grundmann, *Religiöse Bewegungen im Mittelalter* (Berlin, 1935).

10. McDonnell, *Beguines and Beghards*, p. 5.

11. Bolton, *"Vitae Matrum,"* pp. 253–273, esp. p. 256.

12. McDonnell, *Beguines and Beghards*, p. 479. Many of these communities still stand. Street maps of many cities in the Netherlands indicate one or more, termed *beguinhof*.

13. Southern, *Western Society and the Church in the Middle Ages*, p. 32.

14. Ibid.

15. Bolton, *"Vitae Matrum,"* p. 260.

16. The Latin original is *Vita Mariae Oigniacensis*, in *Acta Sanctorum*, June 23.

17. Bolton identifies most of them in *"Vitae Matrum."*

18. Jacques de Vitry, "Preface to *The Life of Marie d'Oignies*," in *Not in God's Image: Women from the Greeks to the Victorians*, ed. Julia O'Faolain and Lauro Martines (New York: Harper & Row, 1973), pp. 140–141.

19. This is the thesis of Walter Simons and Joanna E. Ziegler, speaking of another beguine from the diocese of Liège, Elisabeth of Spalbeek: "Elisabeth was consulted as a prophetess by various important religious and secular figures because of the fame of her revelations. But the primary basis on which her fame rested seems to have derived from her extreme physical manifestations of religion—manifestations which she enacted routinely for audiences. Her hagiographer, Abbot Phillip, describes her enactment of the stigmata and of the Passion, including her own crucifixion and deposition as well as the performance of the roles of Mary and John. Phillip interprets this as an example of women's function in the popularization of *imitatio Christi* in which words and writing (male) are replaced by bodily expression (female)" ("Act, Word, and Image: Elisabeth of Spalbeek and Eucharistic Devotion in the Thirteenth and Fourteenth Centuries" [Abstract, September 15, 1988]).

20. Neel, "Origins of the Beguines," pp. 326–327.

21. The English translation of the works of Hadewijch is Mother Columba Hart, *Hadewijch: The Complete Works* (New York: Paulist Press, 1980).

22. Beatrijs van Tienen, or Beatrijs of Nazareth, wrote an autobiography that

has yet to be translated into English (*Vita Beatricis: De autobiographie van de S. Beatrijs van Tienen, Cist. Ord. 1200–1268,* ed. L. Reypens [Antwerp: Ruusbroec-Genootschap, 1964]); a section of this longer work, known as "The Seven Manners of Loving," is in *Mediaeval Netherlands Religious Literature,* ed. Colledge.

23. Julia Kristeva, *Tales of Love,* trans. Leon S. Roudiez (New York: Columbia University Press, 1987), p. 63.

24. Elissa Gelfand and Virginia Hules, *French Feminist Criticism: Women, Language and Literature* (New York: Garland, 1984), p. xxii.

25. *Meditations on the Life of Christ: An Illustrated Manuscript of the Fourteenth Century,* ed. Isa Ragusa and Rosalie B. Green (Princeton, N.J.: Princeton University Press, 1961). Some editors have suggested that the original creator of these meditations was a woman, an unknown mystic, who dictated them to her Franciscan spiritual director.

26. Judith Oliver has reconstructed and studied a beguine devotional book illustrating the Life of St. Catherine of Alexandria in "Medieval Alphabet Soup," *Gesta* 14 (1985): 129–140.

27. Emilie Zum Brunn and Georgette Epiney-Burgard, *Women Mystics in Medieval Europe* (New York: Paragon, 1989), pp. 71–72.

28. See the account in ibid., p. 72. The trivium included grammar, rhetoric, and dialectic; the quadrivium included music, geometry, arithmetic, and astronomy. This was the same education a young man of similar age would have had at a cathedral school.

29. For a discussion of the contents of her autobiography, along with several excerpts, see the section on Beatrice (Beatrijs) in ibid., pp. 69–94. Part III of *Vita Beatricis* is a Latin translation of the *Seven manieren:* "In one of the last chapters of the Life of Beatrice, the biographer gives a Latin adaptation of her work (III, pars. 246–261). It is thanks to this translation that it has been possible to identify the author of the Middle Dutch (thiosis) text contained in the *Limbourg Sermons* which were rediscovered in 1895" (p. 79).

30. *Beatrijs van Nazareth: Seven manieren van Minne,* ed. L. Reypens and J. Van Mierlo (Leuven: De Vlaamsche Bockenhalle, 1926); there is a French translation by J. B. Porion, *Béatrice de Nazareth: Sept degrés d'amour* (Geneva: Claude Martingay, 1972).

31. Quoted in Zum Brunn and Epiney-Burgard, *Women Mystics,* p. 80.

32. Beatrijs of Nazareth, "There Are Seven Manners of Loving," trans. Eric Colledge, in *Medieval Women's Visionary Literature,* ed. Elizabeth A. Petroff (New York: Oxford University Press, 1986), p. 201.

33. Ibid.

34. Ibid., pp. 201–202.

35. Ibid., p. 202.

36. Ibid., pp. 202–203.

37. Ibid., pp. 203–204.

38. Ibid., pp. 204–206.

39. There are evidently two different poets named Hadewijch whose works have been collected together; recent scholarship identifies a Hadewijch II. According to Paul A. Dietrich, "Included in the *Mengeldichten* of Hadewijch are thirteen poems written by a later poet, Hadewijch II or pseudo-Hadewijch, which differ in style, vocabulary, and theme from the authentic poems. In contrast to the works of Hadewijch the later poems are spare and speculative, reflecting an apophatic moment in Flemish Beguine spirituality at the end of the thirteenth century" (personal

communication, September 15, 1988). The critical editions are edited by Jozef van Mierlo: *Hadewijch: Visioenen,* 2 vols. (Louvain: Vlaamsch Boekenhall, 1924, 1925); *Hadewijch: Strophische Gedichten,* 2 vols. (Antwerp: Standaard, 1942); *Hadewijch: Brieven,* 2 vols. (Antwerp: Standaard, 1947); and *Hadewijch: Mengeldichten* (Antwerp: Standaard, 1952).

40. Hadewijch of Antwerp, "Letter 1," of "Letters to a Young Beguine," in *Mediaeval Netherlands Religious Literature,* ed. Colledge, p. 34. Another translation, by Hart, is in *Hadewijch: The Complete Works.*

41. "Letter 1," in *Medieval Netherlands Religious Literature,* ed. Colledge, p. 34.

42. Ibid., pp. 34–35.

43. "Letter 8," in ibid., p. 55.

44. Ibid.

45. "Letter 9," in ibid., p. 56.

46. "Letter 11," in ibid., p. 59.

47. "Letter 18," in ibid., p. 80.

48. "Letter 19," in ibid., p. 83.

4

A Medieval Woman's Utopian Vision: The Rule of St. Clare of Assisi

On August 10, 1253, the day before she died, St. Clare of Assisi received into her own hands the papal bull approving her Rule for the order of Clarisses, or Poor Clares, founded by her almost forty years earlier.[1] Included in this bull was the "privilege of poverty," by which Pope Innocent IV reaffirmed the right of Clare's own convent of San Damiano to persevere in its commitment to absolute poverty, both individual and collective. A contemporary note written on the reverse of the document says that "the Blessed Clare touched and kissed this Bull out of great devotion many, many times."[2] Clare had good reason to rejoice, both at the "unheard of privilege" of having a pope visit a nun on her deathbed and at the "fulfillment of her most ardent wish."[3]

Papal approval of these texts meant that St. Clare had won a lifelong struggle to create a new kind of community for women in spite of the Church's "deliberate restriction of female initiative," in particular the fact that "the popes and the cardinal protectors found it necessary to provide her own and her sister communities with no less than six rules between 1219 and 1263."[4] This final Rule affirmed Clare's goals in two ways: by what it said (it explicitly confirmed the "privilege of poverty") and by what it did not say (it was not called a Rule, and it did not contain the word *enclosure*).

St. Clare's Rule, which she always preferred to call simply the *Forma vitae*,[5] a form or pattern of life, is the first Rule for a female religious community written by a woman. As we shall see, it is a utopian narrative of a special kind.[6] Furthermore, it was written, and given papal approval, in a time when there was a papal ban on the creation of any new religious orders and consequently on any new Rules.[7] St. Clare's success tells us she was a spirited and innovative religious leader, not merely the sweet and pious follower of St. Francis. Just as Francis had founded an order of Friars Minor (Lesser Brothers) for men, Clare founded a parallel order for women, known variously as the Poor Ladies, the Poor Clares, or the Clarisses. We also know (from St. Clare herself and from her biographer, Thomas of Celano) that Francis had in mind from the beginning that women would be involved in the mission of his order[8] and that St. Clare responded eagerly to his search for a "cooperatrice," a female collaborator.[9]

The popular image of St. Clare has been that she was romantically in love with Francis and with his vision of reform in religious life. To some extent this may be true. Clearly, some very powerful force drew together the fanatical son of a well-to-do cloth merchant of Assisi and the pious and beautiful daughter of one of the noble families of Assisi and called them to lead a powerful—and utopian—movement for spiritual renewal. Class interests kept their families apart, and it may have been the rejection of those very interests that called them together. As Madge Karecki points out, Clare's family was very distinguished: "Clare had seven knights in her ancestry and many others who distinguished themselves in public service."[10] Her father, Favarone di Offreduccio, seems to have been very protective of his family and their interests, and her mother, Ortolana, had a reputation for piety and for concern for the poor. A witness at Clare's process of canonization testified that many of Clare's relatives had urged her to marry,[11] and her beauty and wealth would have enabled her family to make a very good match for her, one that might have raised the family's social standing even higher.

> These were the crucial years during which the commune of Assisi was trying to organize—a task which was not fully realized until 1208–09. Merchants had initiated the formation of the commune and Favarone seemed to have wanted no part in it. Such a movement challenged the place of the nobles within the social, political, and economic areas of life. The merchants insisted that the nobles give up part of their wealth and their privileges. The merchants were motivated not by some magnanimous concern for the welfare of the poor, but rather by a desire to increase their own wealth through trade.[12]

Francis, the son of Pietro de Bernardone, came from one of the most prosperous merchant-class families. Both young people would have grown up "in the midst of this struggle between the nobles and the merchants and could not have been untouched by it."[13] The beginning of their association had the stuff of medieval romance; she sneaked out of her house with a companion to meet with him in private when he was giving a series of Lenten sermons in Assisi in 1211. When she ran away to join him and his followers on the evening of Palm Sunday, March 18/19, 1212, she left through the bricked-up "Door of the Dead" (through which a body was taken from the home for the funeral and burial) and hastened to join Francis at the little church of St. Mary of the Porziuncola.[14]

Throughout their lives, the two leaders continued to influence each other. According to the tradition preserved in the *Fioretti* (*The Little Flowers of St. Francis*), it was Clare (along with Brother Sylvester) who led Francis to commit himself to an active life of preaching and service, when he might have preferred to remain a contemplative, and it was Francis who convinced Clare to accept the restrictions on women's religious lives and the necessity for some kind of enclosure.[15] Whenever Francis was ill, he turned to her to nurse him; in his final illness, after he was almost crippled by the stigmata in his feet, she made slippers for him that protected his wounds and permitted him to walk.

Clare and her sisters at San Damiano remained loyal to Francis's beliefs long after his death, and when Clare died in 1253, twenty-seven years after Francis's death, she was one of the last to hold to a strict interpretation of his idea of evangelical poverty. Indeed, as John Moorman points out, she was a tenacious fighter and an innovative administrator,[16] and it was these qualities, according to her medieval biographer, that brought her thousands of women followers in her own lifetime.[17] Although St. Clare's life has often been seen through the shadow of her spiritual master, St. Francis, in fact she cast a brilliant light herself; in her writings one sees that illumination of Christian truths that for her contemporaries was symbolized in her very name, Clara luce clarior.

What is the ideal female community that Clare wished to institutionalize in her "form of life"? Why was papal approval so difficult to obtain when she "counted Popes and Cardinals among her dearest friends"?[18] Why was she so resistant to accepting any other Rule? Clare wrote the text of her Rule during the last years of her life (probably between 1247 and 1253); she drew on the experience of living in a community of sisters for many years, during which time she was recognized as "the new captain of womankind," according to Thomas of Celano.[19] The years had not dimmed her memory of the vow she had taken with Francis in 1213 or of the Rule that Francis had given her orally in 1215, when she accepted the role of abbess of the small community at San Damiano. These memories, too, became part of her text.

Let us first look at the kind of community Clare wished to create and then examine the text in which she claims that utopian vision as a "form of life," a *forma vitae*. Motivated by the same desires as the beguines, Clare wanted to create a female community based on evangelical service.[20] "Evangelical" meant to her imitating the example of the Gospels, the life of Christ and his disciples.[21] Like them, she wanted to share the life of the poor and to minister to their needs, and she intended her life, and the life of her sisters, to be a contemporary model of Gospel-inspired poverty and charity.[22] Poverty for her had economic, social, and spiritual aspects. Her ideal community was, a response to the conditions of poverty occasioned by the new urban, bourgeois economy, a sharing of the lives of the most disenfranchised. It was also reaction to the aristocratic structure of Benedictine monasticism, which was based on the ownership of property. And it was the means to a deeper spirituality:

> For Clare, a life of economic poverty was the environment in which one could be most attentive to the Lord as well as give credibility to evangelical poverty. It was her way of following in the footprints of Jesus and the way to the kingdom of heaven. . . . Clare had experienced God's love deep within her heart and she knew that no sacrifice was too great to make to keep this love alive. She would have no part of anything that would take her attention away from her Beloved. . . . [I]n order to be open and ready to receive the gifts of the Lord in prayer, one's heart must be free of clutter—the clutter of self and of material possessions and securities. That kind of freedom was also at the heart of love of one's neighbor.[23]

She believed that she and her sisters could support themselves, as Christ's followers did in the Gospels, by the work of their hands and by begging alms; she did not believe that women had to be supported economically by others, and she did not want to own property and live off its income. (These were all women's issues in her time, viewed with much hostility by powerful groups in the Church and in secular society.) She took celibacy for granted as a central foundation of a women's religious community, but she always asserted the necessity of cooperation between men and women for spiritual growth. Cardinal Jacques de Vitry, who visited the early Franciscan communities in Umbria in 1216, described in a famous letter[24] what he observed, and his "evidence is entirely consistent with the indications that Francis originally intended women to play as central a part in his activities as men, and that their role was at first not so different as it later became."[25]

Clare wanted a community that was as close to nonhierarchical as possible; her models for workable female relationships were sister–sister, maidservant–mistress, and daughter–mother, all relationships characterized by emotional closeness, mutual responsibility, and common needs.[26] This conception led to a remarkably democratic community, where most decisions were made by the consensus of all the sisters. The abbess, rather than making unilateral decisions, as Benedictine abbesses were expected to do, was to be advised by a council of "discreets" (Clare's name for an innovative advisory council composed of at least eight older and more experienced sisters). Clare disliked even the term *abbess*, redefining it in her Rule and never using it in her *Testament*, referring only to "the one who shall succeed me."

The physical hardships of Clare's ideal life seemed excessive even in the penitential mood of the thirteenth century. Clare and her sisters, believing that women were as tough as men, saw no reason why they could not share all the austerities endured by their brother Franciscans. The sisters were not to wear shoes unless the climate made it absolutely necessary (they went barefoot in the winter cold of Assisi); they were to sleep on the bare floor or ground; they were to eat only one meal a day on most days, and that meal without meat. But all these conditions were to be modified immediately for anyone who was ill; sisters who were infirm could have mattresses, blankets, and socks in bed and could even eat meat.[27] The sisters' subsistence-level economy could be supported by a small vegetable garden, and the convent buildings were to be geographically isolated, surrounded by only "as much ground as necessity requires for the becoming seclusion of the monastery." Although Pope Innocent, in his prefatory remarks to the papal bull containing the Rule, speaks of Clare and her followers as desiring to live "incluso corpore," a phrase that has often been understood to mean "enclosed," St. Clare avoided using the words for *enclosure* or *cloister* in her writings,[28] and on this topic says only that sisters may not leave the convent unless there is "useful, reasonable, manifest, and approvable cause." This constitutes "une ouverture étonnante," as her recent editors observe,[29] in light of the fact that all the Rules that had been imposed on her required strict enclosure.[30]

The common life envisioned by Clare involved a high level of cooperation and sharing among the Poor Ladies, as the sisters began to be called, and it also demanded cooperation from the male branch of the order. In both her *Forma vitae* and her *Testament,* Clare directly quotes Francis's own words on only two issues: the importance of poverty and the responsibility of the Franciscan brothers for their sisters. Clare saw the possibility for men and women to work together toward the same spiritual goals, each serving the other. Her vision of community is horizontal, not vertical, and collaboration, not hierarchy, is the key. Her ideas here build on Francis's early beliefs. As R. W. Southern observes:

> All earlier religious movements had been guided by a strong sense of order and tradition. Of this there is little trace in the words of Francis that have been preserved. His idea was to cut through all the accretions of monastic development . . . and to live literally the life of Christ. He called for a total surrender, symbolized in following precisely the Gospel precept to sell everything and give to the poor.[31]

Many aspects of Clare's utopian vision were found in other women's communities, especially the beguines in northern Europe.[32] We know that St. Clare was very much in tune with this movement. Cardinal Jacques de Vitry, the self-appointed defender of the beguines, visited her in 1216; his letter about what he observed of her community is the earliest surviving evidence about the Poor Sisters. He notes:

> They [the Fratres Minores and Sorores Minores] live according to the pattern of the primitive church. . . . By day they enter cities and towns, giving practical help that they may benefit some; by night they return to a hermitage or lonely houses, devoting themselves to contemplation. The women live together near the cities in separate hostels; they receive nothing, but live by the toil of their hands, and are greatly upset and troubled because they are honored by clergy and laity more than they wish.[33]

Evangelical poverty was an issue that united many reform groups. Lay people were rediscovering the message of the Gospels, and the simplicity and poverty of Jesus's life seemed to them both an example to live by and an implicit condemnation of the wealth of the Church. Poverty meant something different in the new urban environment of the thirteenth century. As Southern rightly observes, the existence of the mendicant orders, the "begging" orders of Franciscans and Dominicans, is unimaginable outside an urban setting: "Francis was following a pattern of conversion that can be found in all ages; but the sharpness and extremity of his impulse was in some way prompted by the violence, glitter, and instability of the emerging municipal oligarchies of Italy."[34]

The poverty that Clare and Francis espoused was absolute. Franciscans were to own no property, either individually or collectively, except for the clothes on their backs. Their needs, and those of the poor to whom they ministered, were to be provided by the alms of others or by the work of their hands. They were not to own the buildings in which they lived and worshipped, nor were they to acquire land. Their vocation was to pray—as Benedictine monks had done for centuries—but it was also to minister to those in want or in pain—as the secular clergy were supposed to do.

These goals were disturbing enough in a male order, but in a female order they were unheard of. How, then, could a woman compose a Rule (when new Rules were forbidden) that institutionalized many of these tenets? And having composed it, how could she expect papal ratification? Clare had to proceed very carefully; it took Francis eight years to have his Rule approved, and it took Clare thirty years after that to win approval for hers. While waiting for that approval, Clare and her sisters, as we have already noted, lived under six different Rules, most of which merely modified the Benedictine Rule for women, insisting strongly on enclosure and possession of property.[35]

Clare's *Forma vitae sororum pauperum* makes no claim to originality; in fact, it purports to be a written version of the original *forma vitae* that Francis had given her orally when she first accepted the responsibility of leading the small community of sisters at San Damiano. The actual Latin text is a patchwork of quotations from other written Rules: the Benedictine Rule, the Second Rule of St. Francis, the Rule of Hugolino for the Poor Clares, and that of Innocent IV. Less than half of the text is new, and even that seems boringly formulaic. It is not, strictly speaking, a narrative in the modern sense; it is prescriptive legislation. Clare has chosen language that is both powerful and nonthreatening; the words are not her own, she claims, but those of her masters. The twelve-part structure (not marked in the original manuscript, but clearly discernible in the categories treated) imitates the structure of the Second Rule of St. Francis. The "radical" portions of the text, the sections on poverty and on the relationship between the Franciscan first and second orders, claim to be transcriptions of Francis' written accounts of his earlier oral instructions and promises to St. Clare.[36]

Unlike Clare's other writings, in the *Forma vitae* narrative is suppressed in favor of prescription. Clare is choosing a male voice, a male rhetoric, to safeguard the existence of her communities. For this is a revolutionary text intended to guide utopian communities of women in new roles for women in the Church. We may read it as a constitution setting forth the conditions under which a female community is to be formed and demonstrating the authority that grants such a community the right to exist. And when the text of the Rule is seen in the context of the other writings by St. Clare, her autobiographical *Testament* and *Letters,* we can see how her vision of an ideal community differs from that of St. Francis and, more important, from that of more traditional women's communities.[37]

Chapter 1 defines, almost aggressively, Clare's ongoing relationship to St. Francis. Chapter 1.1 identifies the "Poor Sisters" as "the order . . . which the Blessed Francis founded"; 1.2 defines the "form of life" as the commitment "to observe the Holy Gospel of our Lord Jesus Christ by living in obedience, without property, and in chastity"; and in 1.3, "Clare, the unworthy handmaid of Christ and little plant of the most Blessed Father Francis, promises obedience and reverence to the Lord Pope Honorius and to his successors canonically elected, and to the Roman Church." In 1.4, Clare herself promises obedience to Francis's successors, "as in the beginning of her conversion she and her Sisters promised obedience to the Blessed Francis," and 1.5 obliges the sisters to the same obedience to the successors of St. Francis and of St. Clare. This identification of her goals with those of Father Francis is rhetorically effective, for Clare's voice disappears behind that of her "father," disguising female authorship and only indirectly asserting female authority. By appearing to be the loyal follower of St. Francis, Clare masks her own innovations.

Chapter 1 provides the authority for the existence of this new community, and Chapter 2 tells how sisters may join it. They must be accepted by the majority of the sisters (a democratic innovation) and examined in the faith. Sisters must be unmarried (or sworn to a mutual vow of chastity with husbands who are already in religious orders) and must have no impediments to the observance of a celibate life. If a sister-to-be meets these standards, she is to follow the Gospel commandment to sell all her goods and distribute the proceeds to the poor. If she is worried about this requirement and needs advice, the sisters can send her to discreet advisers who will help her in the distributions of her goods.[38] The Rule then details the clothes that sisters may wear: Clare allows more clothing than Francis had done: three tunics, a mantle—all "poor garments . . . for the love of the . . . Babe . . . wrapped in swaddling clothes"—and shoes for the extern sisters (lay sisters who ran errands for the community and dealt more with the outside world).

In the context of the vestment of a sister, the Rule notes, "Thenceforth it shall not be allowed her to go outside the monastery save for some useful, reasonable, manifest, and approvable cause." Clare's other innovations are that girls admitted to the monastery too young to profess are to have their hair cut like the sisters and to wear the same garments; when they have reached the right age, they should profess. She adds, "No one may reside with us in the monastery unless she is received according to the form of our profession." The abbess should provide a teacher for the younger ones; the teacher is to direct their behavior and teach them the "form of our life." The thrust of this section is toward uniformity of commitment; a collective is being formed, to which all sisters belong equally and the goals of which all understand clearly.

Chapter 3 spells out the performance of the divine office and prescribes the specific conditions of the penitential life in community. We are told how the divine office is to be read (humbly, "according to the custom of the Friars Minor . . . without singing"), how and when the sisters are to fast, how often they should confess and receive communion. Those sisters who can read may own breviaries and should recite the Office of the Dead, but in special circumstances, they, like the unlettered sisters, may substitute the Our Father and Hail Mary. The rules about confession and fasting are Clare's own, and the other advice about reciting the divine office is a modification of Francis's Rule. (Francis himself was strongly opposed to allowing brothers to own breviaries, for he felt such ownership created differences in power among the group members.)

Chapter 4 turns to more constitutional issues, outlining the election and responsibilities of the abbess, the convent's other officers, and the "discreets." Most of this chapter is innovative, as we would expect, since Clare's idea of structure is horizontal rather than vertical, collective rather than hierarchical. The sisters and the abbess are to meet weekly, to confess their faults to one another and to make decisions about the welfare of the group; the abbess should consult with everyone, "for the Lord often reveals to the lesser among us that which is best." Any debts the sisters may incur must be approved by all the sisters; no valuables are to be kept in the convent; all officers are to be chosen "by common consent" (*de communi consensu sororum*) and can be removed from office by the common will of the sisters. All these legislative details communicate the special community spirit of this order; the abbess "stands in the midst of the community rather than above it."[39] In Benedictine communities, there were also weekly chapter meetings, but the abbess was an authority figure to whom all the sisters owed obedience. She was not obliged to explain her decisions, much less participate in collective decision making. Clare's prescriptive narrative creates the image of a community based on love and service, in which roles and responsibilities are clear for everyone.

Chapters 7 and 8 tell us more about the daily life of the sisters. We learn that all sisters who are physically able are to perform manual labor each day, assigned to them in the presence of all. The emphasis on manual labor goes back to the Benedictine Rule, but the emphasis on the public assignment of tasks by the abbess and her advisers is new, as is the fact that these assignments are to be made not unilaterally but in consultation with the discreets. This is congruent with Chapter 8, which is truly remarkable among monastic texts for the confidence it shows in the sisters' personal decisions:

> Perhaps the most striking element in Clare's Rule is the freedom it allows to the individual. . . . Clare had no intention of forcing her sisters to sacrifice their personality for the sake of the Order; on the contrary, it was precisely through the perfecting of their God-given personality that they could best further the interests of the Order. . . . Reverential love, therefore, is to be the guiding spirit of Clare's Order. Like Francis, Clare had reached a deep understanding of human dignity, and from this understanding was born her love and respect for the personality of each member of her community.[40]

For example, even though all sisters are to imitate Christ's poverty, they may be sent gifts, and they may choose whether to keep such gifts for their own needs or to share them with other sisters whose need may be greater. If the sisters are given money, the abbess should use it to provide for their needs. (That the abbess can touch money is a departure from Francis's original ideas.) The provisions for caring for the sick reveal what Clare meant by sisterhood: each sister "should make known her needs with confidence to the other: for if a mother love and nourish her child according to the flesh, how much more lovingly must not a Sister love and nourish her sister according to the Spirit." This flexibility in the treatment of the sick and the troubled is Clare's own vision, and she is clear that each sister is responsible for the physical and emotional comfort of each member of the group.

All communities need some way of maintaining order and dealing with dissension. Women's houses with both enclosed sisters and extern sisters needed specific guidelines for their behavior to ensure that the concerns of the secular society did not distract the convent from its collective spiritual function. Chapters 9 and 10 deal with these issues. For example, a sister who sins mortally and does not amend must "eat bread and water on the floor before all the Sisters in the refectory. And if it seems advisable to the Abbess, she shall undergo even greater punishment." Everyone should pray for her and not be angry with her. If there should be any scandal between sisters, the one who caused the trouble should immediately go to the other and ask for forgiveness—even before she asks God for forgiveness. The other sister should freely pardon her. All of this is new with Clare. Nothing is said about a convent prison, about the use of corporal punishment, or about lengthy ostracism from the community, all common in other orders. Extern sisters should not "tarry long unless some cause of evident necessity require it." Their behavior should always be a model for others, modest and quiet, avoiding "suspicious meetings" with men. Clare's basic guideline for the behavior of all sisters is simple: "Let them be ever careful to preserve among themselves the unity of mutual love."

Since this is a female order from which men are excluded, careful provision must be made for those times when men by necessity will have to enter the convent: workmen coming to make repairs or to dig graves; priests coming to hear confessions or to give the last rites to the dying. Furthermore, in the interests of cooperation between the male and the female branches of the order, Clare insists that Franciscan brothers be assigned to help the sisters, both spiritually and materially. All these details are worked out in Chapters 11 and 12 so that everyone may know what behavior is expected. Clare is particularly forceful in affirming papal support for the obligation of the Franciscan brothers to their sister order because this issue had often been a source of friction between the two groups and because papal support in the past had seemed lukewarm.[41]

My understanding of the importance of Clare's Rule is that many women's communities desired a similar constitution (I think it likely that many beguine communities practiced similar "forms of life" but did not write them down), but Clare's is the only one that has survived and that obtained the necessary papal approval. This, then, is the utopia that women wanted—they thought it ideal, although the Church thought it foolhardy at best, if not close to heresy. Clare's *Forma vitae* provides a strong model for relationships within the community, encumbered by a minimal amount of hierarchy. Clare herself places much emphasis on mutual love as the way to solve problems. The life envisioned in the Rule is very demanding physically—the sisters are to fast almost continually, to go barefoot, to do without beds and pillows and bed linen, to support themselves by the work of their hands. This was a feminist issue for the medieval period because it asserted the belief that women are as strong as men—a very new and rather shocking idea. Clare's emphasis on poverty was important not only because it signaled a female commitment to the Gospel commandment to sell all that you have and give it to the poor, but also because it said that women do not have to be protected, that they can provide for themselves. The traditional medieval assumption about women was that they were by nature very concerned with material things and possessed much less physical stamina than did men. Even the remarkable abbess Heloise believed that the Benedictine Rule should be modified for women because women were unable to endure as much hardship as men, although she did assert in her discussion of fasting that women need less food to survive and are much less susceptible to drunkenness than men.[42] For St. Clare, it was very simple: women can practice poverty as well as anyone.

St. Clare's idealism shows up in two other ways in her Rule—her sensitivity to those who were guilty of sins and her profound faith in women's capacity for loving sisterhood. She is interested in reform, not punishment, so she does not legislate about convent prisons or brutal or humiliating punishments. Her prescription for transgressing sisters of eating bread and water on the floor in the refectory with the other sisters (who were also eating bread and water much of the time) is mild by medieval standards, and in any case she wished her abbesses to try every means of private persuasion and exhortation before resorting to this kind of public humiliation. She is perhaps most eloquent when speaking about sisterhood, which she seems to have viewed in the same light as the mother–daughter relationship. She seems never to have tired in exploring this theme; it is central to her autobiographical *Testament* and is luminously portrayed in her letters of love to St. Agnes of Prague.

Notes

1. So precious was this document containing the first written text of the Rule, and so fearful were Clare's sisters of having its authenticity denied, that they immediately hid the original copy. It was not discovered until 1893, when it was found "by the Mother Abbess of Santa Chiara . . . wrapped in a habit of Saint Clare hidden in a reliquary box" (*Legend and Writings of Saint Clare of Assisi,* ed. and trans. Ignatius Brady [St. Bonaventure, N.Y.: Franciscan Institute, 1953], p. 4).

2. In Latin, "Hanc beata Clara tetigit et obsculata est pro devotione pluribus et pluribus vicibus" (ibid., p. 8).

3. Ibid., p. 6.

4. Christopher N. I. Brooke and Rosalind B. Brooke, "St. Clare," in *Medieval Women,* ed. Derek Baker (Oxford: Basil Blackwell, 1978), p. 276.

5. We may wonder whether she termed it a *forma vitae* because of modesty, because she did not want to draw attention to it as a (forbidden) rule, or because she wished to emphasize its originally oral form, as dictated by St. Francis. The editors of a recent edition of her works suggest that she may have used the term *forma vitae* to disguise the fact that she actually was writing a Rule: "Par une sorte de fiction—diplomatique ou juridique?—, elle n'est jamais appelée règle mais forme de vie; par ailleurs sa création est mise sur le compte, non de Claire, mais de Francois. . . . Quel cardinal, quel pape pourrait ne pas approuver, en 1252–53, ce qui est censé être l'oeuvre de Francois?" (Introduction to *Claire d'Assise Écrits,* ed. Marie-France Becker, Jean-François Godet, and Thaddée Matura [Paris: Editions du Cerf, 1985] p. 30).

6. Strictly speaking, medieval writers did not compose utopias, but there are clearly utopian elements in the courtly romances that circulated in the twelfth and thirteenth centuries. For example, one could examine the utopian threads in the narratives of Marie de France's Breton lais, or *romans bretons,* composed in the mid-twelfth century. I would conjecture that utopian ideas surfaced in medieval narrative in the form of otherworldly or heavenly visions and that women's ideas about a better world were determined in part by their depictions of heaven or the otherworld. In any case, there is very little literature by women writers prior to the writings of St. Clare and no surviving written text sketching out the social and economic structure of a new kind of community prior to Clare's Rule. For more on literature by women in the Middle Ages, see the bibliography in Elizabeth A. Petroff, ed., *Medieval Women's Visionary Literature* (New York: Oxford University Press, 1986), pp. 373–391.

7. See the Introduction to *Claire d'Assise Écrits,* p. 30. The ban on any new Rules may be viewed as an instance of well-organized and powerful resistance to the spiritual women's movement of the twelfth and thirteenth centuries; such resistance meant that Clare had to proceed very intelligently if she wished to succeed in her goals.

8. Brooke and Brooke, "St. Clare," pp. 278–279.

9. Albina Henrion, "Santa Chiara d'Assisi: La cooperatrice di San Francesco," *Archivum Franciscanum Historicum* 19 (1926): 579–609.

10. Madge Karecki, "Clare: Poverty and Contemplation in Her Life and Writings," in *Medieval Religious Women*, vol. 2, *Peace Weavers*, ed. John A. Nichols and Lillian Thomas Shank (Kalamazoo, Mich.: Cistercian Publications, 1987), p. 167.

11. Ibid., p. 168.

12. Ibid., pp. 167–168.

13. Ibid., p. 168.

14. Thomas of Celano, "The Legend of Saint Clare of Assisi," in *Legend and Writings of Saint Clare of Assisi*, ed. Brady, pp. 17–61. Clare was greeted by Francis and his followers with lighted torches at the same place where the male branch of the order had its beginnings. For more on Clare's introduction to the Franciscan community, see Karecki, "Clare," pp. 169–170.

15. Brooke and Brooke, "St. Clare," p. 280.

16. John Moorman, *A History of the Franciscan Order from Its Origins to the Year 1517* (Oxford: Clarendon Press, 1968), p. 204.

17. Thomas of Celano, "Legend of Saint Clare," pp. 25–26. But recent scholarship has questioned whether Clare's influence really accounts for the large number of women's communities whose founding has been attributed to her. R. Rusconi demonstrates that many houses supposedly founded by St. Clare or her early followers actually existed prior to St. Clare as informal communities of beguines or female penitents; they later adopted the Rule of St. Clare, probably because, of all the Rules available to them, only this one was close to their original values ("Espansione del francescanesimo femminile nel secolo XIII," in *Movimento Religioso femminile e francescanesimo nel secolo XIII* [Assisi: Studi Francescani, 1979], pp. 265–313).

18. *Legend and Writings of Saint Clare of Assisi*, p. 129.

19. Thomas of Celano, "Legend of Saint Clare," p. 18.

20. For an exploration of other concerns she shared with the beguines, such as her devotion to the Eucharist, her practice of contemplation, and her use of the bridal imagery of the Song of Songs in her contemplative practices, see Fidelis Hart, "Following the Poor Christ: Clare's Spirituality," in *Peace Weavers*, ed. Nichols and Shank, pp. 175–195.

21. For more information on how the evangelical or apostolic life was defined during this period, see M.-D. Chenu, *Nature, Man and Society, in the Twelfth Century: Essays on New Theological Perspectives in the Latin West*, ed. and trans. Jerome Taylor and Lester K. Little (Chicago: University of Chicago Press, 1968), pp. 202–269.

22. As she says in her autobiographical *Testament*, "The Lord has placed us as an example and mirror not only for other men, but also for our Sisters whom God has called to our way of life, that they in turn should be a mirror and an example to those living in the world" (*Legend and Writings of Saint Clare of Assisi*, p. 183).

23. Karecki, "Clare," p. 171.

24. Brooke and Brooke, "St. Claire," pp. 281–282; *Lettres de Jacques de Vitry*, ed. R. B. C. Huygens (Leiden, 1960), pp. 71–78.

25. Brooke and Brooke, "St. Clare," p. 282.

26. The fact that Clare thought of all these relationships as nonhierarchical tells us something of how she perceived bonds between women, that mothers and

daughters and mistresses and maidservants were linked not by authority and subservience but by friendship and mutual caring.

27. Specifically, as St. Clare's third Letter to St. Agnes of Prague details, the sisters were to fast daily except for Thursdays, Sundays, and major holy days— Christmas, Easter week, and the feasts of Mary and of the apostles; on nonfast days, they could eat two meals.

28. *Claire d'Assise Écrits,* p. 122. Gloss on word *incluso:* "Litt. 'incluses': cf. 1 LAg 2. C'est l'unique occurrence de ce mot dans la Règle et encore est-ce dans le texte de la bulle et non dans le texte de la Règle elle-même. Que Claire et ses soeurs vivent sédentaires dans un lieu retiré, cela découle de toutes les sources primitives. Elles n'en vivent pas pour autant isolées ni enfermées. Le mot *clausura,* clôture, n'existe pas dans les écrits de Claire."

29. Ibid., p. 43.

30. It is difficult today to imagine the emotional energy devoted to the issue of strict enclosure for women. The male hierarchy in the Church was always trying to impose more strict claustration, which at its most extreme meant a woman could never leave her convent once she had entered it, and complained that women were always trying to circumvent the rules for enclosure.

The history of enclosure is summarized by Jane Tibbets Schulenberg, "Strict Active Enclosure and Its Effects on the Female Monastic Experience (ca. 500– 1100)," in *Medieval Religious Women,* vol. 1, *Distant Echoes,* ed. John A. Nichols and Lillian Thomas Shank (Kalamazoo, Mich.: Cistercian Publications, 1984), pp. 51– 86. She argues that the early use of enclosure was "essentially an external, physical defense" to "protect nuns and their chastity from barbarian invaders and local violence." By the time of the reforms of the twelfth century, "the basic rationale for narrow enclosure seems to have been the desire of *controlling* women's sexuality through enforced isolation, not guarding her autonomy." She goes on to suggest that women showed less enthusiasm for the religious life when it was associated with strict enclosure and supervision and that perhaps one of the reasons so many women were attracted to pious lay organizations and groups like the beguines was that these groups were not enclosed (pp. 78–79). In any case, the legislation enforcing enclosure, according to Jean Leclercq, "was always made by men who did not share the life-style of enclosed women and who did not consult them" (p. 79). It seems clear to me that while Clare accepted enclosure, she did not endorse it. The fact that she was an invalid for the last twenty-odd years of her life, from shortly after the death of St. Francis, may be relevant to this issue. I like to think of her as smiling when she thought that this final testament of hers was approved even though it did not mandate strict enclosure.

31. R. W. Southern, *Western Society and the Church in the Middle Ages* (Baltimore: Penguin, 1970), p. 281.

32. On the beguines in general, see Eugene W. McDonnell, *The Beguines and Beghards in Medieval Culture* (New Brunswick, N.J.: Rutgers University Press, 1953; New York: Octagon, 1969), and Southern, *Western Society and the Church in the Middle Ages,* esp. pp. 309–331. For *vitae* of several early beguines and texts of beguine writings, see Elizabeth A. Petroff, "New Styles of Feminine Spirituality— The Beguine Movement: Marie d'Oignies, Christina Mirabilis, Hadewijch of Brabant, and Beatrijs of Nazareth," in *Medieval Women's Visionary Literature,* ed. Petroff, pp. 171–206.

33. Quoted in Brooke and Brooke, "St Clare," pp. 281–282.

34. Southern, *Western Society and the Church in the Middle Ages,* p. 281.

35. Brooke and Brooke, "St. Clare," p. 276.

36. These two quoted passages constitute much of Chapter 6 of the Rule:

6.2   But when the Blessed Father saw that we feared no poverty, toil, sorrow, humiliation, or the contempt of the world, but rather that we held these in great delight, moved by love he wrote for us a form of life as follows: "Since by divine inspiration you have made yourselves daughters and handmaids of the Most High and Sovereign King, the Heavenly Father, and have espoused yourselves to the Holy Spirit by the choice of a life according to the perfection of the Holy Gospel: I will and promise for myself and my Friars always to have for you as for them the same diligent care and special solicitude." As long as he lived he faithfully kept this promise and wished it always to be kept by the Friars.

6.3   And that we and those who were to come after us might never fall away from the highest poverty which we had chosen, shortly before his death he again wrote to us his last will, saying, "I, little Brother Francis, wish to follow the life and poverty of our Lord Jesus Christ most high, and of His most holy Mother, and to persevere therein until the end. And I beseech you, my Ladies, and counsel you always to live in this most high form of life and poverty. And guard well, lest by the teaching or counsel of anyone you ever in any way depart from it." (*Legend and Writings of Saint Clare of Assisi*, p. 73)

37. Elizabeth A. Petroff, "Women and Spirituality in Medieval Italy: St. Clare of Assisi, St. Agnes of Assisi, St. Umiltà of Faenza, Blessed Angela of Foligno, and St. Catherine of Siena," in *Medieval Women's Visionary Literature*, ed. Petroff, pp. 231–235.

38. For an example of the importance of this preparation to take Franciscan vows, see ibid., pp. 236–238, and Blessed Angela of Foligno, "From the *Liber de Vere Fidelium Experientia (The Book of the Experience of the Truly Faithful)*," in *Medieval Women's Visionary Literature*, ed. Petroff, pp. 254–263.

39. *Legend and Writings of St. Clare of Assisi*, p. 145.

40. Ibid., pp. 145–146.

41. This is a complicated issue. For an introduction, see Brooke and Brooke, "St. Clare," pp. 280–282, and Moorman, *History of the Franciscan Order*, pp. 34–39, 206–207.

42. *The Letters of Abelard and Heloise*, ed. and trans. Betty Radice (Baltimore: Penguin, 1974), pp. 159–179.

II

THE TRADITION OF HOLY WOMEN: CHANGE AND CONTINUITY

5

Eloquence and Heroic Virginity in Hrotsvit's Verse Legends

The Saxon canoness Hrotsvit of Gandersheim (ca. 935–1000) is the earliest known poet in Germany and the first dramatist since classical times. She wrote eight sacred legends in verse, six dramas in rhymed prose, two historical poems or epics, three lengthy prose prefaces, and a number of shorter works.[1] Her knowledge of classical and religious literature is evidence that Gandersheim had a rich collection of manuscripts, and the library must have been the center of intellectual life in the cloister.

We must not think of Hrotsvit as a cloistered nun knowing little of the outside world. Gandersheim was a royal foundation, and its abbesses were members of the ruling family. As Peter Dronke reminds us:

> [I]n Hrosthvitha's lifetime . . . Gandersheim was a small, proudly independent principality ruled by women. . . . All who belonged to Gandersheim (except for the servants) were of noble birth, some taking vows as nuns, others remaining canonesses. It is almost certain that Hrotsvitha, born ca. 935, was one of the canonesses. It seems likely, too, that she was related to the earlier abbess of Gandersheim, Hrotsvitha I (919–926), and hence was at least a distant relative of the royal house.[2]

Hrotsvit's collections of poetic legends and plays are linked in a kind of double cycle (the term is Dronke's), carefully and symmetrically constructed to unite the two groups of works around certain themes. In this chapter, I explore how the themes of virginity and eloquence resound in the collection of verse legends, focusing particularly on *Agnes,* the final legend in the group. In fact, virginity is one of Hrotsvit's central themes. Of the fourteen narratives (eight verse legends, six dramas), four deal explicitly with the martyrdom of virgins: the two legends presented here and two plays, *Dulcitius* and *Sapientia*. Exemplary virginity is extolled in many other works, most notably in *Maria* and in the character of Constantia in *Gallicanus*. Female characters do not have a monopoly on virginity or celibacy, because for Hrotsvit virginity is not a gender-linked quality. St. Jerome's observation that through virginity a woman becomes like a man has little place in Hrotsvit's thinking, for in her legends and plays she does not view gender as implying moral hierarchy. Models of virginity may be male or female. In *Maria,* when the child Mary argues her desire for virginity, the models she points to are Abel, who for her is a virgin martyr and who for the audience of the Middle Ages was a type of Christ, and Elijah, whose virginity is associated with visionary gifts.[3] The *Apocalypse,* which concludes the cycle of plays, invokes another virgin visionary, St. John the Evangelist.[4] All these symmetries imply a perception of virginity that is as ancient as the Hebrew prophets, as old as creation, in fact, free from gender limitations and Christlike or prophetic.

The verse-legend cycle begins with the narrative of one virgin saint, the Virgin Mary, and ends with the story of another, St. Agnes. The opening lines of both these stories (*Maria* and *Agnes*) stress the importance of virginity as an active choice, as a vocation, and as an emblem of spiritual leadership, both for the saints themselves and for the women of Hrotsvit's own time. The fourth story in the group of eight legends, *Pelagius,* gives us a male virgin martyr who, like Mary and Agnes, is beautiful, brave, and eloquent.

The prologue to the opening legend, *Maria,* illustrates the restorative power and beauty of virginity, invoking the Virgin with a series of descriptive titles:

> Unica spes mundi dominatrix inclita caeli
> Sancta parens regis, lucida stella maris,
> Quae parens mundo restaurasti, pia virgo,
> Vitam, quam perdiderat vetula.[5]

> [To you, unique hope of the world, illustrious lady ruler of the heavens,
> Holy mother of the king, resplendent star of the sea,
> You who by obedience restored to the world, pious virgin,
> That life which the old virgin had lost.]

In this prologue to her life, the Virgin Mary is the "dominatrix," a lady ruler, and a "parens . . . parens," an obedient parent. In her virginity she is both "inclita" and "pia" (illustrious and pious), capable of restoring what the "virgo vetula" (the old virgin, Eve) had lost.

"Virgo" [virgin] is the first word of *Agnes,* the closing legend in Hrotsvit's collection. Agnes's legend too begins descriptively, with an evocation of the timeless beauty of virginity itself, a kind of Platonic form that provides a model for anyone who chooses virginity.

Virgo, quae, vanas mundi pompas ruituri
Et luxus fragilis cupiens contempnere carnis,
Promeruit regis vocitari sponsa perennis,
Si velit angelicae pro virginitatis honore
Ipsius astrigera sponsi caelestic in aula
Addita caelicolis nitida fulgere corona
Atque sequens agnum carmen cantare sonorum,
Conservet pure sincero cordis amore
Signum laudabilis, quod portat, virginitatis.[6]

[A virgin who is desirous of despising the vain pomp of the world
And spurning the luxury of the weak flesh,
Is worthy of being called the bride of the eternal king,
If, for the sake of the honor of angelic virginity,
She wishes to shine in the starry court of the heavenly bridegroom,
Wearing a brilliant crown,
Joined with the citizens of heaven and following the Lamb, singing a resounding hymn,
Let her preserve with a completely genuine love of her heart
The token of praiseworthy virginity that she bears.]

Such a person will be like Agnes herself, "meritis clasissima virgo," a virgin of the brightest merit.

Midway between these two legends that have as their theme heavenly and earthly virginity, we encounter the other virgin martyr of the legends, Pelagius, addressed as "martir fortissime Christe" [bravest martyr of Christ], "inclite" as Mary is "inclita" [illustrious]. Yet his virginity is not mentioned until he has been killed and is rewarded in heaven for his well-preserved virginity, "[oro] bene servata . . . virginitate."

When we examine the legends of Agnes and Pelagius, we see that virginity has three outstanding qualities: it is beautiful; it is heroic or victorious; and it is eloquent. The beauty of virginity and of these virgins attracts others, whom it has a compelling power to transform. The active choice of the virgin's life brings about an inner transformation, resulting in extraordinary strength, perseverance, and eloquence. The virgin is stunning in appearance and persuasive in speech. Pelagius, for example, is released from prison because

> (. . . cum vidissent vultum capti speciosum)
> Necnon praedulcis gustassent ipsius oris
> Verbula rhetoricae circumlita melle loquelae,
> Optabant speciem vinclis absolvere talem.[7]

> [(. . . when they had seen the lovely face of the captive)
> And had tasted the words from his most sweet lips,
> Words flavored with the honey of rhetorical speech,
> They chose to free such a beautiful youth from chains.]

Beauty is a positive quality, a visible sign of virtue, and a source of personal power that the saint will know how to use. It is completely unlike the role of beauty in later hagiographical accounts:

But beauty plays a remarkably different role in the portrayal of the saintly heroine, for this particular motif . . . in fact hinders her spiritual progress. . . . [B]eauty and nobility combine to induce her transformation into an object of desire. . . . These saintly maidens seek, in principle, to remain invisible; yet the logic of the narrative goes counter to this aspiration, and their ordeal can be best described as a process of forced visibility.[8]

In Hrotsvit's legend, Pelagius's beauty and eloquence are consistently paired in all descriptions of him; his "praenitida . . . forma" [outstanding beauty of form] and "mellita . . . loquela" [honeyed speech] commend him to the king, and the entire court marvels "tum faciem iuvenis, tum dulcia verbula fantis" [now at the face of the youth, now at the sweet speech of the boy].[9]

As the stories of both Agnes and Pelagius witness, virginity is neither a cloistered nor a passive virtue. Rather, in the public domain virgins convert others, not so much by their stoic endurance of torture as by their eloquence in defending their choice of a freer and more exalted life and by their liberty and courage in attacking the forces of evil. (This eloquence and this liberty are much like Hrotsvit's purposes in writing, as her prefaces to her abbess Gerberga imply.) Hrotsvit's virgin martyrs submit to testing and to torture, but, within the space allowed them for action, they actively defend their freedom of belief and utilize every possible opportunity to teach others by word and example.

To assess properly the significance of Hrotsvit's treatment of virginity, it is useful to contrast her legends with the typical pattern of a virgin martyr's story. By Hrotsvit's time, a familiar model existed for martyrdom tales, a model so familiar that it was readily evident in both oral and written sources. Events were expected to take place during a time of trials for Christians; the chief protagonist was likely to be a beautiful virgin who has attracted the notice of a pagan noble who is sexually excited by her. The virgin's Christian identity is revealed by her insistence on maintaining her virginity; once she has rejected her noble suitor, the pagan authorities step in (the suitor and the authority figure may be the same person, as in the legend of St. Margaret of Antioch). This authority figure, who may share the lecherous designs of the younger suitor and who certainly promotes them, feels his authority threatened by the recalcitrant virgin and applies tortures to compel the virgin to make the necessary sacrifices to the pagan divinities. When torture fails, due to the steadfast faith of the virgin, mass conversions result. The tale ends with the exemplary death and apotheosis of the virgin and the moral defeat of the pagans.

In the hands of male writers, such a story may imprison the female characters in a male discourse that allows them neither movement nor speech:

Whether adolescents or viragos, the female martyrs of hagiographic romance undergo the same basic drama, a drama that pits a defenseless heroine against a powerful male protagonist. Within these narratives, space is manipulated in a way that focuses on this unequal confrontation, proving that, indeed, "the stake is everywhere." In the portrayal of the female heroines of hagiographic romance, trial by exposure results in their being simultaneously excluded by, and enclosed within, the circle of male power.[10]

Hrotsvit confidently deploys her sources to produce a new model of virgin sanctity, and she must have been well aware of the kind of folkloric models with which her audience would have been familiar. She does not limit herself to written sources, but is free to adapt her stories wherever she finds them. *Pelagius,* unlike the other legends chosen by Hrotsvit and unlike her plays, was based not on a written source but on an eyewitness's oral account of the saint's recent martyrdom in Spain.[11] Pelagius was a noble Christian youth from Galicia (now part of Spain) who ran afoul of a lecherous Moorish despot, the caliph Abderrahman, and who was martyred in Córdoba. Some of the traditional themes of the martyr's tale are recognizable here. Hrotsvit identifies the historical moment in the Spain of her tale as a time of persecution for Christians, who are expected to sacrifice to idols associated with the Muslim religion.[12] The figures of suitor and ruler-judge are combined in one person, the sensual ruler who is sexually attracted to the virgin saint, and the sexual dynamic becomes more dramatic since both lover and beloved are male. Pelagius is a model son; he volunteered to come to Abderrahman's court as a hostage for the tribute owed by his father, the ruler of Galicia, and it is this act that has brought him to the attention of the caliph. The other Christian martyrs who form the background to the confrontation between Abderrahman and Pelagius are obligatory in such a tale, but in Hrotsvit's version they too are active rather than passive or victimized. The Spanish Christians who figure in the story prior to the introduction of Pelagius have a history of aggressively insulting the idols and the emperor. Pelagius himself, although he tries to remain tactful when brought before the caliph, using persuasive speech to protect himself, also acts aggressively. He protects his virginity and his Christian identity by smacking the caliph in the mouth when the latter tries to kiss him:

[E]t dextra compressis martiris ora,
Astrictim laeva complectens colla sacrata,
Quo sic oscillum saltem configeret unum.
Callida sed testis confudit ludicra regis
Osque petit subito pugno regali vibrato
Intulit et tantum pronis obtutibus ictum,
Sanguis ut absque mora stilans de vulnere facto
Barbam foedavit necnon vestes madefecit.[13]

([A]nd when he had grasped firmly with his right hand the face of the martyr,
He encircled that holy neck with his left,
So that he might plant a quick little kiss.
But the witness to the faith confounded the practiced sport of the king
And with a swinging fist sought the mouth of the ruler,
And brought such a blow to that downturned face

That with no delay blood produced by the wound he had made
Dirtied his beard and soaked his clothes.)

The only blood that is shed in the story is shed by the caliph, not by the martyr. This underscores another contrast between Hrotsvit's narrative and traditional accounts of martyrdom; the sadism and voyeurism of most of the early virgin-martyr legends is completely absent in her poem. There is no emphasis on the vulnerability of the saint and no interest in tortures that may be inflicted. The attempt to violate Pelagius's body by hurling it from a catapult fails, and so he is undramatically beheaded and his body given to the waves.

It is impossible to say what the narrative focus of this legend was when Hrotsvit heard it. In the legend she has created, initial emphasis falls on summarizing the political history of Spain, on placing this martyr's death both historically and politically. In contrast to this rather "realistic" concern, her representation of Pelagius is unabashedly idealized. He is gorgeous, verbally skilled, intensely loyal to his father, fearless in facing the consequences of his repudiation of Abderrahman. The poem moves quickly, with rapid shifts in narrative viewpoint and in the location of the observer. Of the 412 lines of the poem, 143 are devoted to giving the background of the political history of Spain and of Abderrahman's motives; the central third of the poem introduces Pelagius with his father and shows his imprisonment as hostage for his father's debt, his presentation to the caliph, and their confrontation. Pelagius's death and the testing of his body (in order to establish his genuine sanctity) take up the final third. This remarkably broad and swift narrative has the effect of reinforcing the impression of historical accuracy and of underlining the concern with establishing political, as well as spiritual, truth.

The cast of characters in *Pelagius* is not divided into good and evil, Christians and Muslims. Instead, we meet a very specific villain, who has specific motivations for putting Pelagius to death. All Arabs are not perceived as evil; for instance, although members of the Muslim court recognize and condone the caliph's homosexuality, they are not perceived as vicious.[14] They are shown to be genuinely pained by seeing Pelagius in prison, and they bring him to the attention of the caliph because they wish to save his life. Pelagius is perfect, and yet his gesture of striking the caliph contradicts any stereotypical notion of Christian perfection. In this situation, it is not for him to turn the other cheek.

As John Boswell notes, "Hroswitha does not suggest that homosexual acts are either praiseworthy or especially despicable." He continues:

> Hroswitha meant to make no theological statement about homosexual acts, but her casual tone is revealing. She recognizes that Muslims are more given to such behavior than Christians but seems to feel that the major issue in her story is that of bearing witness to the Christian faith and not cooperating with lustful pagans. . . . It was not "unnatural" for men to relate sexually to men but simply "unseemly" for Christian men to relate in any personal way to pagan men.[15]

The word that Hrotsvit uses to describe Pelagius in this scene, as he repudiates the advances of the caliph, is "testis" [witness (to the faith)], for this is what is at stake for her. Her hero's virginity is not a rejection of sex so much as it is an affirmation, a witnessing, to one's being as a Christian.

As her source for *Agnes,* Hrotsvit employed a text believed in the Middle Ages to have been written by St. Ambrose.[16] This epistle is a traditional hagiographical account and is the most detailed of the legends concerning the virgin martyr that were available to Hrotsvit. Here, too, Hrotsvit marks the legend as her own by celebrating the beauty, eloquence, and courage of virginity. Agnes is a "meritis clarissima virgo,"[17] a virgin renowned for her merits, her active virtues. Of noble birth, she is "pulchra . . . facie fideique decora nitore" [lovely of face and charming in the splendor of her faith],[18] celebrated everywhere for her outstanding virtues. Sophronius, the son of the prefect of Rome, falls in love with her and "stultus speravit" [the stupid man hoped][19] to marry her and corrupt her with his vile love. But as Hrotsvit tells it, the beautiful virgin rejects the false beauty of the gifts he offers her and insists that he leave her alone—forcefully using three verbs of backward motion in telling him where to go: "Discedens a me citius fugiendo recede" [Back off, depart from me in swifter flight].[20]

Agnes rejects Sophronius because she has a more beautiful husband, whom she describes in the erotic language of the Song of Songs. She adds:

> Affectu quem secreto [cum] cordis amabo,
> Nulla puellaris patior detrimenta pudoris;
> Ast ubi forte sui merear complexibus uti
> Eius in thalamum, sponsarum more, coruscum
> Duci, permaneo virgo sine sorde pudica.
> Cui debebo fidem soli servare perennem:
> Ipsi me toto cordis conamine credo.[21]

> [When I shall love him in the secret affection of my heart,
> I shall suffer no detriments to girlish modesty;
> But when I shall merit experiencing his embraces in my wedding bed,
> When I am led [to him] as a bride,
> I will remain a pure virgin, without defilement.
> Only for him must I preserve eternal troth;
> To him I give myself with all the support of my heart.]

This is a strong and eloquent statement, expanding considerably on the Pseudo-Ambrose Epistle; Ambrose's style has a lapidary eloquence, emphasizing the paradox of chaste love for Christ.

Sophronius, who can recognize the truth when he hears it, gives in to bitter sorrow at this rejection and feigns illness. When his worried father learns the real cause of his son's malady, he rages at Agnes. To him it is a question of power: How dare this maiden prefer someone over his son? Finding that she is a Christian, he believes he can compel her to worship idols. First he tries persuasion, suggesting that she become a Vestal Virgin

if she likes virginity so much; she is unmoved by this threat and enthusiastically attacks such false beliefs and false images. But when the prefect
swears that he will bring her first to the temple of Vesta and then to a
brothel if she refuses to sacrifice, she becomes genuinely frightened. Yet
she maintains a brave demeanor, asserting that he could not voice such
threats if he knew the true God, whom she trusts will prevent her from
giving in to sin:

> At sacra virgo, minis nimium trepidans super istis,
> Audacter mox praefecto dedit ista responsa:
> "Si tu namque Deum scires hunc, quem colo . . .
> Talia verba tuo nolles profundere rostro
> Nec mihi terrores toties praeponere tristes.
> Hinc ego, quae sectando fidem Christi meliorem
> Illum cognosco necnon cognoscor ab illo,
> Ipsius dextra me defendente superna
> Spero delicti numquam maculis violari,
> Carnis spurcitias fragilis sed vincere cunctas."[22]

> [But the holy virgin, although she was very frightened by these threats,
> Still swiftly gave back this brave response to the prefect:
> "If you knew the God whom I worship . . .
> You would not want to pour out of your mouth such words,
> Nor would you show me so many frightful terrors.
> So I, by following the better faith of Christ,
> Acknowledge him and am acknowledged by him.
> I hope, with his right hand protecting me,
> Never to be violated by spot of sin,
> But will conquer all the filthiness of frail flesh."]

Her fear, then, is not so much what may be done to her, but what she
may do. Yet she expects to triumph [vincere]. At this the prefect has her
stripped naked; a crowd has gathered, through which he plans to lead her
to the brothel that is expected to contaminate her. But she cannot be so
easily exposed; her hair miraculously grows long enough to cover her
nudity, and as soon as she reaches the threshold of the brothel an angel
greets her and clothes her in a white garment. The dark place is filled with
light, and Agnes immediately perceives a "suavis odoris" [delicious
odor].[23] The young men of Rome, who have rushed to the brothel eager
to see whether she will persevere in her vow, are blinded by the light and
thrown backward by the energy that surrounds her. They not only desist
from their evil intentions, but willingly confess the true God: "Sique locus
scelerum domus efficitur precularum" [And thus was this place of sin
transformed into a house of prayer].[24]

This is Hrotsvit's Agnes, a powerful role model for the young women
in her community, one would think. Her convent of Gandersheim was
spared hearing of a very different Agnes, the Agnes of French hagiographical romances discussed by Brigitte Cazelles. As Cazelles describes these
later narratives,

Agnes' vulnerability increases as the young and beautiful maiden is exposed to a gradually larger number of onlookers. At first, a single mode of voyeurism is at play, as Agnes endures the unchaste gazing of the tyrant's son. This mode turns pluralistic when additional characters (the prefect's servants) enter the scene. Then, the scenes of trials and tortures, set in public places such as the bordello, induce the presence of an even wider crowd. Finally, all the people of Rome, pagan priests included, are invited to the spectacle of her tortures at the stake. As Agnes' experience of space diminishes, the quantity of onlookers expands, signaling that her ordeal is proportional to her increasing visibility. The greater the number of spectators, the more melodramatic the theatrics of female exposure.[25]

Hrotsvit, keeping female subjectivity at the center of her story, shows us a Sophronius who, although he does not seem to be impressed by the light and the new mood in the place, falls dead as soon as he gets near Agnes. His father comes running and accuses Agnes of having an un-womanly heart and a cruel will and of practicing witchcraft besides. But Agnes, no longer afraid, responds "eloquently, with a well-constructed argument" [dixit facunde, bene composita ratione].[26] Although she did not cause Sophronius's death, she says, for he brought it on himself by foolishly denying the true God, she will try to bring him back to life. In response to her prayers, an angel appears and commands the dead man to live. As soon as Sophronius starts breathing again, he praises God. He has been restored to his earlier beauty, and he begins to convert others. Even the prefect is transformed by these events and feels truly happy. He, too, is converted.

It is especially in this section of her verse narrative that we can see Hrotsvit at work. She departs from her source in several significant ways, all in the direction of giving more freedom and authority to Agnes, allow-ing her to demonstrate her eloquence, and of realizing dramatic possi-bilities not exploited by the Pseudo-Ambrose letter. In the letter, the as-sorted youths who come to the brothel are blinded by the light and immediately converted; only Sophronius steps *into* the light and touches Agnes. He falls dead immediately. When the prefect accuses Agnes of using witchcraft to kill his son, she explains that it was the angel who did it; the hurt father then responds that she should pray for her angel to bring him back to life. She prays for Sophronius outside the brothel, and the angel who comes to her aid revives the dead man where he is lying within the brothel. As Sophronius leaves the brothel, he praises God. His father is stunned at this and is saddened that he cannot help "to free her after the resurrection of his son" [Ipse autem tristis abscessit, quod eam non potuit post resurrectionem filii sui liberare].[27]

The use of narrative space underscores the centrality of a female sub-ject. As Hrotsvit chooses to represent these events, Agnes is standing in a world of light, clothed in a white *stola* and protected by her angel; Sophronius does not penetrate into that light, but collapses as he comes near. Agnes insists that he has killed himself by his denial of God, but

agrees to pray to God (not to an angel) for his life. When Sophronius
returns to life, it is within the bright enclosed space where everyone is now
happily Christian, and even his father is converted. Light is contrasted first
with the darkness of the interior of the brothel and now with the hostile
Roman world, where Agnes still has enemies, for the pagan priests see this
event as an example of sedition and sacrilege. Hrotsvit's dramatic imagination has located Agnes's initial triumph on a stage that, in its alternation of
light and darkness, suggests the battle between good and evil. The Ambro-
sian text had an entirely different focus, for there the power of Agnes'
virginity elicits three accusations of witchcraft: first by the prefect, then by
the pagan priests as they condemn her to the fire, and a third time after she
has turned the flames of her pyre on the crowd of bystanders.[28]

Unlike the Pseudo-Ambrose's unrepentant prefect, the prefect in
Hrotsvit's text, now a Christian but still a member of this outer world, is
conflicted: "He did not like to lose her, but he could not defend her"
[Perdere non placuit, sed nec defendere quivit].[29] He abdicates his authority to a certain Aspasius, "learned in profane rites" [dictus rituque pro-
fanus], a man with "a wolf's ferocity" [feritate lupina].[30] This man commands that Agnes be thrown into a fire, but physical flames cannot touch
her who has remained untouched by the flames of passion. Instead, the
flames devour the executioners and the bystanders. As the flames burn out
to cinders and Agnes is left standing there unharmed, she praises God for
keeping her from succumbing [numquam subcubui] to the "uncleanness of
the flesh" [carnis spurcitias] and the "punishments of the sacrilegious tyrant" [poenas sacrilegi . . . tyranni].[31] Framed by the apocalyptic image
of a world in ashes, Agnes declares her willingness to die. The enraged
judge stabs her in the throat with his sword, and an angelic host descends
to meet her.[32] Her soul is borne to heaven by this beautiful and tender
company, where she is crowned as a martyr-hero:

> Martirii palmam sumpsit sine fine gerendam,
> Quo martir felix, duplici certamine victrix,
> Corporis et mentis carni semper renitentis,
> Utens aeterni bravio decoris duplicato,
> Inter virgineas fulgeret clara catervas,
> Lilia ceu, pulchre roseo permixta rubore,
> Inter delicias florum rutilat variorum.[33]

> [She took up the palm of martyrdom to carry without end,
> So that the happy martyr, the victor of a double battle
> That tested the body and the mind that always resists the body,
> Might experience eternal glory for the double victory,
> And might shine brightly among the virgin throng,
> As the lily, when mixed gracefully with rosy reds,
> Glows crimson among the charms of varied flowers.]

Hrotsvit here has chosen to combine the martial vocabulary of this
earth to honor the virgin hero's physical bravery and conquest of self with a

baroque metaphor for Agnes in heaven, a lily reflecting the rosy tones of other flowers. Her victory is not made to seem easy; Agnes has been tested grievously and has earned her presence in this timeless garden. The poem concludes with a return to earth, where Agnes's parents are solemnly burying her body and keeping vigil at her tomb. During the night they see a beautiful virgin throng, and "among these, shining in the same splendor, they saw their own Agnes, martyred for Christ." Their grief is real, and so is their joy at seeing their daughter. And Agnes is allowed to speak with them, telling them to rejoice with her because she is now with her lover, and they are consoled.[34]

This concluding section of *Agnes,* where she is received into heaven as a *victrix* and made part of a highly aestheticized heavenly choir, from which she comforts her parents by showing them "their own Agnes" now safe and happy, illustrates many of Hrotvit's techniques in her heroic treatment of virginity. Virginity embraces those qualities of beauty and bravery that are ordinarily polarized and sex-typed in literature and folklore. Both Agnes and Pelagius are as beautiful as they are brave, and this union of qualities in virginity creates a particular form of heroism—eloquence, the ability to persuade, to convince others. Eloquence for Hrotsvit is not beautiful or decorative speech, it is irresistable speech, language that converts, that changes behavior. Because they can use language in this way, her virgin martyrs are never victims.

Other scholars have noted that Hrotsvit is not particularly interested in describing war or violence; she is also not interested in describing the tortures applied to martyrs. One of the striking differences between Hrotsvit's *Pelagius* and *Agnes* and other virgin-martyr stories is the refusal to show her virgin heroes as passive victims. We never see their bodies being violated; the ground is not drenched in their blood; their limbs are not broken, as they are in conventional martyrs' stories. Neither does she surround them with supernatural help. Their virtue protects them, but they remain the subjects of their own narratives. The possibility of action is not taken away from them by divine rescues. Even in their most threatened moments, when Pelagius is in prison and when Agnes is brought to the brothel, they are perceived as bathed in an aura of personal power, an appealing combination of beauty and strength, that allows the audience to hope that they cannot really be harmed, that somehow they will not permit themselves to be harmed.

Because Hrotsvit avoids presenting martyrs as victims, she can demonstrate their tenderness and their temptations without becoming sentimental. Agnes and Pelagius are idealized, of course, but, unlike many legendary saints, they do not repudiate their parents but instead show their attachment to them and wish to reassure and to comfort them. They have human fears that they may be tempted. Compared with many saints, Agnes and Pelagius live a remarkably sensual existence; virginity is not a negation of erotic desire, but a creative sublimation of it. The reverse of this is that in Hrotsvit's writings, sexuality, passion, may be portrayed as mad or stupid, but not disgusting. Even Calimachus (in the play *Drusiana and Cal-imachus*), driven by such passion for Drusiana that he wants to violate her dead body, is not presented as disgusting or horrifying. Virginity is heroic because temptations to surrender to passion are also on a heroic scale. For this reason, Hrotsvit's virgin martyrs must be killed with heroic weapons, the instruments of personal combat. Pelagius is beheaded by the sword, and Agnes is stabbed in the throat; in the plays, Hirena is killed by an arrow, and Sapientia's daughters, Faith, Hope, and Charity, can be be-headed only by the sword, although every possible kind of execution is attempted and fails.

Notes

1. Original Latin texts are in *Hroswitha Opera,* ed. Karl Strecker (Leipzig: Biblioteca Teubneriana, 1906, 1930). For a summary of recent scholarship, see two works edited by Katharina M. Wilson: "The Saxon Canoness: Hrotsvit of Gandersheim," in *Medieval Women Writers,* ed. Wilson (Athens: University of Georgia Press, 1984), pp. 112–165, and *Hrotsvit of Gandersheim: Rara Avis in Saxonia?* (Ann Arbor, Mich.: MARC, 1987). For an assessment of Hrotsvit's literary gifts, see Peter Dronke, *Women Writers of the Middle Ages: A Critical Study of Texts from Perpetua to Marguerite Porete* (Cambridge: Cambridge University Press, 1984), pp. 55–83.

2. Dronke, *Women Writers of the Middle Ages,* pp. 55–56.

3. *Maria,* in *Hrotsvithae Opera,* ed. Helena Homeyer (Munich: Schoningh, 1970), lines 394–400.

4. Dronke, *Women Writers of the Middle Ages,* p. 62.

5. *Maria,* lines 13–16. [My translation] This invocation is composed in elegaic couplets; the poem proper in leonine hexameter, with clausulae rhyming with homoeoteleuton.

6. *Agnes,* in *Hrotsvithae Opera,* ed. Homeyer, lines 1–9. [My translation]

7. *Pelagius,* lines 199–205. I quote from Mary Gonsalva Wiegand's text, which utilizes a line supplied by Celtes, an early editor of Hrotsvit's works ("The Non-Dramatic Works of Hroswitha" [Ph.D. diss., St. Louis University, 1936], pp. 140–141 [My translation]). Homeyer, in *Hrotsvithae Opera,* shows a lacuna at line 199.

8. Brigitte Cazelles, *The Lady as Saint: A Collection of French Hagiographic Romances of the Thirteenth Century* (Philadelphia: University of Pennsylvania Press, 1991), p. 50.

9. *Pelagius,* lines 213–214.

10. Cazelles, *Lady as Saint,* p. 59.

11. On the sources and background to *Pelagius,* see the notes in *Hrotsvithae Opera,* ed. Homeyer, pp. 123–126, and Wiegand, "Non-Dramatic Works of Hros-witha," pp. 152–154.

12. The reference to idols makes one question how well informed Hrotsvit's source was, since he did not recognize the implausibility of associating the Muslim religion with idols. But the medieval world in general was not interested in under-standing Islam, and Hrotsvit was writing well before the Crusades, when some-what greater familiarity with Muslim customs may be supposed.

13. *Pelagius,* lines 268–275.

14. On the practice of homosexuality in Spain at this time, see John Boswell, *Christianity, Social Tolerance, and Homosexuality* (Chicago: University of Chicago Press, 1980), pp. 194–200. He observes: "Idealization of intense relationships between persons of the same gender was even more notable in the one area of Europe in which a dynamic and influential urban culture survived through the early Middle Ages. . . . Cordoba was the largest city in the West in the ninth and tenth centuries, and its wealth and sophistication dazzled not only the Muslim but also the Christian world. . . . Although the Qur'an and early religious writings of Islam display mildly negative attitudes toward homosexuality, Islamic society has generally ignored these deprecations, and most Muslim cultures have treated homosexuality with indifference, if not admiration. . . . In early medieval Spain this tendency [to idealize homosexual love in love poetry] was if anything exaggerated. . . . Erotic verse about ostensibly homosexual relationships constitutes the bulk of published Hispano-Arab poetry."

15. Ibid., pp. 199–200.

16. On the various versions of the legend of St. Agnes, see Pio Franchi de' Cavalieri, *Santa Agnese nella tradizione e nella legenda* (Rome: Römische Quartalschrift für Christliche Alterthumskunde, 1899). For the account attributed to St. Ambrose, see *Patrologiae cursus completus, series latina,* vol. 17, ed. Jacques-Paul Migne (Paris, 1849), Sp. 456–459 (the sermon on St. Agnes), and Sp. 479–483 (Epistle on St. Agnes). For the figure of St. Agnes in French hagiographical romances, see Cazelles, *Lady as Saint.*

17. *Agnes,* line 25.

18. Ibid., line 31.

19. Ibid., line 54.

20. Ibid., line 63.

21. Ibid., lines 104–110. Compare the Pseudo-Ambrose Epistle: "Quem cum amavero, casta sum; cum tetigero, munda sum: cum accepero, virgo sum."

22. *Agnes,* lines 193–205. The Epistle states that "Tunc beata Agnes cum ingenti constantia dixit."

23. *Agnes,* line 221. No odor is mentioned in Hrotsvit's source, but the odor of sanctity is a hagiographic commonplace.

24. Ibid., line 253.

25. Cazelles, *Lady as Saint,* p. 51.

26. *Agnes,* line 288.

27. Pseudo-Ambrose, Epistle on St. Agnes, Sp. 482, par. 12.

28. Ibid., Sp. 480, par. 4–Sp. 483, par. 13.

29. *Agnes,* line 354.

30. Ibid., lines 356–357.

31. Ibid., lines 380–383.

32. There is nothing in the Pseudo-Ambrose Epistle that corresponds to the descent of the heavenly host here, just as Agnes dies. At the comparable point in the Epistle, Agnes's strength in martyrdom is compared to the sufferings of two Old Testament saints, Elijah and Daniel, and of two Christian saints, St. Lawrence and St. Thecla. Following this, we are told of the martyrdom of St. Emerentiana, who was stoned to death by a pagan crowd while praying at Agnes' gravesite (Pseudo-Ambrose, Epistle on St. Agnes, Sp. 483, par. 15).

33. *Agnes,* lines 443–453.

34. Ibid. The tender sympathy for the parents' grief is absent in the Epistle; instead, the emotional tone is one of awe at the beauty of the angelic army, and the

concluding image is of heaven, not of earth. While keeping vigil at her grave, Agnes's parents see an "exercitum virginum, quae omnes auro intextis cycladis indutae cum ingenti lumine praeteribant: inter quas etiam vident beatissimam Agnem similiter fulgentem, et ad dexteram ejus Agnum stantem. Haec dum viderent parentes ejus, et qui simul erant, quasi stupore mentis detenti sunt. Sed beata Agnes rogat sanctas virgines parumper gradum figere, et stans parentibus suis dixit: Videte ne me mortuam lugeatis, sed congaudete mihi et congratulamini, quia cum his virginibus lucidas sedes accepi, et illi sum juncta in coelis, quem in terris posita tota devotione dilexi. Et his dictis, pertransiit" (Pseudo-Ambrose, Epistle on St. Agnes, Sp. 483, par. 16).[A virgin army, all of whom had come there garbed in stately robes woven with gold, and they shone with a great light; and among them they saw the most blessed Agnes, similarly shining, standing at the right hand of her Lamb. When her parents saw this, and those who were with them likewise, they were overcome as if by amazement of mind. But the blessed Agnes asked the holy virgins to stop their procession for a moment, and standing next to her parents she said, "You see me whom you mourned as dead, but rejoice with me and give thanks for I have taken my shining seat with his virgins, and I am joined to him in heaven whom I loved with complete devotion on earth." And when she had said this, she went away.]

6

Transforming the World: The Serpent-Dragon and the Virgin Saint

In Florence, in the Casa di Dante, there is an illustration taken from a late medieval manuscript,[1] of the church attended by Dante's family. In the foreground of this sketch of a typical Romanesque parish church, we see a large, rather languid, green dragon, dominated by the tiny figure of a woman with a cross in her hand. This is all that is needed to identify the church of St. Margaret of Antioch, for the iconographic attribute of the dragon is consistently associated with the legend of this virgin martyr of the early centuries of Christianity.

This particular image of the dragon and the woman attracted my attention because it is contemporary with the narratives of late medieval saints' lives in which a holy woman is confronted by and overcomes a monstrous serpent. What I intend to do in this chapter is to trace the iconographic development of the confrontation with the serpent in hagiography about women, by first looking at various versions of the legend of St. Margaret and then turning to the lives of several women saints who lived in the thirteenth century in Italy.

The basic outline of St. Margaret's story is similar to many legends of the first Christian martyrs.[2] Said to be the daughter of a pagan priest, Aedisius of Antioch, she became a Christian, was turned out of her home, and lived as a shepherdess. She was discovered by the pagan Olybrius, governor of Antioch, who kidnapped her and attempted to seduce or marry her. Proclaiming herself a Christian and a virgin, she refused Olybrius's attempts to convince her to renounce her religion. She was then tortured and tempted in various frightful ways, including being swallowed by a dragon that later burst asunder. Through her preaching she was invoked, especially by pregnant women, to whom she promised safety in childbirth and health for their children.[3]

It is unlikely that St. Margaret was a historical person, although details in her legend point to her being beheaded during the persecution ordered by Diocletian. No ancient text of her life exists, although stories about her were certainly in circulation in the fifth century, for in A.D. 494 Pope Gelasius declared her legend apocryphal. She was a saint in the Eastern Church first; only in the ninth century was her name included in a Western martyrology. The real flowering of her cult came in the high Middle Ages, in the footsteps of the Crusaders.[4]

The major part of the narrative of her life, whichever version we read, emphasizes the violence of her tortures. At the command of Olybrius, she is suspended from a beam and whipped with rods. This fails to make her abjure Christianity, so she is strung up again and her flesh torn with hooks. Still recalcitrant, she is thrown into prison, where she prays to see the true agent of her persecution. A huge, frightful dragon suddenly appears before her; she makes the sign of the cross, but he swallows her anyway. The dragon, however, cannot digest her; his belly splits open, and she emerges, unharmed, cross in hand. One manifestation of evil having been vanquished, a second one appears, a dark man who menaces her sexually. She throws him to the ground and steps on his neck. Light fills the prison as the demon confesses his defeat. The next day, further tortures are applied, but the attempts to burn her or boil her are unsuccessful and only give her the opportunity to convert the pagans gathered around. Finally, the frustrated Olybrius gives the order for her to be beheaded. The flight of her soul to heaven is observed by many.

What happened to this already fantastic story when it was retold in the later Middle Ages? The most widespread and popular version was the late-thirteenth-century telling by Jacobus de Voragine in the *Legenda Aurea*, a collection of saints' lives and pious tales for every day of the year.[5] While the *Legenda* is for us a rich source of magical and legendary material, Jacobus himself makes it clear that he does not believe all of it. He is not comfortable with the dragon episode and gives alternative readings of it:

> [A]nd lo, there appeared before her a great dragon, who was seeking to devour her; she made the sign of the cross and he vanished. Or, as one reads elsewhere, placing his tongue under her feet, he thus swallowed her. But Margaret, when she perceived that he wanted to swallow her armed herself with the sign of the cross. Consequently the dragon, by virtue of the cross, burst open, and the virgin issued forth unharmed.[6]

Jacobus adds that the business of the dragon's devouring her, then bursting open, is clearly "fabulous." The second satanic attack, in which the demon appears in the likeness of a man, seems more probable to him. It is a distinctly comic scene. Margaret swiftly throws the demon to the ground, stands on his neck, and insults him. The demon is reduced to whining: "O blessed Margaret, I am overcome. If a young man had overcome me, I wouldn't mind, but I am overcome by a mere slip of a girl. And what grieves me more—her mother and father were my friends."[7]

While Jacobus da Voragine's Version of St. Margaret's martyrdom was extremely influential, it was not the only version of the story in circulation. More revealing about tensions concerning women and sexuality is an anonymous fourteenth-century Tuscan legend.[8] The traditional narrator of St. Margaret's story is a certain Teotimo, a converted Christian and a learned man. He becomes the husband of Margaret's *balia,* or wet nurse; it is with this couple that Margaret has been living when she is kidnapped by Olibrio. The nurse and Teotimo visit Margaret in prison to bring her bread and water; this gives Teotimo the opportunity to overhear Margaret's prayers and her dialogue with her demonic visitors. After her death, it is Teotimo who collects her relics and brings them to Antioch. Like a contemporary notary in a case for canonization, he does not merely summarize what happens—he transcribes the saint's exact words.

That St. Margaret is brought up not by her own parents but by foster parents, and that she leads a pure pastoral life rather than a corrupt city existence, indicates her affinities with the heroes of folk legend and fairy tales. But these attributes, too, have been rationalized to accord with fourteenth-century standards of behavior and with popular fourteenth-century notions about saints' lives. Thus Margaret has become attached to her *balia* and prefers to remain in the countryside with her, tending the animals, instead of returning to a more materially comfortable life in the city with her father, who does not share her religious values and does not appreciate her vow of virginity. Even in the countryside she is not safe; she can still be kidnapped by a powerful figure like Olibrio. "Kidnapped virgins" may be found in indexes to folklore, but they are also to be noted in medieval historical documents.

As we shall see shortly, the sexual tension and violence in this Tuscan story are undisguised. This in itself in not new. Even in narratives as early as those of Eusebius, we find the same polarization of good Christian virgins and evil lustful pagans. The fact that the early Christian saints, particularly the women, chose virginity rather than active sexuality or marriage was clearly very threatening to their society, and the kinds of tortures supposedly inflicted on them by their pagan persecutors were obviously someone's sadistic fantasies. The young heroines of early saints' lives are publicly stripped naked and dragged to whorehouses, where the attempt is made to violate them; their breasts are slashed, their nipples torn off, their teeth pulled. Their sufferings seem to be brought about directly by their choice of virginity and only indirectly by their identity as Christians, for they are revealed as Christians only because they each refuse to marry an influential pagan official. Thus the essence of female sanctity in these stories is to be found in the heroic defense of virginity. But it is virginity defined more by the pre-Christian sense of emotional independence than by an intact hymen. The virgin saints are physically violated, even though

they may still technically be virgins, but they are never emotionally violated. This is the theme that particularly interests St. Margaret's
anonymous fourteenth-century hagiographer.

In his version, the Roman prefect Olibrio becomes God's competition
for Margaret's sexual favors. Like the hero of a medieval romance, he is
riding from the east when he spies the beautiful Margaret tending her
flock. he is struck with blind love immediately: if she is a slave, he will buy
her; if she is free, he will marry her. But Margaret, with equal swiftness,
reveals that she is a christian by declaring that she has already vowed her
virginity to God and has no intention of marrying anyone. Olibrio's offers
to make her the most powerful woman in his entire household, more
important than even his mother, fail to move her. Olibrio then has her
taken to the city, where he gives orders for her to be whipped while
suspended from a beam until she agrees to sacrifice to the empire's gods,
but he cannot bear to look at her sufferings. Enraged and threatened by her
resistance, respectful of her strength, Olibrio cannot retreat now without
losing political control, as well as self-respect. In the course of his dealings
with the saint, he becomes more and more obsessed by his need to violate
her, to possess her body. If he cannot literally rape her, he can find legal
pretenses to brutalize her body, to expose her physically and emotionally,
to force her to surrender to him and to his gods.

Of course, the saint does not surrender, for she sees too clearly what is
at stake in these events. It is in this highly charged sexual context that the
dragon and the demonic man appear to her. Suddenly, we are told,

> a most cruel and horrible dragon issued forth . . . of various colors, with a
> beard and hair that seemed of gold, and teeth that seemed of iron, eyes sharp
> and brilliant as kindled flame, his tongue hanging out of his mouth; and he
> appeared to shoot forth fire from his nostrils and his mouth, and he gave off a
> stink of sulfur that filled the whole prison.[9]

Margaret, who has endured terrible things already, almost becomes hyster-
ical at this apparition, forgetting that this is what she had prayed to see.
Trembling and shaking, she prays to the "Creator and Orderer of the
Abyss" that this dragon not harm her and that she overcome it. She admits,
"I cannot see how I might harm him, if he does battle with me, for he is
hastening to swallow me up."[10] The beast (in this passage called both
"leone" and "dragone," words used earlier to describe Olibrio) does swallow her, but she so "grows" inside him that he splits apart, "and St.
Margaret came forth without any blemish, cross in hand." Her body has
been healed, so that she now senses herself "completely filled with pleasant-
ness and perfume."[11]

Next, in the left part of the prison, she sees a demon, "black and cruel,"
"sitting in the manner of a very dark man," who "says things to make her
afraid." She prays for help as he starts to close in on her, and he tells her
what the dragon's purpose has been:

[M]y brother Rostone . . . came to you in the likeness of a dragon to take away your beauty and to swallow you up and take away your memory and to reduce you to dust—and you with your prayer killed him, and now you want to confound me in the same way.[12]

Margaret recognizes that she has already won, and she wastes no time in proving it:

She . . . took the demon and put him on the ground and placed her foot on his neck and said to him: "Evil one, give up on my virginity, for I have Christ for my helper, and I am Christian and his bride."[13]

At these words, a light fills the prison, the cross appears, and a dove speaks: "Blessed are you, Margaret, for you have killed the dragon and shattered its teeth." Even the demon understands that the saint has been transformed by her union with Christ—a curious insight on his part, but consistent with the theme of virginity and the images of transformation:

Because Christ dwells in you, you can do what you will, but before he dwelt in you, you were merely earth; but since you have had the heavenly discipline, you have in you another form, and the fruit of Christ appears in you, which makes you completely filled with justice and with all agreeableness.[14]

Images of transformation and rebirth dominate the rest of the story. The next day, Margaret is brought out and strung up again, "with burning plasters . . . applied . . . to her tender and most lovely body." Margaret prays to God to use this fire to so burn her body and heart "that there be in me no iniquity and no pride." She is next thrown into a cauldron of boiling water, and again she consciously transforms her torment into further purification: "May this water be for me health and sanctification and light for my soul, so that it cleanses me of every sin, and is for me a font of baptism."[15]

Divine approval is signaled by an earthquake and by a dove bearing a golden crown. Margaret acknowledges her transformation:

Lord . . . you have clothed me in the garment of strength and beauty, of mildness and of openness, and you have illuminated my consciousness of the truth, and you have washed my soul clean of every stain and sin, and you have sent me your holy spirit.[16]

The prefect Olibrio, by now hoping only to cut his losses, seeing that thousands have been converted to Christianity by Margaret's example, gives orders for her to be led out of the city and decapitated. The saint's final prayer is a special plea for benefits for all those who read or hear the book of her martyrdom, especially women in childbirth, that they do not die in labor and that their children be born neither deformed nor deficient.

Despite the anonymous writer's attempts to lend verisimilitude to his story, the exotic manifestations of the supernatural, such as the appearance of the dragon and the excesses of torture, were no longer quite credible to his audience, at least not as physical facts of daily life. The monsters and torments endured by the thirteenth- and fourteenth-century saints were more banal and, consequently, less clearly supernatural. Yet there were events in the lives of contemporary saints that gave medieval people more reason to believe in the truth of the older stories. Let us turn now to two thirteenth-century Italian examples of visitations by serpents believed to be incarnations of Satan. The first is from the life of Blessed Umiliana de' Cerchi, who, after the death of her rather brutal husband, had converted her noble family's tower and dungeon into a hermit's cell and oratory, where she remained until her death. When these episodes took place, Umiliana was in her early twenties. Satan had been attempting to stop her prayers by sending various hallucinations to her to distract her attention. Since these attempts did not succeed,

> the serpent, the enemy of human nature, . . . took on his real form, that of a snake, of which women are generally terrified. . . . [H]e appeared enormous, staring at her with terrible eyes, thinking thus to break down her constancy. . . . Seeing him, she was struck by the great fear that she would not be safe in that cell, whether in prayer or not. Several days passed without his being able to disturb her praying. She spoke to the serpent, saying, "I conjure you, horrible snake, in the name of my Lord Jesus Christ, that if you are corporeal you depart without delay and do not return, and if you are incorporeal, my enemy, disappear from my sight, and do not molest me from now on."
>
> At these words, little by little the snake turned into smoke, but he left such a stink that she could not remain in the cell.[17]

After Umiliana insulted the snake for his foul odor, "the stink went away, and a pleasant smell remained, so much so that it seemed the agreeableness of paradise." But Satan did not give up, and his next attempt was more physically threatening:

> A few days passed, and there was Satan again, and he brought with him a great serpent, not incorporeal as he was, nor an imaginary creation, but truly corporeal, terrible and terrifying. This produced great terror and fear in her, but still she paid attention to her praying. When she rested, he wrapped his tail around her feet, and leaned his head against her cheek. This frightened her so much that she could neither pray nor sleep securely. When she went to lie down, she wrapped her clothes around her feet and tied them with a belt, so that the serpent couldn't enter from below, at her feet, and get to her nude body.
>
> Although she trusted fully in God, she did not want to take such a risk and tempt God by overconfidence, so as much as possible, when the snake was watching her, she was careful not to touch him with her hands. As she knew that this situation had been given to her as a teaching, she was unwilling to reveal it to anyone.
>
> She endured this patiently for three days, and then, not wanting to have her prayer disturbed any further, she said to the serpent that was next to her: "I command you, by virtue of the name of my beloved Christ, to coil up at once, without delay, right here next to my hands." At these words the snake tucked his head under and coiled up his whole body immediately; the holy Umiliana

put both hands under his body, lifting him up from the ground, praising and blessing God, saying "Blessed be that most potent Love that created you." And so, bringing him to a window of the tower, she commanded him, saying "Go on your way, and stay no longer with me, for you are useless and fruitless." Constrained by these words, the serpent departed.[18]

St. Verdiana's technique for dealing with serpentine evil was similar. Like Umiliana, she was living a recluse's life. Her cell was attached to the church of St. Anthony in Castelfiorentino. Her biographer, who had been taken to see her when he was a small boy, introduces the snakes with heroic language from the Laocoön episode of the *Aeneid,* but the snakes are quickly domesticated:

> Behold, two awful serpents, both of equal magnitude, entered her cell through the window. . . . Day and night over a long space of time those serpents remained; and if they ever went out, they came back again after a short while, and they never left during the time that the virgin was accustomed to eat her food. They ate with her from the same dish, in which she had a little broken bread in water, or milk and beans, without any condiments like oil or salt.[19]

The beasts are strong enough to knock her down with a slap of their tails, and after one such blow Verdiana spends eight days lying on the ground, unable to get up. She has to keep reminding herself about the crucifixion and the suffering of the martyrs to maintain her patience, but she neither acts in a hostile manner toward the snakes nor tries to force them to leave. In fact, she makes friends with them. When some of the townspeople try to kill them and succeed only in cutting off their tails, the snakes flee to their "nurse." Not only are their wounds healed, but their tails are restored as well. After thirty years, one of the snakes is killed, and the other runs away. Verdiana is saddened; she makes a basket in which she preserves the head of the dead snake. (Basket and snake's head are included among her relics in Castelfiorentino.) Her biographer says that she was unhappy at losing "the occasion of such great merit in divinely granted companionship." He seems to have forgotten his earlier conviction that the snakes were satanic beings. Verdiana sees the snakes' loss as a portent of her approaching death, for they had been with her for almost the entire time of her enclosure. She does indeed die shortly thereafter.[20]

There can be little doubt that for most medieval persons the serpent and dragon imagery in these female saints' lives was symbolic of the threat of sexuality. In an anonymous dramatic version of the St. Margaret story, for instance, Margaret states directly that the dragon is lust.[21] Yet when one reads the texts of these saints' lives attentively, it is apparent that the narrators, and the women about whom they are writing, are trying to examine the process of transformation that comes about through the confrontation with evil.

Jacobus's intention in writing the *Legenda Aurae* was primarily to codify and to transmit inherited legend, making these devotional tales accessible to a wider audience. He is interested in distinguishing fact from fable; for him, a saint's life is more true, and thus more useful morally, if it is historically probable. The unknown Tuscan writer of St. Margaret's story, however, is highly conscious of how he is shaping and commenting on the pious legend in order to provide a teaching on evil. He is interested in exploring the truth of symbol, not of fact; he sees Margaret's story as one of transformation, and the prayers he ascribes to the saint explicate the process of transformation she is undergoing.

Vito da Cortona, the Franciscan friar who wrote the life of Blessed Umiliana, knew her personally and witnessed her death. He supplemented his personal knowledge by witnesses' accounts of Umiliana's saintliness. Verdiana's biographer also interviewed those who had known her and to verify the events mentioned by his informants. Like Jacobus, these two writers tried to distinguish between fact and fable, attempting to present the most concrete evidence possible of the women's sanctity. Thus the serpent episode must be realistic by late medieval standards; the snakes must be living, fleshly creatures, as well as symbolic revelations of evil. The writers also saw themselves to be composing works of spiritual instruction, yet I suspect that much of the wisdom in Umiliana's and Verdiana's lives was not apparent to them. It is the very transparency of the biographers in presenting what they have established as true that allows us to see the saints' wisdom for ourselves.

The women's ability to remain self-possessed and to act despite their own fear is impressive. There is no pretending to special bravery, no heroics; although afraid, Umiliana and Verdiana stand their ground without making judgments, continuing what they have begun and waiting for the proper response to reveal itself. Because they do not panic, there is no violence in their responses. Nor does their fear turn into hatred. Umiliana does not like her visitor, but the way she picks up the coiled thing tells us that she does not shrink from touching it.

Her reason for not handling the snake earlier is significant: she does not want to tempt God by being overconfident, by taking it for granted that he will rescue her. She expects herself to put limits on the situation— no touching; this snake is not going to crawl under her skirt if she can prevent it. When we read this scene as the medieval audience undoubtedly did, as an attempted satanic rape, we can see how enlightened Umiliana's response is. She is not going to wait for God to save her from anything worse than has already happened; she will minimize and control the situation in a self-protective but nonaggressive and noninflammatory way so that she can continue with her business, which is prayer.

What is critical is that she understands and deals with the situation not as an attack or a temptation (although from Satan's point of view it is both these things), but as an occasion for her own growth, given to her as a teaching. Looking at apparently hostile events as teachings eliminates the need for a negative response that only feeds the hostility; it gives one the space to stand back from one's initial fear and to ask, "What is this situation presenting me with? What is the appropriate way to respond?" Umiliana tries to bring no preconceived notions to the event—she simply looks at it. Looking at it transforms it, and herself, so that in the end she can say, "Blessed is the Love that created this snake."

St. Margaret learns the same lesson in her serpentine encounter, for when she is next tortured, with burning plasters and with boiling water, she is not simply trying to endure. She consciously "reads" these events, not as hostile acts, but as metaphors for self-transformation, as agents of purgation. Her ability to read the divine in the apparently evil gives her three rebirths: she is expelled from the monster's belly like Jonah; like the fabled phoenix, she is renewed rather than destroyed by fire; for her, the cauldron of boiling water becomes a font of baptism.

As the serpent iconography reveals, both Umiliana and Verdiana have studied the evil within themselves. When confronted by the unknown, alien aspects of the world, they do not recoil but act with respect for themselves and for this new situation, which can teach them something. They treat the "enemy" with respect, too, and he thus loses the ability to harm them. Had the women been passive or masochistic, rather than watchful, these situations would have brought them great suffering. They were afraid, but they did not act in stereotypical female fashion by cowering or by flight; neither did they act in conventionally male ways by attacking or trying to kill the beasts.

Umiliana's and Verdiana's attitude may have been acquired from meditating on the story of St. Margaret. The fact that Margaret had triumphed over a dragon-serpent was in itself significant and provided an archetypal image by means of which they could interpret events in their own lives. Margaret's specific behavior was equally instructive: she armed herself with the sign of the cross before surrendering to the greater physical power of the dragon, remembering meanwhile her own inviolate virginity. Thus even when the dragon engulfed her bodily, he could not make her lose her memory, her self-consciousness. In fact, she "grew" in his belly until he was forced to expel her. She did not die; he did.

Similarly, Umiliana and Verdiana submit to being enveloped bodily by their snakes while maintaining a high level of self-consciousness, never permitting the snakes to be more than peripheral to their life of prayer and meditation. As a result of such encounters with evil, all the women are transformed, gaining the ability to "read" the events in the world around them. Having survived such encounters, the saintly woman takes harassment less seriously and can even be amused by events that frighten others. For example, having passed through a series of encounters with Satan, including discovering him in his chilly, serpentine form lying next to her in bed, and learning through experience that violence and aggression on her part only provoked more suffering, Blessed Benevenuta of Friuli learned to preserve her self-consciousness while acknowledging satanic power. Benevenuta was bedridden for some time, and friends who were nuns in the nearby Dominican convent came to keep her company. One dark night, some very alarming things began to happen in the house. Large rocks sailed through the air and landed in the midst of the group, having passed through the expensive glass windows without breaking them. The heavy bar on the door jumped out of its sockets, and something that sounded like a bear seemed to be under the bed, noisily gnawing on a bone. The sisters huddled around Benevenuta in terror; she laughingly comforted them, saying it was "only Satan" harassing them and assuring them that they would come to no harm.[22]

For a woman to be recognized as a saint, as St. Margaret, St. Verdiana, and the Blessed Umiliana were, she must exhibit moral goodness and exceptional heroic virtue, exceptional power to transform the world.[23] To achieve this, her behavior must transcend sex roles and sexual stereotyping. If we read the encounter with the serpent as a sexual attack, a confrontation with the dark, obsessive aspect of sexuality, we see the woman saint's victory as the triumph of moral purity.

But if we further examine the way in which the women confront this kind of attack, their reading of the situation as a teaching, their willingness to be transformed, we can see them escaping sex roles, moving into a new kind of freedom of action that is neither passive nor aggressive, female nor male. This new transformative vision allows them to act in totally unconventional ways when the situation seems to demand it—the woman saint may act as either a man or a woman, or as both or neither. The power of the saint–serpent configuration to symbolize and to catalyze non-sex-typed behavior is clearly revealed in the legend of Joan of Arc.[24] Saintly figures appeared to her while she was tending the village flocks and told her that she must lead her country to freedom; when she was later forced to reveal the identity of her divine advisers, she said that one of them was St. Margaret.[25] It was St. Margaret who counseled her to dress as a man in order to escape sexual harassment, and the trial records indicate that it was St. Margaret who expounded on the power of self-conscious virginity in an aggressive male world.

Women from St. Margaret to St. Joan recognized that essential to being accepted as a spiritual leader was their escape from the categories of male and female. The virgin in armor who led the dauphin's troops to victory was visibly neither male nor female—but she was clearly a saint. The trial documents for Joan indicate that the Burgundians were very aware of this psychological basis for Joan's charisma. Consequently, their mode of attack was to induce doubts about the inspiration by St. Margaret and to try to convince Joan that by wearing male clothing, she was keeping herself in a state of sin so that she could not receive the sacraments.

It would have been very useful to the Burgundians for Joan to lose her virginity, so she was kept in a men's prison where she was repeatedly harassed sexually. In prison, her method for dealing with the situation was the same as that employed by Margaret, Verdiana, and Umiliana: to read the total situation as a teaching, rather than as an attack; to refuse to act hostilely and aggressively; to remain watchful; and to limit the possibilities for physical harm or violation. When Joan wore male clothing as a warrior-maiden, her armor was a sign of the transformation of her sexuality, but in prison, she said, she wore male clothing just so she could not be raped. So strongly had Joan identified with her saints that she expected, like St. Margaret, to be beheaded. Instead, as we know, she was burned at the stake, but even then, according to witnesses, St. Margaret was with her, and Joan seemed to be visibly transformed by the final flames.

Notes

1. The manuscript is the Codice Rustici of 1448; the original is in the Biblioteca Nazionale in Florence.

2. For a summary of the legend of St. Margaret of Antioch, see *New Catholic Encyclopedia* (Washington, D.C.: Catholic University of America, 1967–1979), s.v. "Saint Margaret of Antioch." A convenient handbook of saints' lives is Donald Attwater, *The Penguin Dictionary of Saints* (Baltimore: Penguin, 1965). Central to the study of hagiography are René Aigrain, *L'Hagiographie: Ses sources, ses methodes, son histoire* (Paris: Bloud et Giroy, 1953), and Hippolyte Delehaye, *Les Legendes hagiographiques* (Brussels: Bureau de la Société des Bollandistes, 1905). For further discussion and bibliography on St. Margaret, see Marie Delcourt, "Female Saints in Masculine Clothing," in *Hermaphrodite: Myths and Rites of the Bisexual Figure in Classical Antiquity,* trans. Jennifer Nicholson (London: Studio Books, 1961), pp. 84–102. In this chapter, I have limited myself as much as possible to discussing images of transformation, especially those connected with the image of the dragon-serpent, in the St. Margaret of Antioch legend. But the identity of St. Margaret for the medieval audience is actually more complicated than I make it appear, for there were two St. Margarets: St. Margaret of Antioch, virgin and martyr, and St. Margaret, virgin and martyr. This second Margaret is now identified with St. Pelagia and St. Marina; because these three are all associated with the sea, and because their feast days follow the dates of pagan rites for Aphrodite, some scholars have believed that their saint cults were survivals of the cult of Aphrodite (for further references, see Delcourt, *Hermaphrodite*). The other characteristic shared by these women, called by some the "transvestite saints," is that in each of their legends, the young woman, fleeing marriage, disguises herself as a monk, is accused of having seduced a nun, and is vindicated only at her death. What interests me here is that the stories of these two Margarets are linked by the imagery of transformation and rebirth; wearing male clothing in these legends is indicative of abandoning the old life and entering on a new life with a different sexual identity. It would seem that Joan of Arc's St. Margaret was a conflation of the two Margarets and was for her the symbol of strength, independence, and the transcendence of sex-typed behavior.

3. Her connection with childbirth seems to derive from the facts of her own "birth," unharmed, from the dragon. Her cult is in some ways the perpetuation of the cult of Lucina, the protectress of childbirth.

4. *New Catholic Encyclopedia,* s.v. "Saint Margaret of Antioch." Her story was very popular in the high Middle Ages. According to Brigette Cazelles, "For example, more than one hundred manuscripts preserve one particular rendition of the story of St. Margaret" (*The Lady as Saint: A Collection of French Hagiographic Romances of the Thirteenth Century* [Philadelphia: University of Pennsylvania Press, 1991], pp. 30–31).

5. The most accessible English translation of the *Golden Legend* is that by Granger Ryan and Helmut Ripperger, *The Golden Legend of Jacobus de Voragine* (New York: Arno, 1969). My translation is based on the Latin edition: *Jacobi Voragine: Legenda aurea vulgati storia Lombardica dicta*, ed. Th. Graesse (Osnabruck: Zeller, 1846, 1969).

6. *Legenda aurea*, p. 777.

7. Ibid., p. 778.

8. "La Leggenda di Santa Margarita," in *Leggende del Secolo XIV* (Florence, 1863), vol. 1, pp. 497–525. This is a nineteenth-century collection of anonymous hagiographical legends popular in northern Italy, especially Tuscany, in the fourteenth century.

9. Ibid., pp. 510–511. [My translation]

10. Ibid., p. 512.

11. Ibid., p. 513.

12. Ibid., p. 514.

13. Ibid., p. 516.

14. Ibid., p. 517.

15. Ibid., p. 518.

16. Ibid., p. 519.

17. *Vita Major Sanctae Humilianae*, chap. ii, par. 20, in *Acta Sanctorum*, May 19. [My translation]

18. Ibid., par. 21.

19. *Vita Sanctae Verdianae Virgine*, chap. iii, par. 2, in *Acta Sanctorum*, February 1.

20. Saints Umiliana and Verdiana are two out of fifty Italian women saints of the thirteenth and fourteenth centuries whose lives I have studied and written about. See Elizabeth A. Petroff, *The Consolation of the Blessed: Women Saints in Medieval Tuscany* (Millerton, N.Y.: Alta Gaia, 1979), and "Medieval Women Visionaries: Seven Stages to Power," *Frontiers: A Journal of Women Studies* 3 (1978): 34–45. See also Chapter 7.

21. "Anonimo del XV secolo: Rappresentazione di Santa Margherita," in *Le Sacre Rappresentazioni Italiane, Raccolta di testi dal secolo XII al secolo XVI*, ed. Mario Bonfantini (Milan: Einaudi, 1942), pp. 433–454. Margaret tells the audience: "I see a great dragon coming toward me, who seeks to try to devour me; I feel great temptation in my body, and I would not want to fall into lust. This is the demon who opposes himself to everyone who wants to persevere in virtue." In this version, Margaret has no difficulty in getting rid of the monster; she makes the sign of the cross after this speech, and the dragon vanishes (p. 449).

22. *Vita B. Benevenutae*, chap. iv, pars. 35–36, in *Acta Sanctorum*, October 29. Blessed Benevenuta lived in Friuli, in the Veneto region of Italy; her confessor was a Dominican from Pisa who read devotional literature to her. The day before the Feast of St. Margaret he told or read to her the story of St. Margaret, and that night she had a vision in which Satan appeared to her with a foaming mouth, boar's tusks, flaming eyes, and the body of a dragon. Benevenuta overcame him by first sitting on him, then insulting him while keeping one foot on his neck (Chap. ii, par. 21–25).

23. There is an inherent paradox in female sanctity, for the woman saint must be a good woman, and she must exhibit exceptional heroic power to transform the world. For a fuller discussion of this, see Elizabeth A. Petroff, "The Paradox of Sanctity: Lives of Italian Women Saints, 1200–1400," *Occasional Papers of the*

International Society for the Comparative Study of Civilization 1 (1977): 4–24. See also Chapter 9.

24. For the complete texts of Joan's trial, see *Jeanne d'Arc: Proces de condemnation, par la Société de l'histoire de France,* ed. Pierre Tisset, 3 vols. (Paris, 1960–1971). In English, see T. Douglas Murray, *Jeanne d'Arc, Maid of Orleans, 1429–1431* (New York, 1902), and Williard Trask, *Joan of Arc: Self Portrait* (New York, 1936); both are translations from the original French and Latin documents recording the trial of condemnation and the later trial of rehabilitation. For the text of the articles of accusation, quoting Joan's description of the voices that advised her, see Murray, *Jeanne d'Arc,* pp. 366–371. For a new viewpoint relating her to French hagiographical romances, see Cazelles, *Lady as Saint.* Nadia Margolis has compiled a bibliography on Joan: *Joan of Arc in History, Literature and Film: A Select Annotated Bibliography* (New York: Garland, 1990).

25. The voices were those of St. Michael, St. Margaret, and St. Catherine. Margaret and Catherine almost always appeared to her together; it was to them that she vowed her virginity, and they who specifically advised her to wear men's clothing. St. Michael's influence seems to have been important for her primarily when she was leading the army; once she was in prison, and during her trial, it was St. Margaret and St. Catherine who supported her. Delcourt points out: "For Joan St. Michael was the transfiguration of her martial dreams. Margaret and Catherine represented Joan herself, as she would have wished to be, able to win over by her arguments the haughty doctors who treated her with frightening contempt. They were both women freed from family ties, eloquent and self-confident, strong enough with God's help and in his cause to make men respect them: exactly Joan's *Wunschbild*" (*Hermaphrodite,* p. 98).

7

"She Seemed to Have Come from the Desert": Italian Women Saints and the *Vitae Patrum* Cycle

The *Vitae Patrum* as a Literary Cycle

The concept of a literary cycle dates back to the collection of poems in Greek known as the epic or Homeric cycle. Modern studies of literary cycles have focused on two crucial elements: multiplicity of parts and unity of theme.[1] The idea of a cycle has proved to be particularly helpful for medievalists viewing large collections of narratives, such as those associated with King Arthur or with secular drama. But medieval cycles need not be limited to drama and romance. In this chapter, I argue that the *Vitae Patrum* (the name given to the collection of literary materials about the Desert Fathers' movement) constitutes a literary cycle and that this cycle gives shape and coherence to a secondary, or satellite, cycle that concerns Umbrian and Tuscan female saints. This secondary cycle includes narratives explicitly constructed according to the rhetorical model provided by the *Vitae Patrum*. The authors of works in the latter cycle presume audience familiarity with the *Lives of the Fathers,* and they structure their narratives in accordance with the earlier material.

Seen in this light, the *Vitae Patrum,* the collection of lives and sayings of the Desert Fathers (and of a few Mothers, such as Amma Sarah and Amma Syncletica), constitutes a tale cycle given coherence by a shared ethic, expressed in a rhetoric that utilizes particular tropes, themes, and exempla that highlight the spiritual and social values epitomized by that ethic. Although the *Vitae Patrum* includes numerous *Vitae* of holy individuals (lengthy biographies of several of the fathers of desert monasticism, such as St. Antony, St. Paul, Pachomius, Macarius, and Simeon Stylites, as well as by middle-size and pocket biographies of large numbers of others), along with several collections of the *Verba Seniorum* (the sayings and teachings attributed to various leaders in the desert movement), this material exhibits the circularity identified by Fauriel, as quoted by David Staines: "[T]he romances of each class revolve . . . in a similar circle, around a common, fixed point. In this sense, they can be regarded as distinct parts, as isolated episodes of a single and similar action."[2]

The protagonists of the *Vitae Patrum* are the Desert Fathers, and the holy life they exemplify is a radical turning away from the public and secular world in order to live the life of the angels while still in the body. The model of behavior they exhibit is based on the practice of prayer, fasting, and vigils; it is characterized by extreme asceticism and miracle-working capacity. For the Middle Ages, the *Vitae Patrum* cycle provided a mode of seeing experience as a whole, given coherence by narrative repetition, by the utilization of returning themes, and by exemplary episodes that demonstrated the establishment of self in the face of otherness.

Since the *Vitae Patrum* collection is much too extensive to cite as a whole in an essay of this length, I propose to refer to Athanasius's *Life of St. Antony Abbot* as a paradigm of the larger cycle.[3] There is medieval precedent for such a paradigmatic view of the *Vita S. Antonii*, for St. Antony was the foremost Desert Father, and his life is explicitly cited in many of the thirteenth-century biographies of women. In Italy, the *Vitae Patrum* cycle, including the *Life of St. Antony Abbot*, was translated into the vernacular in the early fourteenth century by Domenico Cavalca (ca. 1270–late 1342), a Dominican who lived in Pisa.[4] Earlier translations undoubtedly existed, and episodes from the *Life of St. Antony* often made their way into sermons. Manuscripts of Latin and vernacular versions were part of private libraries as well as of convent libraries, and the stories of the Desert Fathers undoubtedly influenced women saints as well as their biographers.

The *Life of St. Antony Abbot* as Paradigm

Although the text of the *Life of St. Antony Abbot* had an enormous impact on its readers, Antony himself was not literate, and he knew only one text, Scripture, which he learned by hearing others read. He did not attend school, where he would have learned Greek; he spoke only the vernacular, Egyptian or Coptic. His wisdom came not from philosopher's books but from the heart, from a deep knowledge of himself and others gained during his long life, yet this wisdom enabled him to defeat Greek philosophers at their own game, as anecdotes in the *Vita S. Antonii* make clear.

In telling of the beginning of Antony's spiritual path, Athanasius describes Antony's activities in tropes that will become commonplaces of desert rhetoric. Following his conversion, Antony's spiritual life was characterized by asceticism: "All the desire and all the energy he possessed concerned the exertion of the discipline [*ascesis*]." He willingly sought out poverty and supported himself by manual labor: "He worked with his hands, though, having heard that he who is idle, let him not eat." Anything he earned beyond his immediate needs he devoted to charity: "[H]e spent what he made partly on bread, and partly on those in need." All his actions and thoughts were accompanied by prayer: "He prayed constantly, since he learned that it is necessary to pray unceasingly in private."[5]

At the beginning of his spiritual path, Antony was physically and spiritually beseiged by demons: "The demons, as if breaking through the building's four walls, and seeming to enter through them, were changed into the form of beasts and reptiles. The place immediately was filled with the appearances of lions, bears, leopards, bulls, and serpents, asps, scorpions and wolves, and each of these moved in accordance with its form."[6] The saint conquered them "by being in control of his thoughts and as if mocking them," and at the end of this episode, God spoke to him out of a great light, promising to be his helper and to make him famous.

At the age of thirty-five, Antony went to dwell in a fort, where he pursued even stricter discipline. Here he was not troubled by animals, demonic or real; the serpents that had inhabited the place prior to him left as soon as Antony moved in: "[A]t once the creeping things departed, as if someone were in pursuit."[7] Serpents are often mentioned in Antony's sermons to his followers, almost always in accordance with the metaphor found in Luke 10:19: "And now you see that I have given you the power to tread underfoot snakes and scorpions and all the forces of the enemy, and nothing will ever harm you." This is seen as the fulfillment of the prophecy in Genesis 3:15 addressed to Satan: "I will put enmity between you and the woman, between your brood and hers. They shall strike at your head, and you shall strike at their heel." But the battle between the good man and the forces of evil was not conceived of as merely metaphorical; the spiritual struggle was manifested materially and could be observed by others.

At the end of twenty years, Antony's friends, still fearful for the saint's life, broke down the door of the fort, and Antony came out, looking exactly as he had when he entered, "bello and fresco come di prima,"[8] not old and emaciated, as they had expected. "'He seemed,' says Athanasius, 'to have learned the secrets of the Temple of the Lord and to be endowed with the breath of divinity.'"[9] He was now a healer; although he continued to seek out ever more solitary locations for devoting himself to prayer, he also accepted the call to a public career: "Athanasius shows us Anthony going at his task with full energy, crossing the canals, climbing and descending the mountain, preaching to groups and exhorting individuals, returning quickly to keep up his backlog of silence and prayer, only to set forth again on visits to those who needed his help: he was the father of the new monks."[10]

One of the characteristic motifs in the *Vitae Patrum* is the relationship with animals.[11] When Antony went to live in the Inner Mountain late in his career, he planted a garden in the oasis; when animals came for water, they trampled it. Antony negotiated with them, much as St. Francis was to do later: "But gently capturing one of the beasts, he said to all of them, 'Why do you hurt me, when I do you no injury? Leave, and in the name of the Lord do not come near here any longer.' From then on, as if being afraid of the command, they did not come near the place."[12]

Animals in the *Vitae Patrum* do not simply represent demonic temptations in a material form. They are ambiguous beings, like the animals of ancient myth, both more and less than man. They often appear in liminal situations,[13] as animal companions or animal helpers that arrive near the end of an era in a holy person's life, sometimes at the conclusion of a lengthy retreat, just before the holy person returns to a teaching role, sometimes just before or after death. They are the legendary beasts associated with magical power, such as lions and deer, and they often represent a change in status for the saintly protagonist. Such beasts may also be guides, as deer and lions are for Macarius the Roman in his sojourn in the earthly paradise, helping him to see paths when he could not discern them by himself.[14] They may help the holy man by carrying out functions he is unable to perform. According to Jerome's *Life of St. Paul the First Hermit,* when Antony returns to find that Paul has died in his absence, he is saddened because he is unable to bury him. Suddenly he sees two lions running toward him, their manes flying. Antony, unafraid, watches them as they manage Paul's burial:

> They came straight to the body of the holy dead, and halted by it wagging their tails, then couched themselves at his feet, roaring mightily; and Antony well knew they were lamenting him, as best they could. Then, going a little way off, they began to scratch up the ground with their paws, vying with one another in throwing up the sand, till they had dug a grave roomy enough for a man: and thereupon, as though to ask the reward of their work, they came up to Antony, with drooping ears and downbent heads, licking his hands and feet. He saw that they were begging for his blessing; and pour[ed] out his soul in praise to Christ for that even the dumb beasts feel that there is God.[15]

Animals may be used to represent an aspect of the holy person that has not been seen before, imaging a new aspect of his personality that is about to be integrated with the previous sense of self. A story told about the cave-dwelling Abbot Macarius of Egypt and a female hyena with cubs brings out a tenderness in Macarius that he may have felt ambivalent about in other circumstances:

> While he was at prayer the hyena suddenly appeared and began to lick his feet. And taking him gently by the hem of his tunic, she drew him towards her own cave. He followed her saying, "I wonder what this animal wants to do?" When she had led him to her own cave, she went in and brought out to him her own cubs, which had been born blind. He prayed over them and returned them to the hyena with their sight healed. She in turn, by way of a thank-offering, brought the man the huge skin of a large ram and laid it at his feet. He smiled

at her as if at a kind and sensitive person, and taking the skin, spread it under him.[16]

The hyena's thank-offering allows Macarius to be uncharacteristically kind to himself. In this context, Helen Waddell reminds us that this anecdote is atypical of the "ruggedness of Macarius, who could be gentler with a blinded hyena-kitten, than with his own kind."[17] The use of animal motifs may be taken as one of the hallmarks of the *Vitae Patrum* cycle, for animals, whether helpers or disguised demons, reveal to the reader or auditor the spiritual prowess and discernment of the holy person.

Italian Women Saints' Lives: "Desert" Holiness

The biographies of a number of holy women of thirteenth-century Italy are cast in the rhetoric of the desert. They describe a new kind of female vocation, narrated in a style that recalls the images and the rhetoric of the *Vitae Patrum*. I am not the only scholar who has noticed the unusual lifestyles depicted in this group of texts,[18] although I am the first to suggest that many of these biographies are linked by a common purpose and a shared literary form. Donald Weinstein and Rudolph Bell draw on some of the same hagiographical material in their study *Saints and Society*,[19] and their observations about the *Vitae* of these Tuscan and Umbrian women give us another perspective on the unique qualities of the group of saints' lives I intend to discuss in this essay. For instance, they point to the importance of what they term "guilt-ridden piety" in accounts of the childhood and adolescence of female saints from northern Italy: "[I]n the thirteenth century, perhaps a bit earlier, guilt-ridden piety began to appear in much more dramatic and personal forms. Pioneering this new religious sensibility—for it clearly was more than just a shift of hagiographic style or conventions—were Italian girls, particularly girls from the regions of Tuscany and Umbria."[20]

As evidence of this childhood piety, Weinstein and Bell cite the image of childhood in the *Lives* of Bona of Pisa, Gherardesca of Pisa, Fina of San Gimignano, Chiara of Montefalco, and Sperandea of Gubbio. They note the occurrence of the same kind of piety during adolescence in the *Lives* of the fourteenth-century saints Catherine of Siena, Umiliana de' Cerchi of Florence, Umiltà of Faenza and her disciple Margherita of Faenza, Margherita of Cortona, Panacea of Lombardy, Giuliana Falconeri of Florence, Filippa Mareri of Assisi, and Rita of Cascia and in the fifteenth-century saints Francesca Romana and Catherine of Genoa.

This piety is important not only for its own sake; I have argued elsewhere that such piety is intimately connected to the fierce asceticism practiced by these girls and young women and takes visual form in the early penitential visions and demonic visitations experienced by them.[21] Piety is the first sign of a new kind of spiritual vocation shared by this group of women, a vocation that resulted in a new public role for holy women. Thus "guilt-ridden piety" is not the only trait shared by these girls and adult women. They were also leaders in the new city-states of central Italy.

> Preaching, fighting heretics, giving spiritual counsel, peacemaking, and help-ing the poor and sick, these young women took a vigorous part in the public, communal world. They were much esteemed and sought after by their com-patriots, and their vigorous activities also led to envy and opposition from other religious activists. . . . Early in life most of these saintly girls began to suffer attacks from demons which they countered with fasting, vigils, and other more extreme austerities. But neither private demons nor public slan-derers could defeat these young women. Rigorous prayer and penance, begun early in childhood, may have weakened their bodies, but they toughened their spirits and steeled their wills.[22]

To be acclaimed as saints, these women could not follow the path of male sanctity: "the female saint had to come by a different route, through the torments of a childhood beset by fears of marriage or of an adolescence ridden by sexual guilt."[23] The story of Umiliana de' Cerchi, the female path of holiness and power, could stand for the experiences of all these women:

> [T]he story of Umiliana's travails became an object lesson in how to live the contemplative life in the world. In her father's house she continually resisted diversions that she understood to be temptations of Lucifer. She took a vow of silence, whereupon the devil sent her daughter to entice her into speaking. She fasted for days and prayed that she might be made deaf and blind so that she could cut out the world. She flagellated herself and longed for martyrdom for Jesus' sake, but God would grant her only the death-to-the-world of long ecstasies. Umiliana levitated, gave off a divine fragrance, had a vision of a dove in her nocturnal chamber, and worked miracles.[24]

Saints and Society uses hagiographical sources as valuable evidence of the reciprocal relations between holy individuals and their communities. In this essay, I explore these hagiographies as literature, as a particular kind of literature. If we examine the *Vitae* of the women mentioned earlier (Bona of Pisa, Gherardesca of Pisa, Fina of San Gimignano, Chiara of Mon-tefalco, Sperandea of Gubbio, Umiliana de' Cerchi of Florence, Margherita of Cortona, and Margherita of Faenza, among others), we see a number of patterns that are atypical of the lives of medieval saints, especially women saints. The *Vitae* assert that these women were exemplars of the ascetic life; all are said to have demonstrated supernatural power to an unusual degree, all were known to be visionaries, and all had teaching and leadership roles in their communities. They were atypical in two other ways as well. Histor-ically, the majority of female saints were virgins, but in this group the majority had been married. Most female saints lived enclosed lives in con-vents, but these women were more likely to be recluses or tertiaries than nuns. In fact, only one of the women—St. Umiltà—was a nun, and even as a nun she behaved in nontraditional ways and did not remain enclosed. All these women could be said "to have come not from the secular world, but from the desert." They were also very popular saints, canonized by popular opinion before they were officially canonized by the Church. Their popularity is reflected in the fact that many of their *Vitae* were either originally composed in Italian or quickly translated into the vernacular.[25]

The theme of the desert common to all these *Vitae*—emphasizing asceticism, demonic temptation, visionary experience, and spiritual leadership—is atypical of medieval women saints' lives, but it is typical of a much earlier style of hagiography, the *Lives* of the Desert Fathers in the *Vitae Patrum* collection. Furthermore, there is another group of female saints' lives, written just a generation earlier than this Italian group, made up of the *Vitae* of the beguines in the diocese of Liège in the thirteenth century. The best known of these *Vitae* are those by Jacques de Vitry (*Life of Marie d'Oignies*) and Thomas of Cantimpré (*Life of Christina Mirabilis*). De Vitry begins his biography of Marie with a description and defense of the new life-style chosen by religious women associated with Marie; in letters written shortly after he composed this *Life*, he compares the activities of the Belgian women with those of the female followers of St. Clare in Umbria (see Chapters 3 and 4). These northern texts exhibit the same relationship to the *Lives* of the Desert Fathers as that evident in the Italian texts.[26] I think it is not accidental that the biographers of women belonging to these two groups, groups that invented innovative and often criticized forms of female spiritual life, follow an earlier and highly respected model (of sanctity and of hagiographical style). In utilizing this older desert rhetoric, the male biographers make their contemporary saints more respectable and more understandable to the Church; at the same time, they point out how these women transcend their biological sex by living virile, masculine, styles of sanctity.

The texts I have chosen to focus on are the lives of four Italian (specifically Tuscan) women saints of the thirteenth century—the *Vitae* of St. Umiltà of Faenza and Florence, St. Umiliana de' Cerchi of Florence, St. Verdiana of Castelfiorentino, and St. Fina of San Gimignano. Although we now must read about Umiltà and Verdiana in Latin, in the fourteenth century their stories, and those of Umiliana and Fina, circulated in Italian.

Each of these *Lives* (like those of all the women saints cited by Weinstein and Bell) in some way re-creates and comments on the fourth-century *Vitae Patrum* cycle; the gender reversal, so obvious to us now, is so rarely commented on that awareness of it almost seems to be repressed (I address this fact more directly later). Most of these Italian women were active in the middle of the thirteenth century, all spent major parts of their lives as hermits or recluses, and many (three of the four) were associated with groups of pious laywomen, possibly connected in some way with the Franciscan order. Few, including St. Umiltà, were professed nuns and abbesses of enclosed communities, and those that were assumed those roles for only part of their religious careers, so they were hardly typical of holy women in traditional roles. All four of the women I discuss here were visionaries, thought to be prophets; all were healers; and all had struggles with demonic forces. Two had been married, and all struggled with sexual temptation, although this struggle is almost always expressed obliquely.

The *Life of St. Umiltà of Faenza*

The fourteenth-century author of the *Life of St. Umiltà of Faenza*[27] tells us of a crucial event in that saint's life that took place at the midpoint of the thirteenth century, in 1250. Rosanese Negusanti, a young married woman of noble birth, obtained permission from her husband of ten years to separate from him and to enter a religious community. Her behavior in this new environment surprised her new sisters. Perhaps they had expected someone worldly but disillusioned who wanted to leave behind a world she had found disappointing. Although still young and beautiful, Rosanese was older than the typical novice, for she had just turned twenty-four. She came from the same privileged world as the other community members, but, unlike them, she had married well and had given birth to several children. Yet since childhood, she had desired a religious life and had never given up trying to persuade her husband to join her in a commitment to celibacy and penitence. She seized her opportunity when her husband was discovered to have a venereal disease that necessitated a chaste life if he wanted to live. Their children had died in infancy, her own parents were dead, and, except for her husband, she felt no ties with the secular world. Upon entering the convent of St. Perpetua in Faenza (a community of canonesses under the Augustinian rule), she took the name of Umiltà [Humility]. Her biographer describes the future saint's entry into the community:

> Subito coepit in feminam alteram transmutari, omnia vilia monasterii suis manibus operari, ac religione taliter informari, quod non ex saeculo, sed quod ex deserto venerit nulli erat dubium: silentii, orationis, solitudinis, obsequii erga sanas pariter et infirmas, abstinentiae atque arduorum aliorum operum ipsis cernentibus iam exemplum.[28]

> [At once she began to be transformed into another woman, to perform the most vile tasks in the monastery with her hands, and to be so knowledgeable in matters of religion that no one doubted that she had come, not from the secular world, but from the desert. To all those who saw her, she was now an example of keeping silence, of prayer, of solitude, of ready and helpful obedience towards the sick and the well equally, and of abstinence and all other difficult works.][29]

Umiltà's biographer gives us specific images of the behavior that was associated with the desert—a transformation that involved willingness to perform the kind of manual labor that dirties hands, a ready obedience to other community members, allied with insight into the spiritual life; and the ability to practice silence, prayer, solitude, and abstinence. With the exception of solitude, these are all monastic virtues, and in fact Umiltà has just entered an enclosed community of women. Yet Umiltà's biographer uses the trope of the desert, not the monastery, as a paradigm of holiness and transformation: Umiltà is *transformed* into *another* woman, *performs* vile (humble) tasks, and is *informed, educated* in religion. This transforming/performing/informing makes her an "exemplum" of asceticism. (The sentence is quite elegant, beginning with three parallel phrases, each modifying the verb "coepit" and each ending in a passive verb form: "transmutari," "operari," "informari.")

This association of Umiltà with the desert directs us to read Umiltà's exemplary behavior in a particular key, as a model of "desert" behavior. This "desert" behavior is grammatically opposed to "secular" (worldly) behavior—she comes "not from the secular world, but from the desert" [non ex saeculo, sed . . . ex deserto venerit]. But there is another set of oppositions at work here; the exemplum of desert behavior is also opposed to good nun behavior. The transformation displayed in Umiltà and the example she represents are distinctly different in focus from the asceticism proposed in the Rule of St. Benedict, for example, where the purpose of manual labor, fasting, and obedience is to wear away self-will and encourage the life of community. Even at this early stage in her religious career, Umiltà is acting out a different kind of life for a holy woman, one characterized not just by practicing extreme asceticism, but also by being alone, solitary, which is the original sense of the word *monachus*. By placing this description here, Umiltà's biographer anticipates and justifies the saint's later escape from the convent in order to become a recluse. He may also have in mind her decision to adopt a stricter Benedictine Rule when she formed a Vallombrosan community after leaving her hermitage.[30]

The penultimate paragraphs of the first chapter of Umiltà's *Vita* summarize the chief events of her hermit stage—her austerities and her nonhuman visitor. The austerities come first, and they are described in detail that is familiar from the *Vitae Patrum*.

Annis duodecim in cella predicta stetit, pane solum et aqua, de coctis herbis amaris intus in solennitatibus, semper usa fuit: et ad tantam abstinentiam devenit, quod die qualibet tribus unciis panis suum corpusculum sustentavit: nec secum, toto tempore quo fuit in cella, in suplici refectione, vel ciborum usem aliter quam sicut dictum, casu aliquo dispensavit. Corpore super nudo setis equinis, aut corio porci, versis setis incisis ad carnem, semper omni casu, modo, et tempore vestita stetit, cum cuculla vilissima, nullis interpositis pellibus aut aliquibus vestimentis. Utebatur interdum loco cilicii veste lanea asperrima, quando casu aliquo condeceret: fatigata vero super genibus, super praedictam assidem se locabat: muro, gravata somno, caput ponebat psallendo, sic somnum sumebat, vel cogitando aliquid de divinis.

[Twelve years she lived in that cell; bread and water alone, with cooked bitter herbs on solemn feast days, this was her habitual diet. She reached the point of such abstinence that three ounces of bread a day were enough to support her thin body. Nor did she ever, during the entire time that she was in the cell, arrange for two meals a day, or for any food other than that mentioned, in any circumstance. On her bare body she always wore a shirt of horse hair, or pig skin with the bristles turned toward her flesh, wearing this in every situation, event, and time, with only a worn and worthless cowl over it, without any warm leather or woven clothing placed beneath it. Sometimes in place of the hairshirt she used a very rough woolen vest, when for some reason that was appropriate. When she tired of being on her knees, she positioned herself on the aforementioned board. When she was overcome by sleep, she would place her head against the wall, and would fall asleep reciting psalms or meditating on some divine matter.]

With no preface or commentary, the next paragraph tells of her strange visitor:

Die quadam mustela quaedam cum pelteolo ad collum in cellam introivit: ceu datam in sociam divinitus care sumit: dum vacabat orationi ad ejus pedes se ponit: de carnibus sibi datis studiose quousque fuit in cella, non gustavit: nec alio cibo umquam nisi, quos Matrem sanctam cui divinitus data in sociam fuit, sua existimatione in cellula uti vidit. Tempore magno sic peracto, cum quas-dam Dominas in cellis, juxta suae Dominae cellam, esse inspiceret; super fenestram ascendit, Dominam suam quasi deridendo inspexit, sonalium ibi deposuit, et quasi valedicens nunquam comparuit.[31]

[One day a weasel with a bell on its neck entered her cell. She received it affectionately, as if it were divinely given her as a companion. While she was occupied in prayer, it sat at her feet. It never tasted of the meat given it carefully while it was there in the cell. Nor did it ever seem to eat any other food, except what it saw the holy Mother Umiltà, to whom it had been divinely given as a companion, make proper use of in the cell. A long time passed in this way, when it perceived that there were ladies who lived in cells next to the cell of its lady. It climbed up to the window, looked at its lady as if in derision, deposited there its bell as if saying farewell, and never appeared again.][32]

This seems a baffling episode. Perhaps Umiltà's biographer included it because it really happened and everyone knew the story. But it is more likely that it was included because this kind of relationship with an animal often accompanies descriptions of the eremetical life and symbolized the internal transformations that had taken place.

Umiltà's weasel seems to be a liminal animal for her. Ordinarily wild, this one is domesticated and already wears a bell. In medieval legends, the weasel has both positive and negative associations.[33] In Umiltà's story, the weasel left her at the same time that Umiltà's decided to end her solitary career and take on the responsibilities of an abbess. It seems most likely to me that the weasel here signals Umiltà's change in status, as animals do in the *Vitae Patrum*. This reading would appear to be supported by the story that Henri Queffélec tells about a weasel associated with Macarius:

One day an ermine entered his hut and took hold of the edge of his tunic; it was weeping because its three young had twisted necks. He cured them for her and she gave them her teats, which they began to suck ravenously. And, the story goes, Macarius watched in silent amazement, forgetting that he had just accomplished something far more difficult.[34]

At the same time, the weasel seems to mirror Umiltà's ambivalence about the decision she is about to make. We know from Umiltà's sermons that she was afraid to leave her hermitage and return to a leadership role in the world, yet she felt divinely compelled to do so.[35] The weasel leaves through the window of her cell, the place of her communication with the outer world, turns to look back at her "as if in derision," and leaves behind its bell, "as if saying farewell," freeing her to say goodbye to this stage of her life. That the weasel mirrors her is also indicated by the fact that although she offers it meat she has specially prepared for it, it will eat only the same vegetarian diet she lives on. Although she believes the weasel was divinely given to her as a companion, and although it is evidently moving on to be a companion to other recluses, its role in her life is more significant than she at first perceives.

The episodes I examine from the three other *Vitae*—those of Umiliana, Verdiana, and Fina—all involve what seem to be demonic temptations in the form of giant snakes. Each represents the threat of sexual sin, and, through the snake image, each women finds her own way of handling temptation.

The *Life of the Blessed Umiliana de' Cerchi of Florence*

St. Umiliana (1219–1246) is a Franciscan saint, associated with the church of Santa Croce in Florence. Recent scholarship sees her as a very important leader of women within the Franciscan movement;[36] St. Francis died when she was a little girl, and St. Clare was still alive when Umiliana died in 1246. Her *Vita* was written by Fra Vito da Cortona, a Franciscan contemporary who knew her well. A vivid Italian translation, the "Leggenda della Beata Umiliana de' Cerchi," was made some time in the fourteenth century.[37]

Two models of sanctity—St Antony and St. Francis—are apparent in the Life that Vito wrote. Like St. Francis, Umiliana embraces poverty in spite of the expectations of her wealthy and powerful family. She sneaks out at night with her sister-in-law Ravenna to distribute food to the poor: "quasi come ancille d'Iddio, non vergognandosi di portare il disonore per l'amore di Cristo, andavano attorno per la città al luogo de' poveri infermi e de' sani, distribuendo i detti cibi" [Almost like handmaids of God, they were not ashamed to bear dishonor for the love of Christ, going around the city to the homes of the poor and the sick, as well as the healthy, distributing food].[38] Like St. Antony, Umiliana courageously stands up to her family, as the earlier saint had stood up to his demonic torments. She despises their threats, and no matter how she is abused by them, her mind remains unmoved.[39]

Such constancy moves Vito da Cortona to ask rhetorical questions that clearly identify Umiliana with the model of St. Antony:

What of the monastic life did she lack, who remained in continual silence and kept watch over herself? Did she have any less than the hermit saints, she who, in the midst of such a great city, took and found solitude in the desert, and turned her chamber into a prison . . . ? This woman, creating solitude in her father's house, and in combat defeated the world, the devil, and the flesh while living in the midst of secular people.[40]

Like Antony, she is tormented by Satan, who is incensed at her virtue.[41] In great frustration, Satan is forced to use the form of a huge serpent to frighten her:

[P]rese la sua forma propria, serpentina, la quale suole spaventare le femmine. E preso ch'ebbe la detta forma, grandissima, l'apparve: ragguardandola con occhi terribili, a ciò che almeno un poco rompendo la sua costanzia, le 'mpedisse la grazia della divozione. Il quale vedendo, fu percossa di grande paura; ché, né in orazione né fuori d'orazione, si poteva in quella cella assicurare. Ma passati alquanti dì, non potendo portare il danno dell'orazione, parlò col serpente, dicendo: — Io ti scongiuro, orribile serpente, per lo nome del mio signore Gesù Cristo, che se tu se' corporale, incontanenti ti diparti, e più non ritornare; ma se tu se' incorporale, mio nemico, disparisci da me, e mai da quinci innanzi non mi molesti.[42]

([He] took on his real form, that of a snake, of which women are generally terrified. . . . [H]e appeared enormous, staring at her with terrible eyes, thinking thus to break down her constancy. . . . Seeing him, she was struck by the great fear that she would not be safe in that cell, whether in prayer or not. Several days passed without his being able to disturb her praying. She spoke to the serpent, saying, "I conjure you, horrible snake, in the name of my Lord Jesus Christ, that if you are corporeal you depart without delay and do not return, and if you are incorporeal, my enemy, disappear from my sight, and do not molest me from now on.)

Umiliana insulted the snake for his foul odor, and "the stink went away, and a pleasant smell remained, so much so that it seemed the agreeableness of paradise." As with St. Antony, Satan was constrained to try more compelling threats:

Passati alquanti dì, ecco Setanasso; e menò seco uno grande serpente, non incorporale come era egli, né composto d'immagine, ma veracemente corporale, terribile e spaventevole: il quale di grande terrore e paura la conturbava, però che sempre l'era presente all'orazione; e quando si riposava, la sua coda teneva a' piedi, il capo alla gota sua; il quale la spaventava sì fortemente, che non poteva sicuramente orare né dormire; anzi, quando andava a posarsi, sempre s'avvolgeva i panni a' piedi, e con una cintola gli legava, perché il serpente non le entrasse sotto, da' piedi, e venisse al corpo ignudo.[43]

[A few days passed, and there was Satan again, and he brought with him a great serpent, not incorporeal as he was before, nor an imaginary creation, but truly corporeal, terrible and terrifying. This produced great terror and fear in her, but still she paid attention to her praying. When she rested, he wrapped his tail around her feet, and leaned his head against her cheek. This frightened her so much that she could neither pray nor sleep securely. When she went to lie down, she wrapped her clothes around her feet and tied them with a belt, so that the serpent couldn't enter from below, at her feet, and get to her nude body.]

Although Umiliana trusted fully in God, Vito da Cortona assures us, she did not want to take the risk of tempting God by overconfidence, so as much as possible, when the snake was watching her, she was careful not to touch him with her hands. As she knew that this situation had been given to her as a teaching ("però che sapeva che le era dato per ammaestramento"), she was unwilling to reveal it to anyone:

> E sofferto ch'ebbe questo, tre dì, pazientemente, non vogliendo portare il danno dell'orazione, contro al serpente, che le stava allato, disse: "Io ti comando, per la virtù del nome di Cristo mio diletto, che tutto t'avvolghi, incontanente, senza indugio, qui, allato alle mie mani." Alla cui parola il serpente méssesi il capo sotto e avvòlsesi insieme tutto il corpo, incontanente; sotto il cui corpo mettendo santa Umiliana amendue le mani, il levò di terra, lodando e benedicendo Iddio, dicendo: "Benedetto sia quello Amore potentissimo che ti creòe." E così, portandolo a una finestra della torre, sì gli commandò, dicendo: "Va alla via tua, e più meco non istare, però che se' inutile e sanza frutto." E detto questo, il serpento, costretto, si partì.[44]

> [She endured this patiently for three days, and then, not wanting to have her prayer disturbed any further, she said to the serpent that was next to her: "I command you, by virtue of the name of my beloved Christ, to coil up at once, without delay, right here next to my hands." At these words the snake tucked his head under and coiled up his whole body immediately; the holy Umiliana put both hands under his body, lifting him up from the ground, praising and blessing God, saying "Blessed be that most potent Love that created you." And so, bringing him to a window of the tower, she commanded him, saying, "Go on your way, and stay no longer with me, for you are useless and fruitless." Constrained by these words, the serpent departed.]

Like St. Antony, Umiliana uses the power of naming to unravel the appearance of Satan, to strip him down to his real identity, the negative of that Love that she invokes in dismissing him. For her, there is never any doubt that his appearance is satanic in origin; she knows that he has been sent to her as a teaching, and through her confrontation with him she demonstrates that she cannot really be harmed by him if she maintains a constant mind and remembers divine love.

The *Life of St. Verdiana of Castelfiorentino*

St. Verdiana (ca. 1180–ca. 1242) was another Tuscan penitent who had to deal with serpentine evil. Like Umiliana, she chose a recluse's life after living in the world and gaining a reputation for sanctity; her cell was attached to the church of St. Antony in Castelfiorentino.[45] She had all the virtues of that saint: even as a little girl, she preferred solitude, prayer, and abstinence to playing with other children ("Ea adhuc parvula aliarum puellarum, etiam aequalium, vitabat consortia, intenta solitudini, precationi, abstinentiae"). At age twelve, when she might be expected to be thinking about marriage, for she was very pretty, she dressed humbly and was committed to poverty and content with the minimum necessary to sustain life. She wore a hair shirt and had an iron chain around her waist, and she practiced a life of prayer, fasting, and vigils ("Nondum duodecim annos nata, cultu speciosa, habitu humilis, studiosa paupertaris, paucis ac vilibus rebus contenta, lumbos vinculo ferreo stringebat. . . . Asperrimo praeterea operta cilicio . . . dedita assidue erat vigilis precibus, jejuniis"). Also like St. Antony, she displayed a divinely taught wisdom ("ita divinitus erat erudita"). In fact, her biographer[46] says that no one who has been inspired by reading the "Egyptian Fathers" will be surprised by what Verdiana experienced in her cell. Her poor family gave her to a wealthy female relative as a maidservant and companion, and when she was in the relative's household she began to perform miracles, multiplying food in a time of famine. She went on pilgrimage with her mistress to St. James of Compostella and to Rome, where she was so beseiged by people seeking advice and healing that she determined to become a recluse when she returned home.

According to her biographer, she consciously sought to model herself on St. Antony. When she heard a sermon about how St. Antony had suffered from the attacks of demons disguised as various kinds of wild beasts, she poured out prayers asking to experience the same kind of temptations he had suffered. About two years after her enclosure, her prayers were answered:

> [E]cce horribiles duos serpentes, aequali ambo magnitudine, in cellam ejus per fenestellam ingressi sunt. Cohorruit Verdiana. . . . At Cruce sese consignans, Divinae acquievit voluntati, ac se precationi dedit. Hic Divinam agnoscens visitationem, nihil humani praesidii procuravit aut expetiit. Mansere illic serpentes per longum temporis spatium die ac nocte; ac si quando egrediebantur, brevi rursus redibant; neque unquam aberant eo tempore quo cibum capere Virgo solebat, cum ea ex eadem patina edendo, in qua illa panem aqua maceratum, lactucasve aut legumina habebat, absque ullo olei salisque condimento.[47]

> [Behold, two awful serpents, both of equal magnitude, entered her cell through the window. Verdiana was horrified, . . . but making the sign of the cross, she accepted the divine will, and gave herself to prayer. Recognizing that this was a divine visitation, she neither sought nor encouraged any human protection. Day and night over a long space of time those serpents remained; and if they ever went out, they came back again after a short while, and they never left during the time that the virgin was accustomed to eat her food. They ate with her from the same dish, in which she had a little broken bread in water, or milk or beans, without any condiments like oil or salt.]

Some details of this episode, such as the mode of entrance of the snakes, may be realistic, but others, such as the fact that the snakes are always home when the saint takes her meals, seem drawn from myth or fairy tale. Verdiana seems able to interpret the snakes both as real creatures and as divine visitations, but the citizens of Castelfiorentino do not seem to share this perception. The beasts are strong physically and evidently very large, for they return her hospitality by knocking her down. At one time, Verdiana is so injured that she lies helplessly on the floor of her cell for eight days ("Si quid vero feris hospitibus deerat, cauda eam verberabant, ita crudeliter, ut se Dei famula nonnumquam octo dierum spatio erigere a terra non valeret"). Reflections on the suffering of Christ and the martyrs help her maintain her patience with such guests. When some of the towns-people try to kill them and succeed only in cutting off their tails, the snakes flee to their "nurse." Not only are their wounds healed, but their tails are restored as well. But they remain serpents, and, "as is the way of serpents" ("pro more serpentium"), they are more savage than they had been before, and Verdiana is even more patient than she had been.

After thirty years or more, unknown to Verdiana, one of the snakes is killed by some townspeople who had observed when it was accustomed to leave Verdiana's cell; the other runs away, never to be seen again. Verdiana is unhappy to lose "the occasion of such great merit in divinely granted companionship" and thinks the episode a portent of her approaching death. She does indeed die shortly thereafter, on a date she had foreseen. It would seem that for her the snakes fulfilled several functions: to the extent that they were demonic visitors permitted by God to test her patience, they advanced her self-control and added to her ascetic program; to the extent that they provided "divinely granted companionship," they functioned as forerunners of a paradisal state in which natural enemies, like lions and lambs, might lie down together.

The *Life of St. Fina of San Gimignano*

Santa Fina (1238–1253) lived in the Tuscan town of San Gimignano. Her *Life* was written around 1300 by Fra Giovanni di Ser Coppo of San Gimignano, a brother in the Dominican order.[48] Serafina de' Ciardi was a serious and pious little girl, who determined to live a solitary religious life. Her town was convulsed by the struggle between Guelfs and Ghibellines, and in 1253, the year of her death, she heard the sounds of hand-to-hand combat in the street before the door of her home. Chapter 2 of her *Life,* "Come si rincluse nella sua casa colla madre sua a fare penitenza," tells how she devoted herself to austerities even though she was an attractive young woman who presumably could have found a husband if she had wanted to:

> Et avvenga a Dio ch'avesse bella faccia e fusse di statura grande, et ogni cosa in lei fusse ben proporsionata, di niuna cosa sua faccia adornava, ma solamente intendea di piacere a Dio e none agli uomini del mondo. Et acciò che el servo dilicatamente nutrito non volesse essere signore, coiè la carna inverso dello spirito, questa santa vergine el corpo suo con digiuni affrigeva, le sue membra domava con ciliccio, come facea la gloriosa vergine santa Cecilia; et ancora continuamente colle sue mane laborava secondo el misterio feminile. E questo

faceva non per grande necessità ch'avesse, ma per fuggire l'ozio; che si legge nella Scrittura santa che gli è pessima cosa al servo di dio. Et ancora lavorava continuamente quando non orava, per seguitare e costumi della nostra madre Vergine Maria, che si legge di lei nelle pistole di santo Ieronimo che ogni dì guadagnava quello che era di bisogno al corpo suo di vivere.

[And although it pleased God that she had a pretty face and was tall and well-proportioned, she never made up her face, for she was only interested in pleasing God, not the men of this world. And so that the servant, being too delicately nurtured, should not try to be master, that is, so that the flesh wouldn't dominate the spirit, this holy maiden used to chasten her body with fasting, and like the glorious virgin St. Cecilia, mortify her flesh with a hair shirt. And she continuously occupied her hands at women's work; but all these acts she would perform, not because she was so needy, but to avoid idleness, which Holy Scripture says is a snare for the feet of the Lord's servants. Likewise when not in prayer, she laboured steadfastly, following thus in the footsteps of our Mother the Virgin Mary, as it is said of her in the epistles of St. Jerome, that she earned each day the wherewithal for the sustenance of her body.][49]

The rhythm of her solitude, shared with her mother and other like-minded women of the town, was severely tested when she became ill, paralyzed from the neck down. She could not get up and could lie on only one side, since lying on the other was too painful. She lived upstairs in the little house she shared with her mother, cared for by a pious lay sister named Beldì. Her torments were truly disgusting and may be intended as an allusion to some of the more disquieting passages in the *Life of St. Simeon Stylites:*

E perchè tanto giacè sopra un lato, la carne venne a infracidare e la tavola a ingenerare vermini, et quali vermini si mangiavano la carne di questa santa vergine. Et ancora, perche era cosa putrida, e topi (perdonimi chi legge) andavano insieme [e] mangiavano la carne sopradetta; e molti, che questo viddeno, rendenno testimonanza. O vera, grande pazienzia nella molle fragile natura feminile ci [sei] trovata! che questa santa vergine, in una parte del suo corpo dolori grandissimi aveva, e d'altra, roda da' vermini e da topi e non-dimeno mai non si rammaricò, nè mostrando uno minimo segno di tristizia; anzi sempre colla faccia lieta e sempre ringraziando Iddio.

[This holy virgin lay on one side only for so long that her flesh had rotted and the board on which she was lying generated worms which ate her flesh. Moreover,—readers, forgive me—because her body was a rotting thing, rats gathered there together and devoured her flesh. There are many people who saw this and gave testimony.

O what true great patience this is, found in the soft fragile female nature! That this holy virgin, who had such great pain in one side of her body, and was being eaten by worms and rats on the other side, nevertheless never complained, never showed the least sign of unhappiness, but instead always had a happy face and gave thanks to God.][50]

She was supported by alms that others gave her, since she could no longer work. Anything she did not need for food she gave away to the poor. Satan, the "nimico dell'umana natura," was naturally incensed at her virtue, and since he could not attack her directly, attacked her mother as she was returning home one day. Her mother never saw what attacked her: "le parve che venisse uno, [e] violentemente la pigliasse per sì fatto modo, ch' ella cadde in terra, e quasi diventò a modo d'una pietra immobile, e per cagione nessuna muovere non si poteva" [It seemed that someone came up to her and struck her so forcefully that she fell to the ground, and became like an unmoving stone, and was unable to move for any reason].[51] Fina, upstairs, heard the sounds of a terrible struggle, and then her mother's moans. When she sent her friend Buonaventura to see what had happened, Buonaventura screamed that her mother was dead.

> E udendo questa boce santa Fina, levando gli occhi verso il tetto, vidde uno serpente grandissimo in sur una trave, el quale era terribilissimo a tutti gli occhi che l'avessino potuto vedere, et ella, ch'era semplice, credette che fusse uno serpente vero, e non visione diabolica, che avesse la madre; per la quale cosa fusse morta.

> [Hearing this cry, holy Fina raised her eyes toward the roof and saw an enormous serpent extended all along the beam, a monster of terrifying aspect for the eyes of anyone who could see him, and she, being a guileless soul, thought this was a real serpent, not a diabolical vision, who had possessed her mother, so that she was dead.][52]

Buonaventura was sent to fetch a neighbor, Master Guglielmo, to kill the snake, but neither she nor Guglielmo could see him:

> Et allora la santa vergine Fina intendendo, che non era serpente vero, anco era il nemico dell'umana natura, el quale ingannò i primi nostri parenti in quella specie e forma, ed ella si fece il segno della santa croce, e subbito sparì: e comprese la santa vergine, ch'era stato per dispensazione divina la morte della sua madre, e ringraziò Iddio, non avendo tristizia, ne dolore di tale morte, ma portando ogni cosa con pazienzia.

> [Thus the Holy Fina learned that he was no actual serpent but the enemy of mankind who had deceived our first parents in the same guise and form. She made the sign of the Holy Cross, and at once he vanished. And the holy maiden knew that a divine dispensation had permitted the death of her mother, and she gave thanks to God, experiencing neither sorrow nor grief at that death, but bearing everything with patience.][53]

Along with her patient endurance of physical pain, this encounter with Satan was the big event of Fina's short life; according to her biographer, all that remained was to prepare herself for death. Like other hermit saints, she was divinely informed of the day of her death. St. Gregory the Great, the saint to whom she was especially devoted, appeared to her to tell her that she would die on his saint's day, March 23. She confided this fact to a few of the sisters in her community, and they testified at her trial of canonization that she had told them this before she indeed passed away on St. Gregory's Day.

It is difficult to know how we are meant to interpret the appearance of this serpent. Was this serpentine illusion some kind of test for Fina, or was it an image of her mother's sins? Or was it an image of what was happening in her world, as has been argued was the case with Umiliana's demonic temptations? The ability to visualize the snake effectively distinguishes Fina's perceptions from those of the other figures in the story, and perhaps we are intended to see in this Fina's exemption from the common human fate. The narrator attributes the appearance of the snake to Satan's desire to deceive the holy Fina:

> El nemico dell' umana natura, vedendo questa santa vergine tanto virtuosa e tanto fruttifera, n'ebbe grande invidia, et immaginossi d'ingannarla, secondo che ingannò la nostra prima madre Eva, e non potendo el suo veleno contro alla santa vergine Fina gittare, il gettò inverso la madre sua, siccome diremo di sotto.

> [The enemy of mankind, seeing that this holy virgin was so virtuous and fruitful, felt great envy over this, and believed he could deceive her, as he had deceived our first mother Eve. Being powerless to throw his poison over the holy virgin Fina, he threw it over her mother, as we shall tell you below.][54]

Weinstein and Bell read the episode of the snake as rooted in a mother–daughter struggle over Fina's asceticism:

> It is difficult to escape the inference that Fina's mother had not approved, perhaps had tried to block, Fina's ascetic practices, and that in the mind of the girl (or at least of the hagiographer) the mother's painful death was divine retribution. Five years later Fina followed her mother to the grave to become an object of intense local veneration, especially powerful in guarding the Sangimignanesi against the plague.[55]

I find this very unlikely.[56] Both Fina and her mother were part of a group of laywomen devoted to healing and to caring for the poor in the city, and the narrative of Fina's story gives no indication of a conflict between them. Weinstein and Bell have overlooked two important influences on the telling of this event: the deaths of innocent bystanders in the civil war then raging in San Gimignano between the Guelfs and the Ghibellines, and the influence of scriptural metaphors indicating the spiritual meaning of this event. As the introduction to a modern edition of Fina's biography tells us:

> Fra Giovanni describes how trembling with apprehension [Fina] heard the fearsome echo of trumpet blast, clash of arms, and tumult of angry voices; powerless to quell, through her gracious presence, the affray between Guelf and Ghibelline, in which her mother, the unfortunate Imperiera, lost her life, whilst standing, a harmless onlooker, at the threshold of her home in the Contrada del Sasso.[57]

It seems likely that the narrator of this story has in mind the scriptural images of the serpent in Genesis and Luke, found in the *Life of St. Antony* but a commonplace in medieval thought. The notion of the feminine is dichotomized, characterized by the traditional Eve–Mary polarity, thanks to the motif of the snake. The snake in the garden (Genesis 2–3:15) is associated with Fina's mother, who is thus associated with Eve, and the promise of Luke 10:19, "the power to tread underfoot snakes and scorpions," is attributed to Fina, who is identified with the figure of the Virgin Mary. This device allows the biographer to include a story of demonic temptation in Fina's life, while exempting Fina herself from temptation.

There are no further instances of Fina's relationship to animals, demonic or friendly, in the narration of her life, but in the section on miracles, we learn that Fina was a healer of animals.

> Ancora degni di fede aviamo udito, che la sposa e serva di Gesù Cristo, Fina, non tanto mostra la sua virtù e potenza nelle creature ragionevoli, rendenso loro sanità, ma ancora in quelle che non usano ragione; imperocchè molti uomini e donne aventi chi buoi, o asini e cavalli, di grandi infirmitadi occupati, raccomandandoli con divozione alla vergine santa Fina, furono d'ogni infermità liberati . . . e non è da meravigliare, se tale grazia le concedette, perocchè lui seguito nella pazienza e nel merito: adunque lo dovea seguitare nella grazia di curare le bestie inragionevoli.

> [Moreover we have learned from trustworthy witnesses that Fina, the spouse and handmaiden of Jesus Christ, not only displays her virtue and potency in aid of reasoning creatures, returning them to health [or sanity], but also displays these qualities for the benefit of unreasoning creatures. Thus many men and women, who had oxen or asses or horses that had fallen ill with serious diseases, commended them to the virgin St. Fina, and they were delivered from every infirmity. And you shouldn't be surprised at this, that God granted such a privilege to her, for she followed him in patience and merit, and thus he should accompany her actions by the gift of healing unreasoning creatures.][58]

Fra Giovanni, in trying to understand why Fina has this particular gift of healing, links it with her willing and Christlike suffering. But he is writing this biography almost half a century after the death of the saint, when her reputation as a healer has led to the building of a hospital dedicated to her. Furthermore, he is writing for a community that is aware of countless miracles of this sort over the intervening half-century, as well as for the male administrators of her hospital. In writing this life, he has emphasized certain details of her life, such as the vision of the snake accompanying the death of her mother, and quickly passes over other aspects of her life. As a child, Fina was evidently a part of a group of lay female healers who lived austere lives in their own homes and tended to the sick. When she became ill (perhaps as a result of the austerities she practiced), she in turn became dependent on that same kind of healing and was cared for by several older lay sisters. The Beldì mentioned early in her story, in trying to ease Fina's final suffering by propping up her head with one arm, lost the use of that arm; restoring health to her was one of Fina's first postmortem miracles. The existence of this circle of *pinzochiere* (the Italian equivalent of beguines) is obscured, for by Fra Giovanni's time, their healing function had been taken over by the male ecclesiastics who managed the hospital of St. Fina.

Conclusion

It is impossible to know to what extent the four holy women discussed here had internalized the stories of the *Vitae Patrum;* it is very clear, however, that the hagiographers who composed these narratives perceived telling parallels between the lives of their saints and the practices of the Desert Fathers. Vito da Cortona, the Franciscan friar who wrote the life of Umiliana, had known her well and had been present when she died. Still, he did not limit himself to personal observation, but gathered a fuller historical base for his narrative by interviewing scores of witnesses to the holy woman's life and death. The biographer of St. Verdiana had seen her only once, but he took care to interview those who had known her and to double-check the events mentioned by his informants. Umiltà's biographer had access to earlier *Vitae* and interviewed all the surviving sisters who had known her. Only Fina's biographer did not know her and had to rely on local legend. He was half a century removed from Fina's time, fifty years of miracle working by the saint, and her legend must have been quite fully formed by the time he came to it. In place of reliable witnesses to her "desert" behavior, he used Scripture to underscore the "desert" meaning of her experience.

All these biographers, in spite of their reminders to the reader that they are writing modern saint's lives with attention to verifiable historical fact, employ a rhetoric shaped by the trope of the desert and the images of demonic temptation from the *Vitae Patrum*. The ambiguous image of the snake is ancient and holy, whether or not real snakes may have been also endemic in Tuscan hermitages. In employing the narrative structures of the older tale cycle, the medieval hagiographers create a polyvalent narrative in which ancient symbols of transformation operate in a contemporary context.

These four women saints, although forgotten for centuries, were important leaders in their own time; in fact, their biographers wish us to believe that their influence on their world was like that of St. Antony in his time. None of the four fits contemporary stereotypes of good women or good nuns. I believe that the Desert Father rhetoric constitutes an apologia for what is transgressive in these women's behavior. Umiltà, for example, continually transgresses good female behavior. As a wife, she prays for something to happen to her husband so she can enter a religious community; as a nun, she runs away from her convent and becomes a recluse; as an abbess, she often finds it necessary to live in the secular world while constructing new communities from the ground up, literally stone by stone.

Similar issues are at stake in Vito da Cortona's life of St. Umiliana. She is transgressive because it is the only way she can live a holy life. Her family forbids her to join a monastic order, forbids her to distribute food and clothing to the poor, and steals her dowry when she returns to her father's home as a widow. When she can no longer go out into the streets to help people, she creates an oratory for herself out of the Cerchi family dungeon and tower and becomes a recluse there. It is in that transformed space that she undergoes demonic temptations like the one cited here. Umiliana belonged to one of the most powerful clans in Florence, and the Cerchi probably did not regard her as a heroine until long after her death. Using the rhetoric of the Desert Fathers is a politically safe way for her biographer to demonstrate her importance. Fra Vito does not speak openly of her leadership of a Franciscan women's movement, although we can read between the lines and see her at the center of a powerful network of influential women. Does Vito avoid this topic because of the power of the Cerchi? Or is he personally unwilling to acknowledge female leadership? Again, the choice of desert rhetoric is useful, for it views Umiliana in the context of male leaders and allows her biographer to ignore the context of a widespread female spiritual renewal in Tuscany and Umbria. Fina, too, is part of a community of extraregular laywomen, but her biographer focuses on her solitude and her asceticism, not her community or her power.

Ultimately, I believe that we can best understand this Italian cycle of female saints' lives as a response to two interrelated issues: the existence of a new model of female spirituality that was gathering adherents all over Europe, and the increased interest in lay piety and in living the *vita apostolica* while in the world. Both movements were problematical to pious churchmen; both seemed to them to demand some kind of centralized or institutionalized control. The institutional Church did not have the resources to contain either movement. The *cura monialium*, the problem of who would supervise the burgeoning women's communities, was a serious issue; no one thought that women could govern themselves as spiritual communities, yet one by one all the male orders issued statements announcing that they would no longer admit women to the communities under their jurisdiction. There were not enough educated clergy—in spite of the efforts of the Dominican order to meet just this need—to supervise the piety of uneducated and pious lay people. The ideals of the *vita apostolica* went against the thrust toward capitalism and were an implied criticism of the wealth of the Church. Yet many men saw firsthand the contributions of women and chose to support them by composing *Vitae* of saintly women that formed a cycle of women's saints' lives, a *Vitae Matrum* testifying to the ancient power inspiring this new movement.

Notes

1. For a discussion of the development of critical approaches to the cycle, see David Staines, "The Medieval Cycle: Mapping a Trope," in *Transtextualities,* ed. Donald Maddox and Sarah Sturm-Maddox, forthcoming. I am indebted to this study for the terminology used in this paper.
2. Ibid.
3. St. Antony of Egypt (251–356) is the most famous of the so-called Desert

Fathers; along with St. Paul the Hermit, he is the originator of the movement for spiritual renewal in the desert during the period of the persecution of Christians. His Life, or *Vita,* written by another Desert Father and a friend, Athanasius of Alexandria (295–373), in Greek, was almost immediately translated into Latin by Evagrius (ca. 371). It was this translation that indirectly brought about the conversion of St. Augustine in 386, for St. Augustine was profoundly moved by hearing of a friend's conversion upon reading the account of Antony's conversion. I am indebted to Helen Waddell, ed. and trans., *The Desert Fathers* (Ann Arbor: University of Michigan Press, 1971), for this story.

4. *Vite dei Santi Padri,* trans. Domenico Cavalca (Turin: UTET, 1936). His translation of Evagrius's translation of Athanasius, *Vita di Sant' Antonio Abate* is also found in *Scrittori di religione del trecento volgarizzamenti,* ed. Giuseppe de Luca (Turin: Einaudi, 1977), vol. 1, pp. 41–95.

5. *Athanasius: The Life of Antony and the Letter to Marcellinus,* trans. and intro. Robert C. Gregg (New York: Paulist Press, 1980), p. 32. This is translated from the Greek text. Evagrius has "[e]t primo quidem incipiens etiam ipse, in locis paululum a villa remotioribus manebat: exinde autem, si quem vigilantem in hoc studio compererat, procedens, quarebat ut apis prudentissima; nec ad habitaculum suum ante remeabat, nisi ejus quem cupiebat frueretur aspectibus; et sic, tanquam munere mellis accepto, abibat ad sua . . . omne etiam desiderium et sollicitudinem erga id coeperat exerceret, operabatur manibus suis, sciens scriptum esse: Qui non operatur, non manducet. Mercedem tamen operis sui, pretio panis excepto, egentibus largiebatur. Orabat frequenter, quippe qui didicerat quod oporteret sine intermissione Dominum orare" ("Vita Beatae Antonii Abbatis," *Vitae Patrum sive Historiae Eremiticae Libri Decem,* in *Patrologiae cursus completus, series latina,* vol. 73, ed. Jacques-Paul Migne [Paris, 1849]).

6. *Athanasius: Life of Antony,* p. 38.

7. Ibid., p. 40.

8. *Vita di Sant' Antonio Abate,* p. 51.

9. Henri Queffélec, *Saint Anthony of the Desert,* trans. James Whitall (New York: Dutton, 1954), p. 129.

10. Ibid., p. 139.

11. This reminds one of the function of animals in shamanic traditions, where an animal may first seem a demonic enemy to the holy man and then become his guide or ally. Mircea Eliade observes that "[s]ometimes the animal who tortures him becomes the future shaman's helping spirit" (*Shamanism: Archaic Techniques of Ecstasy* [Princeton, N.J.: Princeton University Press, 1964], p. 44). His comment on friendly animals is also relevant; friendship with animals, and knowledge of their language, may reestablish the "paradisal" situation lost at the dawn of time (pp. 98–99). I am indebted to Janet Adler for first calling my attention to this connection.

12. *Athanasius: Life of St. Antony,* p. 69.

13. "Liminal" is Victor Turner's term for a sacred state that is neither here nor there, no longer the past and not yet the future, the time of initiation and transition/transformation (*Dramas, Fields, and Metaphors: Symbolic Action in Human Society* [Ithaca, N.Y.: Cornell University Press, 1974]). I am using the term in the sense that Caroline Bynum does, in "Women's Stories, Women's Symbols: A Critique of Victor Turner's Theory of Liminality," in *Anthropology and the Study of Religion,* ed. Frank E. Reynolds and Robert Moore (Chicago: Center for the Scientific Study of Religion, 1984), pp. 105–125.

14. *Vita Sancti Macarii Romani,* in *PL* 73, col. 422, chap. xvii.

15. St. Jerome, "The Life of St. Paul the First Hermit," in *Desert Fathers,* ed. Waddell, p. 38.

16. *The Lives of the Desert Fathers: The Historia Monachorum in Aegypto,* trans. Norman Russell, intro. Benedicta Ward (London: Mobray, 1981), p. 110.

17. Waddell, ed., *Desert Fathers,* p. 16.

18. Caroline Walker Bynum, *Holy Feast and Holy Fast: The Religious Signifi-cance of Food to Medieval Women* (Berkeley: University of California Press, 1987), and Rudolph Bell, *Holy Anorexia* (Chicago: University of Chicago Press, 1985), in their studies of female asceticism and food cite the *Vitae* of many of the women included in this essay. Peter Dronke, *Women Writers of the Middle Ages: A Critical Study of Texts from Perpetua to Marguerite Porete* (Cambridge: Cambridge University Press, 1984), touches on the asceticism and piety of Angela of Foligno, who shares many of the attributes of the women I am studying here.

19. Donald Weinstein and Rudolph M. Bell, *Saints and Society: The Two Worlds of Western Christendom, 1000–1700* (Chicago: University of Chicago Press, 1982), esp. pp. 17–72.

20. Ibid., p. 31.

21. Elizabeth A. Petroff, *Consolation of the Blessed: Women Saints in Medieval Tuscany* (Millerton, N.Y.: Alta Gaia, 1979), pp. 40–48, and "The Visionary Tradi-tion in Women's Writings: Dialogue and Autobiography," in *Medieval Women's Visionary Literature,* ed. Elizabeth A. Petroff (New York: Oxford University Press, 1986), pp. 6–7.

22. Weinstein and Bell, *Saints and Society,* pp. 34–36.

23. Ibid., p. 48.

24. Ibid., p. 54.

25. This observation is admittedly an impressionistic one. I know of no study of vernacular accounts of Italian women saints, but I have noticed that many of the Latin *Acta Sanctorum* texts make mention of Italian versions of individual *Vitae.* For example, the *Life of St. Umiliana de' Cerchi* was written in Italian, as was the *Life of St. Fina of San Gimignano.* The Latin text of Umiltà's sermons in the *Acta Sanctorum* is a translation of an Italian version; the original Latin texts were only discovered later. Although it does not deal with this issue systematically, Giovanni Pozzi and Claudio Leonardi, eds., *Scrittrici mistiche italiane* (Genoa: Marietti, 1988), pp. 61–286, is useful for providing texts that circulated in medieval Italy. This study includes extracts from Latin and Italian texts by or about Clare of Assisi, Beatrice I d'Este, Umiliana de' Cerchi, Umiltà of Faenza, Margherita of Cortona, Angela of Foligno, Benvenuta Bojanni, Vanna of Orvieto, Clare of Montefalco, Villana de' Botti, Catherine of Siena, Francesca Romana, and Catherine Vigri.

26. See Margot King, *The Desert Mothers* (Toronto: Peregrina Press, 1989); her translations of the *Lives* of some of the most famous of these Desert Mothers: the *Life of Marie d'Oignies* by Jacques de Vitry, *Supplement to the Life of Marie d'Oignies* by Thomas of Cantimpré, and the *Life of Christina Mirabilis,* also by Thomas; and King, "The Sacramental Witness of Christina *Mirabilis:* The Mystic Growth of a Fool for Christ's Sake," in *Medieval Religious Women,* vol. 2, *Peace Weavers,* ed. John A. Nichols and Lillian Thomas Shank (Kalamazoo, Mich.: Cistercian Publications, 1987), pp. 145–164. Two articles by Barbara Bolton outline the parallels between the Desert Fathers movement and the beguine movement in the Liège area: "Mul-ieres Sanctae," in *Women in Medieval Society,* ed. Susan Mosher Stuard (Phila-delphia: University of Pennsylvania Press, 1976), pp. 141–158, and "*Vitae Ma-*

trum: A Further Aspect of the *Frauenfrage,"* in *Medieval Women,* ed. Derek Baker (Oxford: Basil Blackwell, 1978), pp. 253–274. Both scholars document the contemporary awareness that the women's movement in Liège paralleled the fourth-century movement into the desert, and both indicate that male biographers of these holy women saw themselves in a position similar to that of St. Jerome and St. Gregory documenting the lives of holy women in their area. Neither King nor Bolton sees the *Vitae Patrum* as a primary cycle and the *Vitae Matrum,* the thirteen biographies of holy women in the Liège region, as a corresponding secondary cycle, but Bolton points out, "It is perhaps now the time to look at these *vitae* again with the hope of reaching a reassessment of what was written in the early thirteenth century. This would make these women more important and would upgrade their *Lives* to make them worthy of the title *vitae matrum"* (*"Vitae Matrum,"* pp. 272–273).

27. *Vita de Sanctae Humilitate Abbatissa,* in *Acta Sanctorum,* May 22. The unnamed author of the *Life* had known Umiltà personally. He wrote his account some years after her death, at the request of sisters who also had known her. He wrote his text in Latin, and there is evidence that he used documents collected for her canonization in 1332, as well as gathering oral recollections of the saint.

28. Ibid., chap. I, par. 5.

29. For more on St. Umiltà, including the translation of her *Vita* and selections from her sermons, see Petroff, *Consolation of the Blessed,* pp. 121–150; St. Umiltà of Faenza, "Sermons," trans. Richard J. Pioli, in *Medieval Women's Visionary Literature,* ed. Petroff, pp. 247–253; and Chapter 11. Cathy Mooney has translated and edited all the sermons of Umiltà: *Umiltà of Faenza Sermons* (Newburyport, Mass.: Focus Library of Medieval Women, 1992).

30. The only justifiable reason for leaving one religious community was to adopt a stricter rule in another community. The Benedictine Rule, which Umiltà adopts when she becomes a recluse, is stricter than the Augustinian Rule, and the Vallombrosan Rule is a more ascetic version of the Benedictine Rule.

31. *Vita de Sanctae Humilitate,* chap. I, par. 12, in *Acta Sanctorum,* May 22.

32. Petroff, *Consolation of the Blessed,* p. 126.

33. In late antiquity, the weasel was thought to be a witch's familiar; in the Middle Ages, in its white winter pelt, the ermine was associated with virginity and chastity. In Chaucer's "Miller's Tale," the simile of a weasel captures Alisoun's sensuality: "Fair was this yonge wyf, and therwithal / As any wezele hir body gent and smal." Near the end of Marie de France's lay "Eliduc," a male weasel, seeing that his mate is dead, revives her by gathering a red flower in the woods and putting it in her mouth. Eliduc's wife is able to restore her husband's lover to life by the same means.

34. Queffélec, *Saint Anthony of the Desert,* p. 188.

35. See Pietro Zama, *Santa Umiltà: La Vita e i "sermones"* (Faenza: Fratelli Lega Editori, 1974); Umiltà, "Sermons," pp. 247–253; and Elizabeth Petroff, "Women's Bodies and the Experience of God in the Middle Ages," *Vox Benedictina* 8 (1991): 91–115.

36. Anna Benvenuti-Papi, "Umiliana dei Cerchi: Nascita di un culto nella Firenze del dugento," *Studi Francescani: Revista Nazionale Italiana* 77 (1980): 87–117. She sees the demonic temptations in Umiliana's *Vita* as related to the political ends of the Franciscans and their allies in Florence. The Cerchi family was Guelf, in a city being beseiged by the Ghibellines. Because of its resistance to the Ghibelline cause in 1246, Florence was placed under a papal interdict, and Umiliana's funeral

had to be performed under this sanction. A number of the temptations Satan offers are attempts to get her to pay attention to disorders in Florence caused by the Ghibellines: "[I]nfatti l'illusor che sovente tenta di condurla a quella finestrella della torre, che costituisce l'unico legame di Umiliana con la vita che si svolge al di sotto, nelle affollate e spesso turbolenti viuzze del centro; gli echi degli scontri, dei tafferugli, degli incendi che si susseguono in città giungono fino a lei, introdotti pressoché esclusivamente dalle argomentazioni diaboliche; un demonio molto in linea, del resto, con il buon senso comune, con una ordinata e tranquilla concezione dell'esistenza 'secolare,' dalla quale Umiliana cerca disperatamente di sottrarsi; così a più riprese troveremo nelle parole del suasor l'invito alle seconde nozze, mentre il disprezzo per le soluzioni verginali in genere si esplica in una serie di pesanti allusioni sulle monache di Ripoli e di Monticelli le quali, nell'interpretazione dia-bolica, rifiutandosi di partecipare alle mondane gioie del matrimonio, contrib-uiscono con responsibilità diretta alle irrequietezze civili della città; infatti gli am-anti delle suore, insoddisfatti nei loro desideri amorosi, si uccidono vicen-devolmente per le strade fiorentine" (pp. 106–107).

37. Umiliana's *Vita* was composed in Latin the year of her death by the Franciscan Vito da Cortona and translated into Italian some time between 1250 and 1350. Vito da Cortona's Latin text, *Vita Major Sanctae Humilianae*, is in *Acta Sanctorum*, May 19, along with two shorter *Lives*, one anonymous, and the other by Raffaelo da Volterra. The fourteenth-century Italian translation, from which I quote, is "Leggenda della Beata Umiliana de' Cerchi," in *Scrittori di religione del trecento volgarizzamenti*, ed. Guiseppi de Luca (Turin: Einaudi, 1977), vol. 3, pp. 365–410.

38. "Leggenda della Beata Umiliana," p. 368.

39. "[D]ispregiando le minacce a loro fatte . . . che 'l santo suo fervore vincea ogni ingiuria e paura e timore e i mali diletti della carne; e di quante ingiurie di parole fu percossa, ripresa da' grandi e da' piccoli della casa, et eziando battuta alcuna volta per l'opere della piatade! Le quali ingiurie tutte dispregiava e dimen-ticava, rendendosi famigliare e trattabile appresso de' detti suoi ingiuriatori; *ed in nulla la sua mente si moveva*" (My emphasis). [Despising their threats . . . so that her holy fervor might conquer every injury and fear and fright and the pleasing evils of the flesh; and how she was battered by so much verbal abuse, picked on by great and small in the household, and even one time was beaten for her works of piety! She despised and forgot those injuries, and comported herself pleasantly and obe-diently toward her abusers; *and in nothing was her mind ever moved*.]

40. "Che a costei mancòe di vita monastica, la quale in continuo silenzio e guardia di sé visse? che meno ebbe che' santi romiti, la quale, nel mezzo di sì grande cittade, prese e trovò solitudine e diserto, e la camera mutò in carcere . . . ? questa, in casa del padre faccendo solitudine, e combattendo vinse il mondo, il diavolo e la carne in mezzo de' mondani."

41. "Ma, ragguardando la sua preziosa grazia, lo nemico, invidioso della nos-tra salute e della umana generazione, e isviatore d'ogni bene, accésesi fortemente d'ira. Non dopo molto tempo la incominciò di molte tentazioni e tribulazioni a faticare, a ciò che per paura cessasse dall'orazione e divozione. Chi potrebbe numer-are quante volte egli apparve visiblemente, e la percosse, come permesso gli fue dalla divina potenzia?" [But, gazing on her precious grace, the Enemy, envious of our salvation and of human kind, and the opposer of all good, was fiercely stirred to wrath. After not much time he began to exhaust her with many temptations and tribulations, so that out of fear she might cease her prayers and devotions. Who

could count how many times he visibly appeared to her, and struck her, as was permitted to him by the divine potency?]

42. "Leggenda della Beata Umiliana," p. 381.

43. Ibid., pp. 381–382.

44. Ibid., p. 382.

45. After spending a number of years in pilgrimages to Compostella and Rome as a maid-companion to a wealthy female relative, St. Verdiana was enclosed (in 1208) as a recluse next to the church of St. Antony in Lucca; she is associated with the Franciscan order in some Franciscan chronicles, but there is no evidence she took vows as a Franciscan tertiary, and in fact the date of her enclosure is much too early, eighteen years before the death of St. Francis. It is of course possible that she became a tertiary sometime after her enclosure, since she lived until 1242.

The church of St. Antony no longer exists; a church dedicated to St. Verdiana was erected in its place in the seventeenth century. There is a tiny Museum of St. Verdiana attached to the present-day church, with a panel painting of St. Verdiana and her serpents, in the style of Segna di Bonaventura; another of the assumption of the Virgin Mary with Saints Antony and Verdiana, from about 1600; and a Madonna and Child with St. Verdiana and other saints, attributed to the school of Ghirlandaio (*Guida d'Italia. Toscana: Touring Club Italiano* [Milan: Garzanti, 1974], pp. 456–457). Her cult must have been an active one for at least four centuries, if a new church was erected in her honor in the baroque period.

46. Her *Vita* was originally written in Italian by Hieronymo Setini, who remembered being lifted up to see her through her cell window when he was a young boy. It was translated into Latin by Bishop Attone, *Vita Sanctae Verdianae Virgine,* in *Acta Sanctorum,* February 1.

47. Ibid., chap. III, par. 11.

48. *Leggenda della Beata Fina Vergine da Santo Geminiano* was written in Italian by the Dominican Fra Giovanni di Ser Coppo of San Gimignano about 1300. In the bilingual edition, *The Legend of the Holy Fina, Virgin of San Gimignano,* trans. M. Mansfield (1908; New York: Cooper Square, 1966), the Italian text is based on that of Francesco Zambrini, *Leggenda di Santa Fina da San Gimignano scritta nel buon secolo della lingua da Fra Giovanni di Coppo della medesima Terra* (Imola: Galeati, 1879), a collation from two early manuscripts: one from the fifteenth century but preserving language of an earlier date, and the other dated 1538. There is also a Latin text by Fra Giovanni exhibiting some differences from the Italian, published in the *Acta Sanctorum,* March 12. It is not known which is the earlier text. St. Fina, who died in 1253, may have been connected with the Franciscan order, since she is mentioned in Franciscan chronicles of the period, but she is also claimed by the Benedictines; according to the *Leggenda,* she was a sister in an association of pious laywomen who supported themselves and the poor by the work of their hands and by begging for alms. Other sources call these women *pinzochiere* (the term is thought to correspond to *beguine*) and attest that both men and women belonged to a lay order that served a hospice for the sick poor (founded in 1220) in San Gimignano. After the death of St. Fina in 1253, the Comune used the wealth that had accumulated at her shrine to construct a hospital dedicated to her. Fra Giovanni addresses his *Life of St. Fina* to Fra Goccio, then the rector of the hospital of St. Fina.

49. *Legend of the Holy Fina,* pp. 50–51.

50. Ibid., p. 52. The Latin text sees her fortitude as the indication of a man's mind and compares her tortures with those of the early martyrs: "O vere patientia

mira et cunctis praeferenda miraculis, quae in fragili foemineo sexu masculinum animum reperit: quo scilicet Dei Virgo, cum ex una parte corporis tam diris torqueretur doloribus, a vermibus vero ex altera et muribus roderetur, sic tamen laeta facie tranquillaque mente manebat, ut numquam vel signum tristitiae in vultu suo monstraverit, vel verbum lingua ejus protulerit conquerentis. Non igitur in ore ipsius resonabat impatientiae murmur, sed semper gratiarum actio et vox laudis. Propter quod sine ferro et flammis quasi Martyr fuisse videtur, quam etsi gladius persecutoris non abstulit, tormentum tamen diutinum multiplicium dolorum afflixit: quod ipsa non cum mentis tristitia, sed laeta patientia toleravit" (*Vita Beata Finae Virginis,* chap. i, par. 5, in *Acta Sanctorum,* March 12).

51. *Legend of the Holy Fina,* pp. 53–54.

52. Ibid., p. 54.

53. Ibid., p. 57.

54. Ibid., p. 53.

55. Weinstein and Bell, *Saints and Society,* p. 32.

56. Bell and Weinstein are in error regarding the time period of Fina's illness. Fina had already been ill for five years; her mother apparently died in January, when the fighting was most intense in the city, and Fina died on March 12, 1253.

57. Mansfield, Introduction to *Legend of the Holy Fina,* p. xxxiv. The introduction gives a history of the cult of St. Fina after her death, the succession of shrines dedicated to her in the next two centuries and decorated by famous Tuscan artists, and an account of the hospital of St. Fina.

58. *Legend of the Holy Fina,* p. 75.

III

WOMEN MYSTICS AND THE ACQUISITION OF AUTHORITY

8

Male Confessors and Female Penitents: Possibilities for Dialogue

Students of medieval women mystics have long recognized that in the absence of approved leadership roles for women in medieval society, mystical or visionary experience gave women an authority they would not have possessed otherwise. Studies of famous women mystics and prophets, such as Hildegard of Bingen, Mechthild of Magdeburg, and Marie d'Oignies, have demonstrated what this authority meant in social terms. What has not been explored as fully is how this authority manifested itself in interpersonal relationships, particularly in regard to men who were in a position of authority vis-à-vis these women.

What I would like to examine in this chapter is the nature of the dialogue between confessors and penitents—what male ecclesiastics learned from the women who were under their spiritual direction. What was it in certain relationships with certain women that turned a clearly hierarchical and power-laden situation into one of equality? Of female superiority in some areas? What did men learn from women that they needed? I can make a few generalizations here and then explore the stories of three male–female relationships in more detail. First of all, the women seem to present men with a compelling image of living faith. Second, the men are attracted by the women's gift of prophecy; they want to know more about themselves and about the future. Third, the women are intercessors with God; the men go to them when something terrible is happening or when someone is dying to request their prayers and their communication with God. Fourth, medieval holy women demonstrate a new kind of teaching in action, apparently spontaneous, compassionate, and nonhierarchical. Finally, women have refreshing new viewpoints; they can react and respond to situations directly (or so it seems to male observers) without recourse to precedents, and thus they can be transgressive in ways a male ecclesiastic cannot be.

On the basis of existing texts, it is more difficult to ascertain what the women get from the men. Official approval and acceptance were certainly primary for many women. Lay penitents were in a vulnerable position in regard to the Church hierarchy, for they were not nuns and they weren't quite laywomen. A loyal and understanding confessor could provide protection for a woman who was living a holy life outside a convent or the regular structure, and the confessor–penitent bond was a connection with the institutional Church that defined the women as good women, even if their status was ambiguous. And, of course, the confessor was the door to the reception of the sacrament of the Eucharist. As Caroline Bynum has pointed out, women—no matter how radical their ideas of God might have appeared in other respects—supported the traditional role of the priesthood when it came to their access to the sacraments.[1] It is likely that the women also received theological instruction, guidance in meditation practices, and advice in cases of conscience. A confessor who was knowledgeable about mystical experience could provide guidance and reassurance in times of doubt. But the hagiographies written by men that I am about to cite, interestingly enough, do not speak about that. Only Margery Kempe's *Book* tells us of both the woman's and the man's view of the teaching that went on in their relationship.

Christina of Markyate

Christina was an Anglo-Saxon recluse, later a prioress, in Anglo-Saxon England, whose *Vita* was probably written for the nuns of her convent. (For more about Christina's life, see Chapters 1 and 2.) However, not all the biography has survived, and the part we have covers the period from her childhood to the 1140s. She was still alive in 1155 and may have lived until 1166. She is believed to have been born between 1096 and 1098, the same time as Hildegard of Bingen. Christopher Holdsworth summarizes what is known about her; our two main sources of information about her are her *Life* and the *St. Albans Psalter,* which was made for her.[2] We know very little about the author of *The Life of Christina of Markyate,* except that he was a monk in the nearby monastery of St. Albans and that he was writing in the monastery itself. The editor and translator, C. H. Talbot, observes: "Whoever the writer was, he was very close indeed to Christina. The whole tone of the story is autobiographical rather than historical. . . . There is in the narrative a frankness, a vigour of expression, and an economy of words that must reflect direct contact with Christina herself."[3]

Although he never says that he was her confessor,[4] he knows things about her that only a confessor would be likely to know, for

[h]e apparently had enough authority to question her about her visions and her gift of foreseeing future events, for besides showing intimate knowledge of her spiritual difficulties, he knew exactly what signs gave her a premonition of some impending supernatural grace. All this is described with such naturalness as could arise only from long familiarity, a familiarity which is emphasized by his reference on one occasion to his having taken a meal with her.[5]

The anonymous biographer never reveals himself, and Talbot has established that the version we have[6] is an edited copy of an original, more detailed, *Vita* he wrote that no longer exists. If there was a story about the relationship between Christina and this biographer, it is not to be found here.

But there is another story—Christina's relationship with the Norman abbot of St. Albans, Geoffrey:

One of his most prolific sources of information must have been Abbot Geoffrey himself, for in his account of the relationship between the abbot and the recluse, he seems to know Geoffrey's side of the story with uncanny precision, what he said and did, his perplexity over the sources of Christina's spiritual knowledge, and his reactions to her teaching.[7]

Geoffrey died in 1147; I think it is likely that he in fact left a written account of his relationship with Christina. At one point in the text, Christina's sister Margaret and Geoffrey's sister Lettice agree that the events in Christina's and Geoffrey's relationship deserve to be recorded, as St. Gregory had done.

The story of Christina and Geoffrey must be seen in the context of the time in England. Christina came from an influential Anglo-Saxon family that had retained its position after the Norman Conquest, and the world she lived in was composed almost entirely of persons of Anglo-Saxon descent. As Holdsworth argues, until Christina met Geoffrey, all the people close to her had Anglo-Saxon or Anglo-Scandinavian names: "The canon who strengthened her resolve as a girl was called Sueno; the first person she fled to was Aelfwen, a recluse; another hermit Eadwin helped her to escape."[8] All were members of the "submerged majority" who "were ministering to the people who were not at home with the Anglo-Norman culture and who may well have found it hard to make themselves understood by their new French-speaking lords."[9] The hermit who trained Christina in meditation must have spoken to her in Anglo-Saxon, for the one phrase in that language in the Latin *Vita* is Roger's name for her: "myn sunendaege dohter" [my Sunday's daughter].

As a hermit, Christina was a representative of an older, native English religious culture. During her lifetime, the aftermath of the First Crusade, the age of conflict between pope and emperor, there was popular mistrust of the established Church and a new interest in an apostolic Christianity based more closely on Christ's life as depicted in the Gospels:

For not only was England in the twelfth century a conquered country where those who might have exercised the functions of lordship were often absent from the village communities who needed them, but it shared with the whole of western Christendom a sense of unease about the old centers of power in the church. Both parish clergy, the bishops, and the old cultic centres guided over by monastic bodies under attack from those who sought new standards of behavior, even though their novelty was often disguised as a return to old, apostolic practice or to the life of the desert fathers.[10]

In this context, it is no accident that Christina was the name the girl Theodora chose as her name in religion, after her father told her in anger, "Si enim Christum vis habere: Christum nuda sequere."[11] Not much later, this became the cry of the Franciscan movement: "naked, to follow the naked Christ."

Geoffrey came from a different world, the world of the overlords of England. He was a Norman and, according to one reader of the Christina manuscript, acted just like a Norman ("more Normanorum" says the marginal note), meaning he behaved arrogantly and thought himself superior.

> He was a man of affairs, a former schoolmaster of Dunstable, who had offered himself as a monk to St. Albans in compensation for the loss of some valuable copes which he had borrowed from the abbey for a play and which had been accidentally burnt whilst they were in his keeping. From the hints dropped by the biographer in the Life one gets the impression that he was a worldly man, rather proud of his success as an administrator and inclined to pay little heed to the opinions and advice of others.[12]

When Geoffrey and Christina came to know each other, Christina lived at Markyate, in a tiny congregation of female hermits that had grown up around her hermitage. Geoffrey was abbot of the male community of St. Albans, a few miles down the road. Everyone seems to have known of the close relationship that developed between these two:

> The biographer is at pains to emphasize the close spiritual relationship that bound these two people together, the gossip to which it gave rise, and the great advantages which both of them drew from it. Christina always called the abbot "her beloved," whilst he on his side referred to her as his *puella*. Her affection for him was such that she was continually preoccupied with his welfare and spent more time praying for him than she did for herself, and it was mainly by his persuasion that she agreed to make her profession at St. Albans.[13]

Christina and Geoffrey met in inauspicious or, rather, confrontational circumstances. He was not known to her personally, but she probably had heard of his arrogance and obstinacy. She had become known in the area as a prophet and a miracle worker and was venerated by many, but she still had enemies in the Church, dating back to her initial refusal to marry.[14] She felt that she needed a protector, someone who could help her to found a women's house affiliated with St. Albans, for, after resolving many doubts, she had recently decided to become a nun.

Her biographer sees their meeting as the beginning of an exchange: "[I]t was through this man that God had decided to provide for her needs and it was through His virgin that He decided to bring about this man's full conversion. And this was how it began."[15] Abbot Geoffrey was about to make a big mistake; he risked offending his community because he had in mind "a project which he knew could not be accomplished without the annoyance of his chapter and offence against God." Alvared, a monk who had been converted by Christina and who must have died not long before, appeared in a vision to Christina and explained that Geoffrey had decided on a dangerous course of action, "for if he carries it out he will offend God." He authorized her to intercede in this delicate matter: "I beg of you not to let him do it. This is the injunction I bring you from God."[16] This put Christina in the awkward position of having to send an unwelcome message to someone who was her superior and whose help she could use. But being more afraid of offending God than of offending a mere man, she sent a messenger to the abbot to report her vision. Geoffrey did not take it well: "He grew angry, considering the message as a piece of nonsense, and sent the man back to the virgin with the advice not to put her trust in dreams. [This is where the marginal note says "just like a Norman."] Nevertheless he was astonished that the virgin should be aware of something that was only in his own mind."[17]

Although Geoffrey ignored his message, Christina did not forget hers, and she doubled her efforts, praying with fasting and vigils for Geoffrey to be diverted from his course. That night, Geoffrey was attacked by "black and terrifying figures" and then confronted by "the aforesaid Alvared, his eyes and countenance blazing in anger." There was a standoff, and "[a]t first neither spoke to the other." When Geoffrey finally asked what he was to do, Alvared replied that Geoffrey knew very well what he was supposed to do, for he had already received a message about it. Geoffrey was very frightened at this and pleaded: "Holy Alvared, have pity on me: I will not continue on my evil bent and from now on will obey her messages promptly." The next morning, his physical bruises convinced him that the night's events had really happened, so he called together his confidants and promised to put an end to the project. He also went to speak with Christina in person. He seems to have known what he needed to say: "acknowledging his debt to her and thanking her for his deliverance, [h]e promised to avoid everything unlawful, to fulfill her commands, and to help her convent in the future: all he asked was her intercession with God."[18]

This first meeting became the pattern for their future meetings: "Ever after the man often visited the servant of Christ, heard her admonitions, accepted her advice, consulted her in doubts, avoided evil, bore her reproaches."[19]

Even if he had to accept her criticisms, the abbot gained something valuable from these meetings, for, as Christina's biographer continues: "if he went discomfited, he returned comforted; if weary of the vicissitudes of the world, he returned refreshed. He withdrew under the shadow of Him whom lovers find, and when he grew cold in divine love, he was glad to realize that, after speaking with her, he grew fervent."[20]

Christina, seeing how much progress he was making, "cherished him with great affection and loved him with a wonderful but pure love."[21] Again, the biographer point to the element of fair exchange in their relationship:

> Their affection was mutual, but different according to their standards of holiness. He supported her in worldly matters: she commended him to God more earnestly in her prayers. . . . Nor did she make a secret of reproving him harshly in his presence, when she knew that in his absence he had sinned, thinking that the wounds of a friend are better than the flattery of an enemy.[22]

A loving and thoughtful dialogue was established; each partner was authoritative in one type of matter. Geoffrey's role as abbot made Christina's life simpler and safer, and Christina's role as prophet and confidante strengthened Geoffrey and made his life simpler and safer, too. Her prayers saved his life when he thought he was dying—she saw him in a vision and knew how badly he wanted her to be there with him. But there is one important area in which the parity confirmed by their dialogues was not shared—Christina's gift of prophecy.

She always seemed to know what he was up to and often used her sister Margaret as a witness of her foreknowledge concerning him. He could never figure out how she always knew when he was coming to visit her. He tried to test her by telling no one of his planned visit to her, but she knew and told the other sisters to be ready for him. He took a long time getting there but finally arrived, saying triumphantly, "This time I know my sudden coming took you by surprise." As usual, she had the last word; she called Margaret and asked her to repeat what she had already told them.[23] This need to test her is probably indicative of his dependence on her insights; since he relied on her in all his decisions, he felt compelled to understand more fully the source of her information. (For another point of view on this episode, see Chapter 3.)

Their relationship was mediated by visions and dreams; she was aware of his visions when they happened and was able to be present in them at times. She also had visions of what he was doing in his life as a priest and saw God's response to his activities. An example of the mutuality of this visionary life is shown in two episodes. The first was a response to Geoffrey's desire to know how he could ask her how she obtained her knowledge of him. In spite of their closeness, he felt he could not ask her directly what he wanted to know. I quote the passage in its entirety, for it is very revealing of his attitude toward her:

> [H]e saw himself holding a flowering herb in his hands, the juice of which was very efficacious for driving away maladies. If he squeezed it strongly, little juice

came out, but if gently and quietly he would get what he wanted. Next morning he hastened to accompany a religious man, Evisandus, on a visit to the hermitage which he loved. And in discussing the dream as they went, the herb was interpreted as Christina, the flower as the honour of her virginity; he said she should be approached not on impulse, but gently and kindly. This we often experienced later on. He told everything to Christina. For at a very early hour, after having heard the divine Office, she came out of the church and walked in a little enclosure nearby filled with flowers, and plucked the first flower, camilla [*sic*] which she found. And taking it reverently in her hands, she went towards the abbot as he approached and as if about to greet him said: "This is the flower, is it not, which you saw in your vision during the night?" And she showed him the plant. For she had been told this by a voice which came to her from above. . . . In this manner God in his mercy solved the problems of the inquirer and made the loved maiden more lovable to the abbot.[24]

Perhaps the abbot was not very good in interpersonal relations. The vision tells him in no uncertain terms that gentleness will work when force will not, something he probably needed to learn. The metaphor of the flower is very telling, for the flower he picks, and the one she holds out to him, is an herbal remedy that must be handled carefully if its healing properties are to be effective.

After this episode, more trust must have been apparent in their relationship, for Geoffrey was able to ask for her intercession with God in some very delicate matters. Three times he was asked by King Stephen to journey to Rome to consult with the pope about matters concerning Stephen. Each of these missions was personally dangerous, for Stephen was notoriously hostile to the papacy and, thanks to the advice of some evil churchmen, was often equally hostile to the leaders of the English Church, among them Abbot Geoffrey. Each time Christina was very worried for him when he reported that he had been chosen for the mission, and two of the three times Geoffrey himself was very reluctant to obey, but was afraid to refuse because of the king's power. Each time Christina prayed for divine counsel, and each time she was given a vision of Geoffrey's divine protection. In all three episodes, the symmetry of their experiences is stressed.

The first time Geoffrey was requested to make this journey, he asked Christina to make him some undergarments for greater comfort while traveling. As she thought about Geoffrey, she heard a voice

> coming to her from above: "Behold the wall." And she saw a wall, in which her beloved friend was, as it were, cemented alive. "As long" (it continued) "as he is firmly fixed in it, the protection of God will never desert him. But the garments you have prepared for his comfort give as quickly as possible to the poor, because Christ will obtain for him more gracious comfort on his journey."[25]

The woven garments were the price of Geoffrey's protection; he did not have to go to Rome, but she had to give the garments away: "So in giving away the garments, she fulfilled the command, whilst He, in keeping back her beloved, confirmed the promise. And she counted it little loss to dispose of the woven stuff so long as he, whom true charity has woven, was prevented from embarking on so onerous a task."[26] Earthly dialogue has been ratified by a celestial colloquy with Christina, in which God and the holy woman exchange valuable objects.

The second time, she saw Geoffrey standing happily in a kind of transparent enclosure with no doors or windows. A voice told her, "This enclosure which you see has but one doorkeeper, God: and that man cannot come out except by divine intervention."[27] She told Geoffrey, "On this account . . . I am confident that you are kept within that enclosure and prevented from setting out on your journey." Encouraged by this, Geoffrey hastened to Oxford to argue before the king's court, while she went "to the Eternal King to pray about the same journey. At the king's court and with the earthly king discussions were held about the abbot's departure. With God and the celestial King she discussed how the same man might be prevented from departing. She who knew how to love to supreme advantage gained the day."[28] Geoffrey's mission was again cancelled. By coordinating their interviews with their respective kings, both parties obtained what they sought; the symmetry of their colloquies underlines their spiritual communion or dialogue.

The third time, Geoffrey's mission was even more dangerous, and this time Christina's vision was even more personal:

> She was rapt in ecstasy and saw herself in the presence of her saviour; and she saw him, whom she loved above all others, encircled with her arms and held closely to her breast. And whilst she feared that, since a man is stronger than a woman, he would free himself from her grasp, she saw Jesus, the helper of the saved, closing her hands with His own loving hand, not by intertwining her fingers with His but by joining them one over the other: so that by joining her hands no less than by the power of her arms she should feel greater strength in holding her friend back.[29]

This time Christina, not Geoffrey, is the subject of the vision. She holds Geoffrey in her arms, but, as if in response to her fear that he might be strong enough to break out of her grasp, Jesus himself shows her how to strengthen her grip by joining her hands. She has received divine reassurance not only that she ought to hold Geoffrey back, but that she is capable of so doing. She has found her center, in the presence of Christ, and now can rest within it.

She continues to be the teacher in the relationship—the very last paragraph of the *Vita* speaks of her being mindful of Geoffrey day and night and constantly praying for him, and the final clause is "sensibly reproving him when his actions were not quite right."[30]

Marie d'Oignies

Marie d'Oignies, the first known beguine, is probably the best known example of a lay penitent who has a deep bond with her confessor, Jacques de Vitry. (For more about Marie's life, see Chapter 3.) But rather than looking at their relationship as described by de Vitry in the *Life of B. Marie d'Oignies*, I would like to look at their relationship as described by a third person, Thomas de Cantimpré, who wrote after Marie was dead but while Jacques de Vitry was still alive.

Thomas wrote the *Supplement to the Life of Marie d'Oignies* about 1230, just about the time that he left his position as an Augustinian canon of Cantimpré to join the Dominican order. His work is addressed to Prior Giles of Oignies (Marie's brother-in-law) and to Cardinal Jacques de Vitry, whom Thomas adored as a young man but of whom he had become very critical. As Hugh Feiss says in his introduction to his translation of the *Supplement,* Thomas "portrays a close interaction between professed religious, holy women, and laity; he manifests a lofty regard for the religious gifts of women."[31] As well as being experienced and well read in the spiritual life, Thomas has the writerly gifts of the novelist; he is superb at finding the telling details in an anecdote and at re-creating the ambiance in which an encounter took place. He also has a gift for reproducing speech patterns; whether or not his characters actually said what he attributes to them, we are convinced by the individual voices we hear.

In the *Supplement,* Thomas's avowed intention is to cite events in the life of Marie relating to Jacques de Vitry that were not included in de Vitry's *Life of Marie.* His covert hope is to use this text to recall his beloved master to Liège—a feat he knows even Marie had not been able to accomplish. As Thomas describes their relationship, both Marie and Jacques knew they were destined for each other. When studying in Paris, Jacques learned of her reputation and "abandoned his theological studies in which he was immoderately interested and came to Oignies where she had recently gone."[32] Marie went out to meet him upon his arrival and "followed in his footsteps, kissing on bended knee the places where he stepped."[33] Urged by a companion to stop this embarrassing behavior, Marie said she could not: "No, no, I can't. I am forcefully impelled by the spirit who now reveals to me interiorly that God has chosen him from among mortals to exalt him gloriously so that through him the salvation of souls will be miraculously achieved."[34]

Marie "*compelled* this venerable man to preach to the people," and her encouragement (that is, her "prayers and merits") was so successful that "he reached in a short time such a pre-eminence in preaching that scarcely any mortal equaled him in expounding the Scriptures and destroying sins."[35] He defended the cause of the holy women in Liège so enthusiastically and effectively that soon news of them extended all over Europe, but Marie knew that his activities would not end there. She foresaw what others were reluctant to admit, that God would "raise this man up to an episcopal see in the holy land across the sea" and that de Vitry would be pulled away from his responsibilities in Liège. As Thomas saw it, she was aware that once she was dead, de Vitry would be seduced by higher positions in the Church. Ironically, de Vitry's famous biography of her, which details the whole movement of feminine piety in the Liège area and his effectiveness as a preacher under her guidance, would be the basis for his rise in the Church.

Jacques says that while he was the master in ordinary matters, in matters of the spirit Marie was master. Marie not only had the gift of prophecy, but was a teacher herself, as Thomas shows in an anecdote about a rich businessman whom she had called to a new life. Although this anecdote is not related to Jacques de Vitry, it furthers our knowledge of their relationship by showing us Marie in action. In this situation, as in the Jacques–Marie relationship, both parties recognized each other immediately—she knew he "was going to be a vessel of election," and he, on seeing her face, "experienced completely unclouded self-knowledge and felt the spirit of God miraculously at work in him."[36] She gave him teaching on purgatory, emphasizing the necessity for purgation and terrifying him by her vivid description of the intensity of the purgatorial flames. At the end of that conversation, she sent him into a nearby church to pray, where he promptly had a vision in which the pyx, in three stages, moved toward him from the altar. After seeing this, "[h]is gazing eyes were suddenly covered by his eyelids and he was rapt to interior contemplation." His consciousness began to return, and he ran to his "mother," "emitting flames of divine fire" and saying, "I will love God without discretion." To this she counseled:

> "No, friend, certainly not." The handmaid of Christ continued, ". . . when the pyx approached you for the third time, like a white dove, He went out of the pyx, encircled you with a gentle, warming flame and thus, through your soul, made his way towards me. *So pay no less attention to what I saw:* for our Lord Jesus, holding a white cross in His hand, gave testimony on your behalf. Because you had wished with a perfect will to suffer for His truth, you were made His martyr. He promised you that after your death you will pass to the heavenly realm with little or no additional suffering in purgatory."[37]

Her teaching on purgatory, and his fear of punishment, brought the merchant to a new and deeper relationship with Christ, one that was mediated by her knowledge. For she not only had precipitated his visionary experience, but had seen it and participated in it, recognizing in it a promise that he had already undergone the flames of purgatory and had found them to be the flames of love.

Marie's expertise was not limited to spiritual direction and healing. She was also capable of physically healing this unnamed man and those he loved. He fell ill on a business journey and crawled back to her, barely alive. He asked for some of her hair, confident that it would "cure him of his sickness." She pulled out "a bunch of hair" as easily as if it were a leaf, handed it to him, and left. When he rubbed himself with the hair, he was cured, and he immediately returned to saying the Hail Mary with many genuflections, a practice he had abandoned during his illness. Marie visited him again, saying that she had left him alone so he could do his spiritual practice. Although he was certainly grateful for the miracle she had performed on his behalf, what evidently seemed perfectly natural to her was understandably disturbing to him. Thomas observes that "[h]e was frightened not only by the speedy cure of his illness, but also that she could know immediately when it happened and what he had done in the meantime." When he returned home to his wife and child, he saw that his little boy had received a terrible head wound. Confident of another miracle, he told his wife to wash the boy's head. When she did so, she saw the gaping wound and could not continue. The father pushed "all the relics of the already tested hair of the holy woman of God into the open wound."[38] While he prayed, the wound closed, leaving only a narrow scar.

If we put this portrait of Marie in action next to the figure of Jacques de Vitry, we can see that Thomas has created a portrait of a very powerful woman, a prophet, a teacher, and a healer, in a relationship with a very powerful ecclesiastic, a cardinal. Their personal power and authority make them equal—but she has the ability to prophesy and to heal, particular strengths that Jacques has learned to rely on. She was never deceived in her discernment of spirits, says Thomas, a gift any priest would devoutly wish to have. So powerful was she in this area of spiritual knowledge that she (after her death, and through the mediation of Jacques de Vitry) healed the temptation to blasphemy of Bishop Hugolino, a close friend of St. Clare of Assisi.

Hugolino had confessed to Jacques that

> a spirit of blasphemy troubles my soul and submerges it with waves of temptations. Almost every day I am driven to desperation. . . . It does not allow me to be refreshed and rested by food, drink, or sleep. . . . I am as fearful as I can be that I will be unable to carry such a burden and will be completely dislodged from the holy faith.[39]

Jacques tried to comfort him as best he could and, when this was not enough, gave him his *Life of Marie* to read and the relic of her finger to wear (a proven relic, for it had saved his life earlier). The bishop found hope in the biography and rest in the relic, for when he was attacked by temptation again, "he grasped the finger of the handmaid of Christ in his devout hands" and prayed for her help. He was instantly "illumined with the heavenly light of interior grace."[40] Thus Marie and Jacques together saved for the Church the future Pope Gregory IX.

Another bishop was also saved by the intercession of Marie, this time without the aid of Jacques de Vitry. Thomas does not reveal his name in the *Supplement,* but in his *Bonum Universale* he is identified as "Conrad, a former canon of St. Lambert of Liège who became abbot of Villiers and finally a cardinal."[41] He had great veneration for her during her life and returned from Italy to pray at her tomb: "Suddenly he was rapt in spirit and saw the venerable Marie, risen from her place of rest, praying with extended hand and bended knees opposite the holy altar, interceding to the Lord on his behalf. The manner of his exceptional vision gave the bishop great joy."[42]

According to Thomas, Marie's relationship with Jacques was not one of uncritical admiration, either in life or after her death. She rescued Jacques from drowning once, but not without using the opportunity to rebuke him. Shipwreck seemed imminent, and everyone on the ship was invoking a favorite saint; Jacques invoked Marie. He seemed to swoon and saw her speaking to him: "Behold I, your protector, am here because you called me. I really did love you in life and since my life ended, I have been ceaselessly praying for your salvation." She promised him that he would not die then and conducted him in spirit to a church in Oignies, where she showed him five altars, the fifth of which he was supposed to consecrate to the Trinity. She concluded with a prophecy and a comment on his character:

> If you wish, before this altar Christ will give you the peace you have sought. . . . But you are a man with a will of your own, and you have never wanted to accede to my counsels and the counsels of those who loved you spiritually. You have always walked according to your own judgments, rather than the judgments of others."[43]

Jacques promptly asked to be released from the episcopate and returned to Oignies. He told no one of his experience until the church of Oignies was completed and the five altars were in place, just as Marie had shown them to him. When he asked Prior Giles to whom the fifth altar was to be dedicated, Giles told him that during a recent illness, he had made a vow to consecrate it to the Trinity. Evidently Marie did not trust Jacques alone with the task, but when "the bishop heard this in great wonderment, he was filled with inestimable joy. He was frightened and wondrously venerated the outcome of divine revelation manifest in all things."[44]

When Pope Honorius III died, Bishop Hugolino was named pope, and Jacques wanted to go to Rome to see him. The prior and the brothers were afraid (quite rightly, as it turned out) that the pope would keep Jacques with him "by entangling him in some dignity." As she had done before at crucial junctures in his life, Marie appeared to him; he dreamed that he was anointing her as if she were ill:

> [S]he looked at him with a stern face, as though indignant, and said, "Since your book of rites does not contain my kind of anointing, you certainly can't anoint me. But anoint our prior and the brothers since, like me, they are gravely weakened by your departure." . . . However, he was not turned back from his plan, but made all the arrangements to begin his journey.

Jacques was not the only one who turned to Marie for aid over this matter. Prior Giles also turned to Marie in prayer, to ask her to block

Jacques's journey. In a vision, she said to him: "You needn't doubt that I am just as opposed as you are to the bishop's journey. Hence, I will not accompany him as he goes; rather, three women will accompany him. He won't escape their hands. So let him do what he wants; you can't turn him from his purpose now."

Thomas, good storyteller that he is, does not end the episode here. Prior Giles was awakened from this vision by Jacques de Vitry's voice and told de Vitry what Marie had just told him:

> The bishop was not impressed by these words. He laughingly rejoined to the prior, "Lady Marie said the same thing to me. I am not moved by such things. . . . I will return faster than you expect. Don't be upset, dearest brother. Truthfully, love, it would be hard for me, and even harder for him, if I didn't visit and see such a good friend in such circumstances. Besides, I don't believe it; indeed I certainly presume that, contrary to your fears, the pope will not detain me with him if I am unwilling."[45]

Of course, Marie knew him better than he knew himself. He did not return to Liège from Rome, and Thomas used the remainder of the *Supplement* (five pages out of thirty-six) to plead with de Vitry to return to Liège, where he was more needed. He concludes with a statement of his own motivation:

> With what charity I love you, with what sincere love I embrace you, He knows who knows all things. When I was not yet fifteen years old and you were not a bishop, I heard you preaching in Lorraine. I loved you with such veneration that I was happy just at the sound of your name. . . . So, holy father, forgive me, especially since I have only recalled to your mind things you saw revealed long ago. I wish that if . . . my love is able to obtain your return, which is the goal of its desire, I will not be charged a big penalty for my foolishness, even though I have presumed to provoke you, a venerable cardinal . . . with rather rude, if loving, words.[46]

For Thomas to make his plea to Jacques de Vitry, he has brought Marie back from the other world to support his goals. So vivid is his portrayal of her that the reader forgets that Marie had been dead for seventeen years when the *Supplement* was written. Yet with this conclusion, it is clear that the female discourse of Marie has become imbedded as narrative in a male discourse and, in fact, has been exploited to serve the needs of that discourse. What is at stake is Thomas's criticism of his one-time mentor, Jacques, and Marie's comprehension and criticism of that same Jacques is not as important in itself as it is as part of a male ideology of leadership. By its existence as a text, the *Supplement* testifies to the incompleteness of de Vitry's work in Liège; Jacques could not finish the *Life of Marie* any better than he could fulfill his task of spiritual leadership there. Of course, Marie may be having the last laugh on both of them, since she knew that Jacques would not be returning to Liège and probably had the prescience to know that Thomas's criticism of him would not count any more than hers did.

Margery Kempe

The Book of Margery Kempe gives us another point of view on the confessor–penitent relationship.[47] Margery Kempe was the daughter of the five-time mayor of Lynne. She was married at twenty to John Kempe, with whom she had fourteen children, only one of whom seems to have lived to adulthood. In order to tell her story, she invented the first autobiography in English, just as in her life she invented a new religious role, a blend of personal asceticism, public apostolate, and pilgrimage.[48] Her first mystical experience took place when she was twenty, when Christ, quite unexpectedly, appeared to her and healed her of severe postpartum depression.[49] More mystical experiences followed, and, as she spoke to various confessors seeking understanding and support for her visions and her lifestyle, someone suggested that she dictate her life story. She did not do so at the time, but twenty years later, when she was in her sixties, she sought out an amanuensis who could help her.

Three kinds of confessor–penitent dialogues are evident in her book. She solicits one kind of dialogue as she confesses her life and narrates her visions and "felynges" to her spiritual advisers. Ecclesiastics solicit another kind of dialogue when, believing in her gift of prophecy, they want to know about themselves, their own spiritual states, and the fates of others.[50] A third kind of dialogue ensues when she is attacked for her behavior and defends herself to male ecclesiastics. All these kinds of dialogue refer to a fourth and higher type, her dialogues with God and the Virgin Mary.

All these successful verbal constructions are counterpointed by an insistent and inarticulate voice—the sound of Margery's weeping. For accompanying Margery's forays into ever more successful dialogue is an increasingly loud and uncontrollable weeping. For most readers of Margery, and certainly for her contemporaries, this weeping characterized her and made her visible (audible). As Dhira Mahoney reminds us, *"The Book of Margery Kempe* recounts many dramatic incidents when its author's recollections of Christ's Passion result in uncontrollable weeping and loud cries, sometimes accompanied by bodily convulsions. These tears and cries exasperate Margery's contemporaries, to the point that they seek to ban her from attendance at public sermons and even from communion."[51]

Mahoney argues that Margery, in seeking a new kind of religious life for herself, needed "to find physical markers that would perform the same function as enclosure, that would announce her separation from society, her holiness, and her link with God."[52] Like the dialogues with those around her, the tears "are signs of the visionary experiences that she alone is privileged to witness."[53] Until she can write her book, her tears are her voice, "in a world which would deny that voice."[54] In this sense, "Margery's tears are a sign of her power, her link with the Other."[55] In the real world, tears accomplish the same thing that her dialogues do in the world of her book—they prove that she is a participant in the divine world. The intensity of her cries may be related in part to the depth of her need to prove her link with divinity, in the face of public scorn and disbelief.

As a married woman belonging to no religious order but having a strong sense of personal vocation, she was very dependent on her various confessors for validation, both of the truth of her visions and of the appropriateness of her life choices. She begins the book with her bout of insanity when she was twenty, caused, she asserts, by her confessor's maladroit handling of her confession:

> When this creature was twenty years of age, or somewhat more, she was married to a worshipful burgess [of Lynn] and was with child within a short time, as nature would have it. And after she had conceived, she was troubled with severe attacks of sickness until the child was born. And then, what with the labour-pains she had in childbirth and the sickness that had gone before, she despaired of her life, believing she might not live. Then she sent for her confessor, for she had a thing on her conscience which she had never revealed before that time in all her life. . . . And when she came to the point of saying that thing which she had so long concealed, her confessor was a little too hasty and began sharply to reprove her before she had fully said what she meant, and so she would say no more in spite of anything he might do. And soon after, because of the dread she had of damnation on the one hand, and his sharp reproving of her on the other, this creature went out of her mind.[56]

This opening page establishes without a doubt that this is a woman's book, about women's experiences and women's spiritual needs. Margery's need for reassurance from a confessor is probably typical of what most medieval women sought. She refers to herself in the third person as "this creature." This device may be a result of the necessity of dictating her story to a male writer who may very well see her this way. It may be a sign of her modesty and insecurity; it may be intended to suggest symmetry between the voice of "this creature" and the creator who also speaks at length, or it may be a way of identifying her experiences with those of all women, who as women are less mind and more body, more "creature," than their male contemporaries.

One episode among many shows the interconnection of her spiritual dialogues and her earthly ones. In Chapter 12, God tells her that she is pregnant again;[57] she is troubled by worries about caring for the child, and she feels "unworthy" to hear God speak to her when she is still having sex with her husband. God reassures her: "I love you, daughter, as much as any maiden in the world."[58] He encourages his mother to verify this, and she too assures Margery, "Daughter, I am your Mother, your lady and your mistress, to teach you in every way how you shall please God best." The only person to whom she can tell this is her spiritual director:

> [The Virgin] taught this creature and informed her so marvellously that she was embarrassed to tell it to anybody, the matter was so high and holy, except to the anchorite who was her principal confessor, for he was most knowledge-

able in such things. And he charged this creature—by virtue of obedience—to tell him whatever she felt, and so she did.[59]

Her marriage and her sexual experience trouble her, because they seem to contradict what she has heard of holy women.[60] She can not believe that she can be holy and loved by God if she is married: "Because I am no virgin, lack of virginity is now great sorrow to me. I think I wish I had been killed as soon as I was taken from the font, so that I would never have displeased you."[61] God comforts her in her despair and convinces her that her married state is not an impediment:

> I have told you before that you are a singular lover of God, and therefore you shall have a singular love in heaven, a singular reward and a singular honour. And because you are a maiden in your soul, I shall take you by the one hand in heaven, and my mother by the other, and so you shall dance in heaven with other holy maidens and virgins, for I may call you my dearly bought and my own beloved darling.[62]

Unlike Marie and Christina, Margery often has trouble interpreting these feelings: "She sometimes had such great trouble with such feelings when they did not ring true to her understanding, that her confessor feared that she would fall into despair at them."[63]

The chapter on her colloquies with God and her confessor is immediately followed by a chapter devoted to dialogues solicited by those who were to exploit or learn by her gift of prophecy. Foremost among them is the priest who wrote down her book; he refuses to write for her unless she tells him about the future:

> [I]n order to test this creature's feelings, [he] asked her questions many different times about things that were to come—things of which the outcome was unsure and uncertain to anybody at that time—asking her, although she was loath and unwilling to do such things, to pray to God and discover when our Lord would visit her with devotion, what the outcome would be, and then truly, without any pretending, tell him how she felt, or else he would not have gladly written the book.[64]

She gives him the information, but in circumstances that reveal his own lack of insight. A young man came to him, claiming to be a priest who had gotten in trouble in his home parish (he had fatally wounded several persons in the course of defending himself) and asking for his aid. The priest told the young man's story to some well-to-do friends in Lynn, hoping that they would give him money for the young man. Margery overheard the conversation and had an immediate intuition that charity would be wasted on the young man and should better be given to others in Lynn who were more needy. She warned the priest: "Don't you get involved with him, for he will deceive you in the end."[65] But the priest gave in to the young man's importunities and lent him money. The young man never returned to repay it. The priest was almost taken in a second time, this time by an old man who wanted to sell him a breviary, "a good little book," but this time the priest went to Margery and asked her advice. She told him not to trust the seller, and when the priest questioned him about where he got the book, the old man was evasive and went away without making the sale.[66]

Other examples Margery provides indicate that she could be a reassuring confessor herself and relieve the doubts of others. A vicar came to her, "asking her to pray for him and discover whether he would please God more by leaving his cure of souls and his benefice, or by keeping it, because he thought he was of no use among his parishioners."[67] Margery kept his situation in mind when she was praying, and Christ provided useful advice she could pass on to the questioner:

> Tell the vicar to keep his cure and his benefice, and be diligent in preaching and teaching to them in person, and sometimes to procure others to teach them my laws and my commandments, so that there is no fault on his part, and if they don't do any better, his reward shall be none the less for it.[68]

Thus encouraged, the vicar kept his cure, and the advice to enlist the help of others in areas where he may have felt inadequate was no doubt useful.

Another priest, who had protected Margery in Rome, accompanied her back to England but was fearful of being killed by certain enemies. She was able to return his assistance to her by assuring him that he would travel safely "by the grace of God." Both parties gained from this exchange, "[a]nd he was much comforted by her words, for he greatly trusted in her feelings, and along their route he treated her as warmly as if he had been her own son, born of her body."[69]

Margery knew when to use her gift of prophecy and when it would be dangerous to do so, and she was quite able to protect herself. She had narrowly escaped being tried as a Lollard in several towns when she came to Lincoln and was approached by the men of a powerful lord in the region, who "swore a great many oaths, saying, 'We've been given to understand that you can tell us whether we shall be saved or damned.'" She met their challenge by asserting:

> Yes, truly I can, for as long as you swear such horrible oaths, and break God's commandment as knowingly as you do, and will not leave your sin, I dare well say you shall be damned. And if you will be contrite, and shriven of your sin, willingly do penance and leave sin while you may, with a will to turn back to it no more, I dare well say you shall be saved.[70]

Like Marie d'Oignies and Christina of Markyate, Margery was a teacher and a corrector of ecclesiastics, even when she was in great danger herself. She was brought to trial before the archbishop of York on charges of heresy. Although she was so afraid that "her flesh trembled and quaked amazingly, so that she was glad to put her hands under her clothes so that it should not be noticed,"[71] she held her own and gave back as good as she got. When the archbishop asked her why she cried so loudly, she said, "Sir, you shall wish some day that you had wept as sorely as I." He examined her in the articles of faith and found nothing to criticize in her ready responses. Not knowing what to do next, for his clerics were very opposed to her, he said, "I am told very bad things about you. I hear it said that you are a very wicked woman." Not to be deterred by this, she rejoined, "Sir, I also hear it said that you are a wicked man. And if you are as wicked as people say, you will never get to heaven, unless you amend while you are here." By this time, the archbishop wanted only to get her out of his district, so he asked her to swear that she would not "teach people or call them to account in my diocese."[72] Her eloquent refusal is a defense of women's rights to be moral teachers:

> "No, sir, I will not swear," she said, "for I shall speak of God and rebuke those who swear great oaths wherever I go, until such time that the Pope and Holy Church have ordained that nobody shall be so bold as to speak of God, for God Almighty does not forbid, sir, that we should speak of him. And also the Gospel mentions that, when the woman had heard our Lord preach, she came before him and said in a loud voice, 'Blessed be the womb that bore you, and the teats that gave you suck.' Then our Lord replied to her, 'In truth, so are they blessed who hear the word of God and keep it.' And therefore, sir, I think that the Gospel gives me leave to speak of God."[73]

In her defense, she invokes the female body as sanctified by Christ's words and parallels this with a woman's voice blessing the body that bore Christ. This new public discourse enables her to sanctify that female body with which she began her book.

All writers of autobiography discover themselves anew when they write their lives, and certainly this is true for Margery. Perhaps her actual statements in court were not as pithy as they are when she dictates them; she has had thirty years to think about what she said. But she cannot have strayed too far from the record, for in her audience were people who still remembered stories about her. For her, the empowerment that came from visions allowed her the luxury of a dialogue with herself, as she orally composed her own story.

Conclusion

In reviewing these three accounts of confessor–penitent relationships, we have seen that visionary authority indeed provided women with a voice and the content for teaching. The three texts are driven by three different purposes. The *Life of Christina of Markyate*, although it presents a great deal of autobiographical material, focuses on the dialogues between Christina and the men who would supervise her, most importantly on the exchanges between Christina and Geoffrey, *dilectus* and *puella*. The *Supplement to the Life of Marie d'Oignies* completes and corrects the earlier *Life of Marie d'Oignies* by foregrounding dialogues between Marie and her first biographer that were not included in the first biography, exploiting Marie's assumption of authority in her relationship with Jacques de Vitry for the ends of a rival biographer. *The Book of Margery Kempe* uses examples of dialogue, themselves made possible by Margery's divine colloquies, to demonstrate the acquisition of a voice subsequent to the acquisition of visionary authority.

One of the elements common to all three discourses is the audacity of the female voice. This audacity is all the more improbable because of the irregular status of all three women. Each had chosen to live out an isolated and self-defined religious role, a dangerous project for any woman; in these three lives, that unique role was the consequence of a deliberate rejection, on the one hand, of marriage and therefore of the social world and, on the other, of typical convent life in an enclosed community. Those were the choices the medieval world offered women, and those were the choices that these women could not and did not make.[74] By shattering the stereotypes of the good nun and the good wife, these women gave birth to themselves, and furthered that growth, and the growth of the men around them, by engaging in dialogue with them.

Notes

1. Caroline Bynum, *Jesus as Mother: Studies in the Spirituality of the High Middle Ages* (Berkeley: University of California Press, 1982), pp. 183–185.

2. Christopher J. Holdsworth, "Christina of Markyate," in *Medieval Women,* ed. Derek Baker (Oxford: Basil Blackwell, 1978), pp. 185–204.

3. *The Life of Christina of Markyate* [*De S. Theodora Virgine, Quae et dicitur Christina*], ed. and trans. C. H. Talbot (Oxford: Clarendon Press, 1959), p. 6.

4. Talbot notes that "it may be that although he was a monk of St. Albans, he was attached to Markyate in some official capacity, such as chaplain or confessor" (ibid., p. 7).

5. Ibid.

6. The British Museum Manuscript that contains the *Life of Christina* is Cotton Tiberius E.I., vol. 2.

7. *Life of Christina of Markyate,* p. 8.

8. Holdsworth, "Christina of Markyate," pp. 202–203.

9. Ibid., p. 203. Christina could read French, for the *Life of St. Alexis* in her psalter is the French *Chançon d'Alexis.* For a fine analysis of this story, and its appropriateness to Christina, see Brigitte Cazelles, *The Lady as Saint: A Collection of French Hagiographic Romances of the Thirteenth Century* (Philadelphia: University of Pennsylvania Press, 1991), pp. 21–27. In fact, an examination of the *St. Albans Psalter* reveals that Christina read French and Latin as well as Anglo-Saxon.

10. Holdsworth, "Christina of Markyate," p. 204.

11. *Life of Christina of Markyate,* p. 72.

12. Ibid., p. 28.

13. Ibid., p. 9.

14. For the story of this period of Christina's life, see "Of S. Theodora, a Virgin, Who Is Also Called Christina," trans. C. H. Talbot, in *Medieval Women's Visionary Literature,* ed. Elizabeth A. Petroff (New York: Oxford University Press, 1986), pp. 144–150, and Chapter 1.

15. *Life of Christina of Markyate,* p. 135.

16. Ibid.
17. Ibid., p. 137.
18. Ibid., p. 139.
19. Ibid.
20. Ibid.
21. Ibid.
22. Ibid., pp. 139–141.
23. Ibid., pp. 143–145.
24. Ibid., p. 153.
25. Ibid., p. 161.
26. Ibid., p. 163.
27. Ibid., p. 165.
28. Ibid.
29. Ibid., p. 169.
30. Ibid., p. 193.
31. Thomas de Cantimpré, *Supplement to the Life of Marie d'Oignies,* ed. and trans. Hugh Feiss (Toronto: Peregrina Press, 1989), p. vii.
32. Ibid., p. 5.
33. Ibid., p. 6.
34. Ibid.
35. Ibid., p. 5.
36. Ibid., p. 7.
37. Ibid., pp. 8–9.
38. Ibid., p. 11.
39. Ibid., p. 22.
40. Ibid., p. 24.
41. Ibid., p. 49.
42. Ibid., p. 26.
43. Ibid., p. 28.
44. Ibid., p. 29.
45. Ibid., p. 31.
46. Ibid., p. 36.
47. The original Middle English text was published in *The Book of Margery Kempe,* Early English Text Society, o.s., no. 212, ed. Sanford Brown Leech and Hope Emily Allen (London: Oxford University Press, 1940). The translation used in this book is by B. A. Windeatt, *The Book of Margery Kempe* (New York: Penguin, 1985).
48. Elizabeth A. Petroff, "Women Writers of the Late Fourteenth Century—Seeking Models: Julian of Norwich, Margery Kempe, Doña Leonor López de Córdoba, and Christine de Pizan," in *Medieval Women's Visionary Literature,* ed. Petroff, p. 301.
49. Maureen Fries, "Margery Kempe," in *An Introduction to the Medieval Mystics of Europe,* ed. Paul Szarmach (Albany: State University of New York Press, 1984), pp. 217–235. According to Fries, Margery suffered "a painful and lengthy postpartum depression (apparently at its unipolar manic phase) following upon a first childbirth" (p. 219).
50. ". . . God gave her great gifts, especially prophecy: she advised a vicar to keep his cure, knew the condition of dead and live souls and who should live and who die, correctly foretold that two men trusted by the priest who wrote her book were con men (this is obviously a future reference) and predicted a Benedictine

Chapel's failure to receive the right to baptize and purify. No wonder she could see the host 'flicker' like a dove, especially with Christ's assurance that St. Bridget 'saw me never in this wise'" (ibid., p. 221). Fries's essay gives a useful summary of Margery's book.

51. Dhira Mahoney, "Margery Kempe's Tears and the Power over Language" (Paper presented at the twenty-fifth International Congress on Medieval Studies, Western Michigan University, Kalamazoo, May 10, 1990).

52. Ibid., p. 3.

53. Ibid., p. 4.

54. Elizabeth A. Petroff, "The Visionary Tradition in Women's Writings: Dialogue and Autobiography," in *Medieval Women's Visionary Literature,* ed. Petroff, p. 39.

55. Mahoney, "Margery Kempe's Tears," p. 7.

56. *Book of Margery Kempe,* p. 42.

57. Ibid., p. 84.

58. Ibid., p. 85.

59. Ibid., p. 86.

60. For her time, she was very right to be concerned. Fries summarizes the patristic attitude toward women: "Margery was a married woman when her mystic experience began, and this state of life was not only inferior to virginity but also to widowhood (no wonder she had so much trouble with widows); her state of life precluded the claims she made to direct revelation from God" ("Margery Kempe," p. 229). Furthermore, she was not enclosed, and she journeyed constantly—the antithesis of monastic stability.

61. *Book of Margery Kempe,* p. 86.

62. Ibid., p. 88. Janel M. Mueller holds that after the experiences detailed in this section of Margery's book (which includes a lengthy and reassuring interview with Julian of Norwich), Margery "attains a level of confidence that never recedes, despite intermittent doubts and challenges" ("Autobiography of a New 'Creatur,'" in *The Female Autograph: Theory and Practice of Autobiography from the Tenth to the Twentieth Century,* ed. Domna C. Stanton and Jeanine F. Plottel [Chicago: University of Chicago Press, 1987] pp. 57–69). What Mueller focusses on in this period is not so much the dialogues as the tears which Margery experiences. Yet she adds, "One major aspect in which female spirituality, selfhood, and authorship come together is in the formation of blocks or sequences of narrative that address the question of giving credence to Margery, to what she says and does" (p. 59).

63. *Book of Margery Kempe,* p. 90. This is not the only time she mentions her doubts and confusion about her "feelings." Just before her trip to the Holy Land, she had doubts about Christ's revelations to her concerning the damned and the saved; as punishment for this doubt, she was tormented by lecherous thoughts about men's members, particularly those belonging to men of religion. This went on for twelve days, until Margery declared that she believed what Christ had revealed to her (Fries, "Margery Kempe," p. 224).

64. *Book of Margery Kempe,* p. 90.

65. Ibid., p. 92.

66. Ibid., pp. 93–94.

67. Ibid., p. 88.

68. Ibid., p. 89.

69. Ibid., p. 138.

70. Ibid., p. 174.

71. Ibid., p. 162.
72. Ibid., p. 164.
73. Ibid.
74. Christina of Markyate did end up turning her hermit community into a convent, but she did this after she had gained a reputation as a holy woman, and she did it on her own terms. In any case, her *Life* is not interested in her as a nun.

9

The Rhetoric of Transgression in the *Lives* of Italian Women Saints

The narratives of medieval Italian women saints in the *Acta Sanctorum,* the official life stories of holy women revered for their austere virtues and miracle-working powers, are not conventional accounts of a life of virtue and self-sacrifice. Instead, these narratives reveal the lives of strong, independent women, most of them tough-minded and gifted with a sense of humor, whose activities shattered the stereotypes about feminine behavior in the Middle Ages. Yet there is also something profoundly disturbing about these *Lives,* for the experiences of these holy women seem caught, deformed, by the felt contradiction between their own sense of mission and vocation and their internalization of the medieval world's institutionalized misogyny.[1] The style in which these narratives were written mirrors these contradictions, perhaps quite unintentionally. These observations led me to what may seem a startling conclusion.

The women saints of the Middle Ages were transgressors, rule-breakers, flouters of boundaries, and yet they were also saints. Of course, in a way all saints are transgressors, in the sense that a saint lives by excess, lives in a beyond where ordinary measure does not hold; all saints, by their lives, stretch the boundaries of what we have conceived of as human possibility, and their zeal in breaking through conventional limitations can be both attractive and repellent, pointlessly mad and unshakeably sane at the same time. Women saints, it seems to me, were doubly transgressors—first, by their nature as saints and, second, by their nature as women. What I wish to explore in this chapter is the rhetoric of the latter transgression, female transgression. I will examine how language presents and mediates and even denies transgression in these transgressive texts. How does transgression get shaped into nontransgression, into, in fact, a virtuous and compelling act? What rhetoric is used to signal this double register of values, to show us that an event is both transgessive and divinely sanctioned? To pursue these questions, it is helpful to have some background on the literary genre of the saint's life.

The Goals of Hagiography

The medieval Christian writer who set out to compose a saint's life had one primary goal: to convince his audience that the person about whom he was writing really was a saint. To do this, he obeyed the traditional rhetorical injunction to teach, move, and delight. His audience included both learned and unlearned folk, and the hagiographer's rhetoric, the choices he made in marshaling his evidence of sanctity, had to convince the Church hierarchy, from the local bishop up to the Papal Curia, in their deliberations on beatification and canonization.[2] The hagiographer also had to appeal to popular taste in saints' lives if he wanted his *Vita* to circulate.

The narratives of saints' lives, although written "to honour the saints, to exalt their virtues, and to kindle a more living spirit among lethargic or discouraged Christians,"[3] as Donald Attwater puts it, also satisfied medieval people's fascination with the bizarre and the excessive and their lust for adventure, all in a pious setting. Collections of saints' lives were among the most widely disseminated of all manuscript books, and even those lives written with attention to historical accuracy to prove the existence of a long-standing cult and for use as evidence in the process of canonization were quickly copied and read by everyone. They seem to have been especially important to women, for they were the most accessible form of spiritual literature available to laywomen and to monastic women who could not read Latin very well.[4]

There were certain agreed-on "components of Christian saintliness":[5] moral elements, including asceticism, contemplation, and active service; and extraordinary manifestations of power, such as miracles and visions. Each of these components came to have its own section in the saint's life, where the hagiographer provided telling examples of his saint's heroic virtue and extraordinary gifts. Although the hagiographer's guiding purpose was to compose "generalized portraits for ethical instruction and exaltation"[6] (for saints were the paradigms of medieval ethics, and their lives, "the book of manners for an age"[7]), it is important to remember that saints are not typical of the medieval population at large. Kieckhefer's observation is well worth repeating in this context: "[S]aints have traditionally stood apart from the ordinary run of Christians. Their virtues might be imitable, but their special charismatic powers have been seen as marks of a special numinous presence upon the earth."[8] The message is a contradiction: imitate/don't imitate these saints.

Saints are an elite group, the outstanding exemplars of moral goodness, of virtuous modes of behavior that may be adopted by any Christian as part of his or her path to holiness. In this respect, a saint's life should move us to follow the saint's mode of life. But the appeal of a saint's life lies not only in the image of ideal behavior it provides; the power manifested by the saint is equally, if not more, compelling. Medieval Christians believed that the power of saints, their ability to perform miracles, was contingent on God's power. In theological terms, saints do not perform miracles—God performs miracles through saints. A miracle is not an imitable event; it is not posited as a model for behavior, even though the same miracles appear in countless saints' lives. Miracles suspend the natural order of things, a business that must be left up to God.[9] Yet miracles were what made a saint famous; miracles were needed by people, and medieval people gratefully honored those saints whom they felt were on their side, interceding with God for them, answering their prayers, and rescuing them from disaster.[10]

The Gospels provide the primary model for what constitutes a miracle. Most of the miracles narrated in saints' lives repeat events ascribed to Christ and his disciples: prophecy (foretelling the future, reading unexpressed thoughts or states of sin), transforming matter (changing water into wine, multiplying food), healing the sick, escaping from captivity, exorcising demons. All these events transcend the normal laws of reality; all imply divine intervention in ordinary life; all are performed by both male and female saints in the Middle Ages, although there is some evidence that women saints were thought to be particularly adept at prophecy and at transforming matter.[11]

Women, Miracles, and Other Transgressions

In her study of thirteenth-century hagiographic romances Brigitte Cazelles examines "visibility, both as an essential component of the portrayal of female perfection and as the locus of a gender distinction regarding the functional role of greatness."[12] The hagiographic romances in her collection are viewed as a "product of a predominantly male discourse that elaborates an idealized representation of female greatness."[13] In this context, the "visibility" of the female saint is dangerous, for it leads to her "loss of freedom and power." "Becoming visible," Cazelles asserts, is "a sacrificial process in the course of which a heroine is transformed into a mute and passive victim."[14] Virginity is the sine qua non of the female saint, but virginity is associated with hiddenness, being invisible. Visibility, then, is equivalent to the loss of virginity and cannot be a part of female sanctity. The problem is body, specifically the female body:

> Inspired by a deep distrust of the body, a number of Church Fathers posited that, in order to be, purity should neither be seen nor described. In their view, a virgin ceases to be a virgin when she becomes the object of sensual love (Cyprian; third century); when she endures unchaste gazing (John Chrysostom; fourth century); and when she is submitted to the adultery of the eyes

(Novatian; third century). Tertullian goes even further when he declares that "every public exposure of a virgin is [to her] a suffering of rape."[15]

Beauty, then, is a dangerous quality in a saint—dangerous for her personally, since it attracts attention, and dangerous for men, because it may seduce them. Learning is another dangerous quality, for it too can bewitch men, can get them to believe things they had no intention of believing. Both beauty and learning are power, and power is not appropriate for women; for a woman to have power is to deny her gender. In the tales that Cazelles discusses, beauty and learning in women lead inevitably to martyrdom or imprisonment. (In real life, they could lead to an accusation of witchcraft, if not to burning at the stake.)

Caroline Bynum outlines the kind of thinking that led to the exclusion of religious women from leadership roles:

> Although some (for example, Aquinas) argued that women were unfit for priesthood because of their natural state of subjection and some (for example, Bonaventure) disqualified women because of Christ's male sex, woman's increased exclusion from clerical leadership and from certain new types of evangelical religious life (for example, mendicant poverty) was connected to the notion of her inferiority—i.e., her fleshliness and weakness. Even the folk tradition, in its carnival rituals of reversed sex roles and its lewd tales of cuckolded husbands, expressed a clear sense of the female as disorderly and sexually voracious.[16]

But Bynum is convinced that real medieval women—unlike the unreal women portrayed by the male authors of the hagiographic romances—found a new way of dealing with body. Their view of the Incarnation saved them, for if they were body, Christ was body, too.[17] Even the most bizarre of medieval women mystics "were not rebelling against or torturing their flesh out of guilt over its capabilities so much as using the possibilities of its full sensual and affective range to soar ever closer to God."[18] In fact, "religious women . . . saw in their own female bodies not only a symbol of the humanness of both genders but also a symbol of—and a means of approach to—the humanity of God."[19]

These two scholars are speaking of two different classes of texts from the same historical epoch. Cazelles presents us with fictional hagiographies, written by men, that promote an ideology of invisibility for women, yet provide a voyeuristic opportunity to see the punishments women call upon themselves by becoming visible, whereas Bynum shows us autobiographical texts by women that make body visible as an *imitatio Christi,* proving the suffering body to be an instrument of transcendence. The texts I will be speaking of fall into a third category; they are written by men, but they are about historical women who are making themselves visible in their pursuit of sanctity. Consequently, I think we can see at work the attitudes delineated by both Bynum and Cazelles.

As my examples show, a particular class of miracles predominates in female saints' lives—events that, because they violate the apparently natural order of things, are categorized as miraculous: having visions, not needing food, learning to read without being taught, escaping from convents, teaching without being learned. These are events that are dangerous because they draw attention to the woman, who is supposed to be invisible to be virtuous. These activities might be termed women's miracles. They are, in fact, transgressions. But because they are acts performed by holy women and because they are "successful" transgressions, not punished by God, they may be viewed not as transgressions but as miracles.

Miracles are not the only area in which we find examples of apparent transgression in women saints' lives. We saw earlier that there are two categories of experience necessary for a person to be classified as a saint: heroic virtue and exceptional power to transform the world. In practice, the dividing line between these two categories of experience is rather artificial, since the practices of ascetism, strenuous piety, and active charity blend gradually into the manifestation of miracle-working power.[20] The asceticism attributed to many saints is so superhuman that it could be explained only as a miracle, as in the lives of the Desert Fathers, for example.[21] Just as we can distinguish a special class of "women's miracles," we can also discern a special class of female asceticism in women saints' lives. Two examples should suffice to show what I mean: women's experiences in fasting and in the care of the sick.

We know that medieval saints often practiced very strict fasting, and several recent studies have established that women's exercises in fasting were even more strenuous than men's.[22] Perhaps the most famous representative of this tendency is St. Catherine of Siena, who beginning in childhood gradually cut back her food intake to nothing except the host. This was regarded by her detractors as very sinful behavior; in order to be viewed as acceptable, her inability to eat had to be seen as a miraculous event not under her own control.[23] Similar attitudes are also apparent in narratives about women's care of the sick, especially lepers. Monastic groups had long been responsible for the care of the sick, and it is not surprising that women, whether nuns, laywomen like the beguine Marie d'Oignies, or tertiaries in the mendicant orders like St. Catherine, would choose to care for lepers as one of their spiritual practices. But we must remember that this choice put women on the boundary of acceptable activity, since in medieval society lepers were feared and shunned. A nice woman could have nothing to do with lepers, who were thought to be both physically repellent and sexually depraved. When Margery Kempe asked her confessor for permission to kiss lepers as a demonstration of her humility and as part of her ascetic discipline, he reluctantly told her that she might kiss only women lepers.[24] Yet in the saints' lives of the high Middle Ages, it becomes almost a commonplace to read of a woman saint washing a leper's sores and drinking the effluvia.[25] Clearly, what is at stake in fasting and in caring for lepers is something that has nothing to do with self-control or good nursing practices. These are transgressions, violations of the proper order of things, and they are troubling events in saints' lives because they are deeply ambiguous—at once heroic, transgressive, compelling, miraculous.

The Contradictions of Female Sanctity

The women saints of the thirteenth and fourteenth centuries whose stories we possess were almost invariably visionaries and healers; their lives tell us of an individual soul's relationship with the divine and show us how that growth was mediated by visionary experience and expressed in the miraculous activities of the saint. The context for becoming a woman saint in this period was different from what it had been earlier, yet the Church was still dominated by tradition, by a need to be true to its own tradition. Perhaps the most intractable tradition of the institutional Church concerned woman, the *janua diaboli*, "the most dangerous of all obstacles in the way of salvation."[26] Although the cult of the Virgin may have tempered somewhat the horror felt toward the daughters of Eve, the medieval doctrine of the good woman held as paramount the Christian and Marian virtues of patience, submissiveness, chastity, strenuous piety, and self-effacement. The good woman was the invisible woman, the silent woman.

Yet the good woman was not the saint. To become a woman saint, one had to transgress somewhere, if only in order to become visible. At the same time, such transgression had to meet with God's approval in some demonstrable way; otherwise, the holy woman would be labeled a heretic, a witch, or a whore. The profound misogyny of the medieval world made it inevitable that any woman who achieved prominence was open to accusations of transgression, of sinning against conventional female behavior, if not against God's will in gender arrangements. This accounts for an over-determined quality in narratives of transgressions that are not transgressions; apparently, the hagiographer did not feel it was sufficient simply to present to us what the saint did and then affirm this event as a miracle because it obviously violated the usual order of things. God's will, and not the saint's will, had to be apparent in the event from its very genesis.

Since the hagiographer's goal is to convince us of the saintliness of his saint, he (for the narrator of these female saints' lives is usually male) must create a compelling portrait of an ideal woman, that contradiction in terms for the medieval mind—a woman leader. The biographer was often the deceased saint's confessor, someone, that is, who had access to spiritual secrets told to no other living person. A holy woman's confessor may have been gathering information about "his" saint for years while she was still alive, and after her death he added to this store of anecdotal material by collecting and recording oral accounts about the woman's life and miracles. Even if the hagiographer had not known the woman saint personally, he was usually given access to earlier accounts written by those who had known her, and when he was composing the *Life* there were still living witnesses to her activities. He could reveal things about her that no one else knew, but he was not free to ignore common knowledge about her; he could not, that is, make up his story out of whole cloth, even if he wanted to.

As a general rule, we can say that women saints' heroism and exceptionality was demonstrated by their leadership roles. This (out)spoken leadership, the spiritual direction of others, was inevitably depicted by male biographers (ecclesiastics) as a miracle, a response to divine commands for action. Behind this interpretive stance[27] lies an unexpressed contradiction. Society told women that they were not to become spiritual leaders, but divine voices told the saintly women that they *must* become leaders. And so they did. But there is evidence in most women saints' lives that female leadership was felt to be transgressive and that women themselves had internalized this belief. There is no doubt that the Church was suspicious of or hostile to spiritual direction by women. St. Paul was the chief authority here:

> Let your women keep silence in the churches; for it is not permitted unto them to speak; but they are commanded to be under obedience. . . . And if they will learn anything, let them ask their husbands at home: for it is a shame for a woman to speak in the church.[28]

> I suffer not a woman to teach, nor to usurp authority over the man, but to be in silence. For Adam was first formed, then Eve. And Adam was not deceived, but the woman being deceived was in the transgression. Notwithstanding she shall be saved in childbearing, if they continue in faith and charity and holiness with sobriety.[29]

Gratian's *Decretum,* written about 1140, made this notion law: "Woman's authority is nil; let her in all things be subject to the rule of man. . . . And neither can she teach, nor be a witness, nor give a guarantee, nor sit in judgment."[30]

The Woman Saint as Transgressor

Since my method requires a close reading of fairly lengthy passages, I draw my sample texts from the *Lives* of only three saints—St. Bona of Pisa, St. Umiltà of Faenza, and Blessed Villana of Florence. My texts are all found in the *Acta Sanctorum.*

St. Bona of Pisa

My first example of the rhetoric of transgression comes from the *Life of St. Bona of Pisa.* Bona (1156–1208) was an Augustinian canoness who lived in Pisa. The unnamed author wrote the *Life* fifty years after Bona's death, using material collected during the saint's lifetime by older colleagues. He knew Bona's closest companions intimately, interviewed many of the people who claimed to have been cured by the intercession of St. Bona, and witnessed some of her postmortem miracles himself. He is a good writer who prefers the humble to the ornate style; his dominant device is the anecdote, and the entire text is a chain of anecdotes only rarely interrupted by brief digressions. There are only a few characters, and each is delineated by a judicious—and often funny—use of a telling gesture or phrase. We meet Bona herself and her almost mute companion, Domina Gaitana; two priests, Johannes Presbyter and Marcus Presbyter; an abbot, Donnus Paulus; and a young boy named Jacobus who adores Bona and wants to accompany her everywhere. After a brief prologue, punning on the saint's name, the *Life* begins.

The text itself, "Legenda sanctae Bonae Virginis," is divided into seventy-eight paragraphs. The first ten swiftly tell us of her pious child-hood. This sequence of events is interwoven with another sequential narra-tive, the story of the divine revelations about her made to Johannes Presby-ter, a Tuscan priest from Mugello who was studying in Paris. These two narrative strands are punctuated by a number of vignettes depicting mira-cles that demonstrate Bona's privileged status and are further adorned by parallels drawn between Bona and biblical figures. Bona's life is quite unusual, even among women saints. Her father was a Pisan merchant who left for the Holy Land when she was three and never returned. Her mother was Corsican (at that time, Corsica was a possession of Pisa). The issue of marriage is never mentioned, perhaps because Bona had no dowry. Bona's vocation is already formed by age seven, when she refuses to sleep in the same bed with her mother, although this is the custom; at ten, she requests permission to join the Augustinian sisters of St. Martin and is accepted in spite of her youth. She is too poor to dress like the other sisters, so Johannes Presbyter gives her his *cappa* to make a *clamyde*. One of the miracles that underscores her chosen status occurs when, returning home one day after doing an errand for her mother, Bona bows to the painting of Christ on the outside north wall of the Church of the Holy Sepulchre and crosses herself; in response, the image of Christ bows to her and extends his hand. Another time, the image of Christ blows in her mouth and infuses her speech and gestures with the Holy Spirit. All these childhood miracles take place out of doors, when Bona is going or returning some-where, never in her own home. And in fact, movement and travel charac-terize the first half of her life.

When she is thirteen, her mother is visiting her in the cell where she lives alone, supporting herself by the work of her hands and giving to the poor.[31] Suddenly there is a visitor, Christ disguised as a pilgrim. He an-nounces to Bona's mother that he has news of her husband; he is alive and well and living overseas. Christ wishes to accompany Bona and her com-panion, Domina Gaitana, to her father. Bona's mother, who has no idea who the visitor is but feels confident about what he is asking, permits Bona and Gaitana to leave; Bona, who knows very well that this is Christ, is overjoyed. Once the ship arrives in Jerusalem, however, Bona understands that her father and her three half-brothers (her father has started a new family in the Holy Land and is now ashamed of his Corsican wife) have evil designs on her; she runs away and takes refuge with a hermit, with whom she dwells for nine months. It is at this point that her pilgrimage career begins; she goes first to Jerusalem, but falls into the hands of the Saracens, who imprison her, Gaitana, and their servant girl. All three are ransomed by some generous Pisan merchants, who accompany the little group back to Pisa, where Bona reenters her "beloved house" [domum dilectam].

The second chapter, paragraphs 18 to 25, details the miracles associated with her pilgrimages; the third chapter is devoted to miracles performed in Pisa, when she seems to abandon her career as a pilgrim to found the church of St. Jacob of Podio (in honor of the saint whose shrine she had visited many times in Spain) and to supervise its activity. It is in this section that we find the passage I wish to analyze:

> There was once an angry dispute among the monks of St. Michael of the Garden, over which of them were supposed to assist at the forthcoming feast of St. Jacob of Podio, and as a result no one attended the vigil of the said feast. The blessed Bona, not wanting to scandalize the church by publicizing the monks' discord, but knowing that the church of her St. Jacob was lacking the necessary ministers for this important feast, set out for St. Michael's on the night of the vigil, and stood in the midst of them in their church. And so that the purpose for which she had come might be accomplished, she began by saying to them: "Is there any one of you who wants to go to St. Jacob's?"
>
> They all made excuses for not going, and they would not discuss it further, since the hour was already late, and by now the street was full of people who were going to St. Jacob's. Again St. Bona said to them, "Will you come if nobody sees you?" Her hearers, hoping to see some sort of miracle, mustered enough men to set out on the journey with her. As they went along, they were seen by no one in the crowd of people who were going to the same place. Going thus invisibly, they arrived at a certain broad flat place. So that from one miracle might grow another, and they might be obedient to the saint in all things, St. Bona said to them: "Would you like to see how I go to St. Jacob's when I want to?" They responded that they would very much like to see this. And at once, in the sight of all, she was raised above the ground, and propelled in an arc through the air, as an arrow flies. And when they saw her travelling in this fashion, they all ran to follow her, no longer feeling constrained by the presence of the crowd accompanying them. . . . Thus by the exhibition of a miracle she restored concord among the discordant monks.[32]

St. Bona evidently knows her monks pretty well and realizes that the only way to motivate them is to go to them herself and seduce them into taking appropriate action. Johannes Presbyter chooses to quote her speech in direct discourse, although he uses indirect discourse in reporting the speech of the recalcitrant monks. This is typical of his privileging of her speech; in recorded dialogue, he usually quotes her words directly and paraphrases the speeches of her interlocutors. Yet here, for the first time in the *Vita*, Bona only asks questions; she asserts nothing and demands nothing. Her questions seem innocent enough: Does anyone want to go to St. Jacob's? Will you go if no one sees you? Do you want to see how I go there, when I want to? (There is a pun in this last question: "[*V*]ultis videre quomodo ad S. Jacobum ambulo, quando volo?" "Quando volo" probably means "when I want to," since she has just asked "Vultis vedere . . ." [Do you want to see . . .], but it might also mean "when I fly.")

This special treatment of Bona's speech suggests that the fact of her speaking is the central issue here, but other transgressions are suggested. She is a woman and a religious; what is she doing going to St. Michael's at night,[33] and how often does she go to St. Jacob's, in this fashion or any other? The biographer allows us to hear a woman merely asking questions of her fellow ecclesiastics, tactfully not telling them what to do, yet motivating them to do what is correct. A double miracle, he calls it: she got the monks to abandon their discord and to get to church on time, and she showed them the miracle of her flight. The biographer is providing evidence of her heroic power to transform the world by showing us how she functioned as a moral teacher of male colleagues, but since her role as moral teacher is a potentially disturbing one, he has to employ a rhetoric that will prevent his readers from focusing on her as a woman who dares to correct the transgressions of male ecclesiastics. In short, he must show her as preventing transgression without transgressing herself. Her intervention, by means of pointed questions, foresees the monks' intention to neglect their duties to God and the Church; she succeeds in preventing this potential transgression by demonstrating not personal authority, but divine authority.

St. Bona is quoted in direct discourse several times, and, in all the other instances I have noted, she does not ask questions but responds, rather acerbically, to unspoken questions. Once on pilgrimage, she becomes so ill that Domina Gaitana thinks that she is dying. Since Domina Gaitana can not bring Bona's body back to Pisa by herself, she plans to decapitate the saint and bring her head back with her. Suddenly Bona wakes up and says:

> Praeparate nobis cibum, Domina, ut peregrinationem nostram perficere valeamus: quia caput meum Pisas non portabitis, quemadmodum cogitastis, sed ego ipsa portabo.[34]

> [Prepare some food for us, my Lady, so we'll be able to complete our pilgrimage. For you're not going to carry my head to Pisa, as you've thought, but I'll carry it myself.]

In another instance of direct discourse, Bona reports that God wishes Donnus Paulus to be in charge of the new church of St. Jacob instead of Abbot Simon, whom the monks have proposed. Donnus Paulus grumbles, saying "Domina Bona de me optime cogitavit, quod ad S. Jacobum acetum bibiturus accedam" [Lady Bona has thought very highly of me, that I should approach St. Jacob's ready to drink vinegar]. When Donnus Paulus dutifully reports to St. Bona the following morning, and she tries to kiss his hand out of respect for the order, he does not let her. She reassures him: "Vade, quia non bibes acetum, ut times, sed de bono vino sufficienter habebis. Beatis etenim Jacobus mihi dixit, quod vult esse tuus amicus et frater, imo te pro Domino vult habere" [Go on, for you won't be drinking vinegar, as you fear, but you'll have plenty of good wine. For St. Jacob himself told me, that he wants to be your friend and brother, and indeed wants to keep you for God].

St. Umiltà of Faenza

In the *Life of St. Umiltà of Faenza,* we find similar transgressions and boundary crossings, again identified as miracles. Like the *Life of St. Bona,* this *Life* was written after the saint's death by a certain Biagio the priest, a monk who had access to witnesses' oral accounts and to written material collected during Umiltà's lifetime (1226–1310). We learn that in her secular life, Umiltà had been a stubbornly pious girl named Rosanese. She resisted the idea of marriage and refused several high-ranking suitors chosen for her by her family. After her father's death, however, she could not be supported at home, so she married the man selected by her relatives. After about eight years of marriage, her husband became ill, and his doctors told him that if he wanted to live he must abstain from sex. This reawakened Rosanese's determination to live a religious life, and she began a campaign to get her husband to agree to a mutual vow of chastity. Successful at this, she set about convincing him to join a monastery so that she would be free to become a nun.

As soon as she entered a Benedictine convent, she became "silentii, orationis, solitudinis, . . . abstinentiae atque arduorum aliorum operum ipsis cernentibus iam exemplum" [an example to all who saw her of keeping silence, of prayer, of solitude, of obedience, and of all other difficult works]—in other words, an example of conventional female virtues, especially for religious women. The narrator's use of hyperbaton reinforces the focus on the ascetic activities, not the person; Umiltà is so self-effacing that she is an 'exemplum,' not an individual. As time went on, she was seen to have the ability to work miracles; one of the first was acquiring literacy. One day she was asked by the other sisters to read during the meal.

> I think they commanded her to do this for their own relaxation. She bowed her head and took up the book so that she might obey. Having picked it up, she carried it to the appropriate place, opened it, and began at this verse: "Despise not the works of God, since they are all true and just." What is more, she spoke such lofty words, keeping her eyes always raised to heaven, that she excited the entire convent, who came running to see this spectacle, . . . marvelling in wonderment. And when the sign was given for her to conclude her reading, by saying, "you, however," as was appropriate, taught by the Holy Spirit, she concluded in the best possible way. Inside that volume no one was ever able to find the passages that she had read, neither before nor after. From that time on, the convent took care to teach her letters—which she did learn—by getting a woman teacher for her.[35]

Umiltà is a paragon of obedience; told to read, she reads—but it is a text known only to her, and she reads it on high: "keeping her eyes always raised to heaven." The evidence, but not the rhetoric, suggests that she is in fact preaching, that the convent had gotten the message that she should be taught to read, but the text states that the Holy Spirit has already taught her to read. The biographer focuses on her gestures of humility and obedience: she bows her head, she takes up the book obediently, she reads with her eyes raised to heaven. We are given not her own words, but only her gestural language and her apposite use of biblical quotations. The miraculousness of the event is fixed in our minds by the gestures of the other sisters: they are excited; they come running; they express wonderment. The scene is silent, except for the implied voice of God—as recorded by her biographer. Again, a rather daring act of publicly enunciating a noncanonical text, an unfindable text, is overwritten by a rhetoric that presents only gestures of humility and wonderment.

But this is only the beginning of the narration of miracles associated with the saint, the miracles that will demonstrate her to be a woman with exceptional heroic power to transform the world. Umiltà began to wish for a more solitary life. She had visions. One day she heard a voice tell her that she would leave the monastery the next Saturday. She dutifully confessed this in chapter, but, we are told, no one, not even the saint, thought the words meant anything:

> After considering the height of the walls and her extern brother outside guarding the door, she decided that what she had heard spoken was fantasy; assuming the thing was impossible, she ignored the words. But when the aforesaid night arrived, a voice spoke: "Sister Umiltà," it said, "arise and follow me." As she was about to obey, she went first to the bed of a certain sister who had been very poor, and hastily snatched up her worn out old tunic, leaving her the better one which she had been wearing. Holding her Psalter in her hand, protecting herself with the sign of the cross, she instantly found herself placed on the top of the convent wall. Now while she was there and thinking anxiously about how to get down, as before, something unseen picked her up again, so that she left behind the Psalter. Since the gates were closed, the unseen being unlocked them with the brother's keys while she was standing there. Then it brought her smoothly outside, depositing her unharmed at a distance from the entire convent.[36]

The Poor Clares were surprised and a bit dubious; they wanted to know how she, a beautiful woman, managed her journey at night without being attacked and, indeed, how she succeeded in escaping such strict custody. As soon as they heard her story, they sent her to a kinsman of hers who could protect her.

In the passage just quoted, the saint does not speak; she obediently submits to being acted upon: she hears a voice speaking to her, and she is physically moved by an unseen being. The only actions she takes are spiritually correct ones: she leaves her good tunic behind for a poor sister, and she prepares to obey by crossing herself and taking up her psalter. My translation cannot show how truly invisible this being is who performs these actions. He is merely a "vox quaedam" [certain voice]; the passive voice is used to place Umiltà atop the wall, and then the active voice is again used for an unnamed subject who acts invisibly: "quidam eam invisibiliter, ut prius, arripuit et . . . firmatis portis, clavibus Fratrum, illas . . . aperuit . . . incolumem ipsam suaviter collocavit." The use of hyperbaton and asyndeton intensifies the strangeness of these proceedings, since neither the word order nor the use of conjunctions is what we would expect.

St. Umiltà seems to have been guided to an unusual extent by divine figures; she also broke more rules than usual. In her sermons, in themselves an unusual activity, even for an abbess, we see a woman who feels herself surrounded at all times by divine beings, angels and saints and invisible forces, protected and advised by them. The narrator goes to great lengths to validate the authority by which Umiltà asserts her teaching role, for this was the activity most frowned upon for women. Her transgression is a triple one: she learned to read as an adult, and she both wrote and delivered sermons in Latin, a male language, and on doctrine, a male territory. Her biographer "reads" her transgression as a miracle:

> It was a thing marvelous in all respects, to see the blessed Umiltà, who had never learned letters, not only reading at table . . . but even discoursing and speaking in the Latin language, as if she had studied much in it, dictating sermons and lovely tractates on spiritual things, in which there appeared profound doctrine, very skilled verbal expression, even when speaking of the more sublime mysteries of sacred theology. . . . It is to be considered, first of all, that her words were not so much accomplished by her, as they were dictated from heaven by the Holy Spirit.[37]

And how does the saint herself express her transgression? In one sermon she says: "I am amazed and fearful and I blush concerning these things which I dare to write and dictate, for I have not read them in other books, nor have I applied myself to learning human knowledge; but only the Spirit of God has spoken in me, who fills my mouth with the words that I ought to speak."[38]

Umiltà's rhetoric is very revealing of the double register of values mentioned earlier. She is embarrassed about her own audacity, yet she is also absolutely confident that God's knowledge is speaking through her. The passage uses seven first-person verbs; the polysyndeton of "miror et timeo atque erubesco" is also an example of the accumulatio that governs the entire paragraph. In effect, the content asserts that she is only a vessel for God's word, but the rhetoric reaffirms a speaking "I."

In another sermon, she reiterates:

> [T]he divine words that I speak are not mine, but come from the Father and God most high. . . . He himself teaches me to ask and to answer, and speaks with me while in hiding: I, however, speak to you openly and publicly. . . . I go to the Lord, that he may help me to do this work; and at once Jesus teaches me by the spirit in me. Then and always I am secure in all things, that I do not speak as one ignorant: but I understand whatever I see, and I am fully instructed concerning that which I think.[39]

Blessed Villana dei Botti of Florence

Compared with the style of the two *Lives* we have just looked at, the Latin style of the *Life of the Blessed Villana dei Botti of Florence* is much more elevated. It was written in 1452, almost a century after the saint's (1332–1360) death, by a Florentine Dominican named Johannes Carolus, or-Giovanni Carlo; the project was suggested to him by another Dominican, Hieronymus Johannes, who wrote the preface to the *Life*. Both men seem to have had access to an earlier Italian *Life* and to other written testimonials; the saint was buried in her parish church of Santa Maria Novella, and her tomb had been the object of a cult since her death. The narrative is brief, its two chapters occupying only six pages in the *Acta Sanctorum*. The first chapter quickly runs through her pious childhood, her marriage and conversion, her kindness to the poor, and "incredibilis patientia, revelationes et praedictiones." The second chapter covers her final illness, her blessed death and the miracles that followed it, and her burial in the Dominican church of Santa Maria Novella.

The opening paragraphs give some idea of the ornate style; the biographer is so concerned to place Villana properly in her city and in relation to her father that the figure of the saint as a little girl almost disappears. Punning on the name of the city (Florence/flourishing), friar Giovanni Carlo shows us a supremely wealthy city, accumulating superlatives to emphasize the richness of his city. Here dwelt a rich merchant named Andreas; effectively employing zeugma to link Andreas's activities, the friar presents him as equally avid in seeking to acquire earthly and eternal rewards. The figure of comparatio relates Andreas to Job, for, like Job, Andreas counts as part of his wealth his children, among them a pious daughter named Villana. She scorns this world, thinking only of releasing her mind from the weight of the flesh to dwell in heaven. This use of periphrasis is supplemented by pleonasm in the next sentence: "[S]he first studied how to castigate her most tender body with the harshest macerations" [tenerrimum corpus suum primo acerrima studuit maceratione castigare]. She sleeps on the bare ground with a rock for a pillow until her parents catch her at it; then she secretly sprinkles sand in her bed at night and sweeps it up every morning. It is pretty clear to all that she wants to be a nun, or, as her biographer expresses it, piling up superlatives along with his fondness for periphrasis and pleonasm, "her mind began to aspire totally to the solitude of the most sacred religion" [ad sacratissimae religionis solitudinem coepit mens illius totaliter aspirare]. One night her room is found to be empty (metonymy), and the entire house is searched for the "lost talent"; Villana is finally found outside hiding near the dustbin. Her father immediately marries her to a very noble young man, "although [she?] was in every way reluctant" [quamvis modis omnibus reluctantem].

She discovers that she enjoys the embraces of her husband, becoming a veritable Magdalene, according to her biographer; this gives him the opportunity to employ a string of antitheses, showing how she abandons herself to the joys of expensive dresses and jewels, rejecting the hair shirts and ashes she had preferred as a girl. One day, elaborately dressed and coifed to attend a festivity at church with her husband, she pauses in front of a mirror to admire her image (I give the Latin text first so that the rhetorical influence of the Vulgate Bible will be more apparent):

> [A]enigmatice prospexit, quantum apud Deum interioris animae plenitudo jam fuisset deformata: nempe, cum iterum atque iterum lumina studiosius infigeret, teterrimi spiritus imaginem se gestare, non hominis, in ipsis vestibus manifeste deprehendit.⁴⁰

> ([S]he perceived as in a glass darkly how deformed her interior fullness of soul was in relation to God; and indeed, when she anxiously fixed her eyes again and again, she grasped very clearly, in those very clothes, an image of a most loathsome spirit, not a human being, presenting itself.)

Struck by the truth of this representation of herself (or rather, of her nonself, her nonhumanity), she tears off her fine clothing, rushes to the nearby church of Santa Maria Novella to confess, and embarks on a new life.⁴¹

What law has Villana transgressed here? She has obeyed the wishes of her father in marrying, although she would have preferred to become a nun. But she has disobeyed the divine law; even God's elect may fall, as St. Peter did, the narrator tells us. She has also disobeyed local law, the sumptuary laws of Florence that attempted to restrict ostentatious dress and jewelry in women. What will prove that she repudiates her transgression? She must dress differently if she is to embark on a new life:

> [S]ince she wished to take on a new life, once she had put aside her previous darknesses, she girded herself around her breasts with an iron chain, which stuck to her body so tenaciously, that at her death it could hardly be removed without [tearing] her flesh. She further donned a gnawing hairshirt, and was content with the most vile and rough clothing.⁴²

But because her transgression was not just in the matter of her dress but also in her pastimes, Villana must also acquire new occupations. She therefore devotes the rest of her life to various penances (fastings, vigils, and prayer) and, when she has any spare time, to reading "the books of holy scripture, the collections of the church fathers, the lives of the saints, and in particular the epistles of St. Paul." She is so absorbed in the latter reading, according to witnesses cited by her biographer, that she neither sees nor hears anything going on around her. When her confessor suggests that perhaps she is transgressing the limits of penitential behavior, she claims to find not discomfort but great pleasure in her readings and her meditations.

Because of her visions and the miracles attributed to her, she acquires a saintly reputation, but she has learned the lesson of her mirror very well and, in response to claims made about her prophetic ability, sees herself as "insulsa mulier, et quaedam fatua" [a bungling and foolish woman]. Nevertheless, although fearful of being labelled "fatua" [foolish] or "insaniens" [raving], she publicly prophesies in the square, and the events she predicts come to pass within a few days. This is one of the few places in her biography where she speaks in the first person; yet we hear not the words of her prophecy, but an apologia in which she expresses her reluctance to speak, saying that she would rather be killed with the tyrant's sword as a martyr. And, in fact, she was physically tormented by illness and pain after her speech, "which she bore with so much patience and eagerness that it is incredible to speak of it" (a very conventional use of aporia, but one that has the effect of diminishing Villana's experience rather than exalting it).

Although the biographer's rhetoric groups Villana's reading with other penitential activities, it seems that in fact she was remarkably literate, even in a city where women had a reputation for reading.[43] The depiction of her as a recluse is contradicted by other information provided by her biographer. Distressed at the sedition current in Florence, she tried to run away, but her relatives prevented her, so she devoted herself even more fervently to reading and the consequent visionary trance states in which she did not move for days. She also worked publicly in the square of Santa Maria Novella, distributing food and clothing to the poor, and volunteered in the hospital run by the Pinzochere, or lay Franciscan sisters.

In summary, then, we can see that although Villana's biographer is concerned to use all the rhetoric at his disposal to create the portrait of an ideally obedient, silent, and immobilized woman, he also must tell us of her frustrated attempts to be more autonomous and mobile. In Villana's story, it is particularly clear that in order to not transgress, the saint must do great violence to herself (beyond the self-inflicted violence that was expected as a part of the penitential path). For example, when she did overcome her scruples about prophesying publicly, she was afflicted with a lengthy illness.

Conclusion

What, then, can we conclude about the "rhetoric of transgression" in female saints' lives? What I hope I have demonstrated is that although there appear to be two different kinds of transgressions for female saints—transgressions of excess in ascetic practices such as any holy figure, male or female, might commit, and transgressions against a specific code of behavior for women—in actuality there is only one real transgression for a woman: to go public, to be a visible, speaking, informed moral leader. In that context, the two most dangerous activities for a woman are literacy and public teaching—to possess the word and to move in public space. Yet because of the requirements for sainthood, in particular the need to demonstrate exceptional heroic power to transform the world, women saints had to be literate, and they had to have a public voice. Since these were disturbing traits in "good" women, biographers found themselves using a rhetoric that denied transgression at the same time that it depicted women saints in fact transgressing the limits on proper female behavior. St. Bona merely asks questions of her male colleagues, but the necessity of her intervention implies a critique of male action, and the intervention itself is carried out by her demonstration of miraculous flight, which rhetorically cancels the fact that she has stepped beyond the boundary of her convent walls. Umiltà preaches to her sisters, and this is "read" as the miraculous acquisition of literacy; she escapes her convent walls, but she does so by obeying an invisible being who not only lifts her over the walls, but enables her to cross over water with dry feet. Villana is not as fortunate; no divine aid helps her to run away, and she cannot do so unaided. She does speak publicly, prophesying future events, but she not only apologizes for this, but immediately becomes ill and suffers in silence. As a general rule, prophecy such as this would have been thought to be a miracle, but Villana's guilt over her action implies not a miracle but a transgression for which she must seek forgiveness by suffering.

It is no wonder that these texts are disturbing. The authors have created a rhetoric that masks but does not deny transgression. The female protagonists are not the subjects of their own lives, for they are captured by the rhetoric that inscribes them in a patriarchal mentality. They are not subjects because they are never responsible; even at their most active, they are portrayed as the bearers of another's message, the means by which God works miracles. They are not even allowed their transgressions, for that would make them truly public figures, and the notion of female sanctity excludes going public. Nevertheless, they did exist, and that fact allows us to read through the rhetoric and catch glimpses of real heroism.

Notes

1. For an introduction to these saints' lives, see Elizabeth A. Petroff, *Consolation of the Blessed: Women Saints in Medieval Tuscany* (Millerton, N.Y.: Alta Gaia, 1979).

2. By the twelfth century, when canonization procedures came under papal control, it was customary to submit a saint's *Vita* as part of the evidence presented in a cause or process of canonization (the official declaration by the Church that a certain person is in heaven) (Richard Kieckhefer, "Imitators of Christ: Sainthood in the Christian Tradition," in *Sainthood: Its Manifestations in World Religions,* ed. Richard Kieckhefer and George D. Bond [Berkeley: University of California Press, 1988], p. 3). On the development of canonization proceedings, see Damian Joseph Blaher, *Ordinary Processes in the Causes of Beatification and Canonization,* Catholic University of America Canon Law Studies No. 268 (Washington, D.C.: Catholic University of America, 1949).

3. Donald Attwater, *The Penguin Dictionary of Saints* (Baltimore: Penguin, 1965), p. 13.

4. Evidence in the texts of saints' lives bears this out. In the *Vita B. Benevenutae,* chap. I, par. 8, in *Acta Sanctorum,* October 29, we see how Benevenuta's entire household gathered in the evenings to hear saints' lives read aloud; Blessed

Umiliana de' Cerchi prescribed saints' lives as healing readings for women who were troubled spiritually (*Vita Major Sanctae Humilianae,* in *Acta Sanctorum,* May 19). For the latter, see "Leggenda della Beata Umiliana de' Cerchi," in *Scrittori di religione del trecento volgarizzamenti,* ed. Giuseppe de Luca (Turin: Einaudi, 1977), vol. 3, pp. 365–410. For more details, see Michael Goodich, *Vita Perfecta: The Ideal of Sainthood in the Thirteenth Century* (Stuttgart: Anton Hiersman, 1982), p. 178.

5. Kieckhefer, "Imitators of Christ," p. 22.

6. C. W. Jones, *Saints' Lives and Chronicles in Early England* (Ithaca, N.Y.: Cornell University Press), p. 75.

7. Ibid.

8. Kieckhefer, "Imitators of Christ," p. 39.

9. On miracles in general, see Howard Clark Kee, *Miracle in the Early Christian World* (New Haven, Conn.: Yale University Press, 1983); Peter Brown, "The Rise and Function of the Holy Man in Late Antiquity," *Journal of Roman Studies* 61 (1971): 80–101, and "Society and the Supernatural: A Medieval Change," *Daedalus* 104 (1975): 133–151; and Ronald C. Finucane, *Miracles and Pilgrims: Popular Beliefs in Medieval England* (Totowa, N.J.: Rowman and Littlefield, 1977).

10. I discuss the image of medieval life provided by the notarized lists of miracles usually appended to a saint's *Vita* in "The Paradox of Sanctity: Lives of Italian Women Saints, 1200–1400," *Occasional Papers of the International Society for the Comparative Study of Civilization* 1 (1977): 20–21. As the hagiographer selected his examples, he would tend to choose the most dramatic and hopeless stories, in order to increase the glory owed to God and the saint. Reading the accounts of miracles, one comes to believe that it was the most difficult and pathetic cases (and those who were too poor to afford any help but the supernatural) who came to the saint. Probably without intending to, the hagiographer presented a desperate and disordered world in which only the saint was effective in healing and consoling people, in redressing wrongs, and in renewing an ordered world.

11. For a breakdown of what saints performed what miracles when, see Donald Weinstein and Rudolph Bell, *Saints and Society: The Two Worlds of Western Christendom, 1000–1700* (Chicago: University of Chicago Press, 1982); on women saints in particular, see Goodich, *Vita Perfecta,* esp. chap. 9.

12. Brigitte Cazelles, *The Lady as Saint: A Collection of French Hagiographic Romances of the Thirteenth Century* (Philadelphia: University of Pennsylvania Press, 1991), p. 43.

13. Ibid.

14. Ibid., p. 44.

15. Ibid., p. 49.

16. Caroline Walker Bynum, *Holy Feast and Holy Fast: The Religious Significance of Food to Medieval Women* (Berkeley: University of California Press, 1987), p. 217.

17. I have discussed this in "The Visionary Tradition in Women's Writings: Dialogue and Autobiography," in *Medieval Women's Visionary Literature,* ed. Elizabeth A. Petroff (New York: Oxford University Press, 1986), pp. 12–18. On the cross, Christ suffers as women suffer; if his body is transcendent, so are our bodies.

18. Bynum, *Holy Feast and Holy Fast,* p. 295.

19. Ibid., p. 196.

20. I trace the development from ascetic practices to visionary experience to miracle-working power in "Visionary Tradition in Women's Writings," pp. 5–20.

21. For recent studies on the Desert Fathers, see the works written and translated by Sister Benedicta Ward, especially *The Sayings of the Desert Fathers* (London, 1983). My favorite translation remains Helen Waddell, *The Desert Fathers* (1957; Ann Arbor: University of Michigan Press, 1971). Several *Lives* of the Desert Fathers were translated into Italian in the thirteenth century and became widely used as devotional reading, thus reinfusing ascetic practices with new vitality. For the texts, see *Scrittori di religione,* ed. de Luca, vol. 1.

22. Several recent studies explore this phenomenon: Rudolph Bell, *Holy Anorexia* (Chicago: University of Chicago Press, 1985), and Bynum, *Holy Feast* and *Holy Fast,* look at the phenomenon of women saints' inedia from two very different viewpoints. Bell and Weinstein, in *Saints and Society,* verify that fasting was particularly severe among women saints. Richard Kieckhefer, *Unquiet Souls: Fourteenth-Century Saints and Their Religious Milieu* (Chicago: University of Chicago Press, 1984), discusses the role of fasting in his fourteenth-century exemplars. Sister Benedicta Ward, in *Harlots of the Desert: A Study of Repentance in Early Monastic Sources* (Kalamazoo, Mich.: Cistercian Publications, 1987), discusses fasting in light of the role of repentance in the lives of the Desert Mothers.

23. There is a letter by St. Catherine in which she defends her inability to eat as God's will: "As to your special fear, father, concerning my behaviour about eating, I am not surprised; for I assure you, that not only do you fear, but I myself tremble, for fear of devilish wiles. . . . You sent me word to pray God particularly that I might eat. I tell you, my father . . . that in all ways within my power I have always forced myself once or twice a day to take food. And I have prayed constantly . . . that in this matter of eating He will give me grace to live like other people, if it is His will—for it is mine" (*Saint Catherine of Siena as Seen in Her Letters,* trans. Vida L. Scudder [London: Dent, 1927], pp. 77–78). See also *The Letters of Catherine of Siena,* ed. and trans. Suzanne Noffke (Binghamton, N.Y.: CEMERS, 1988).

24. *The Book of Margery Kempe,* Early English Text Society, o.s., no. 212, ed. Sandford Brown Meech and Hope Emily Allen (London: Oxford University Press, 1940), p. 177.

25. Lepers were feared because of their physical repulsiveness and because leprosy was thought to be highly contagious; women's intimate contact with lepers was even more shocking, outside the proper scheme of things, because leprosy was thought of as a sexually transmitted disease. In his aptly titled study, *The Disease of the Soul: Leprosy in Medieval Literature* (Ithaca, N.Y.: Cornell University Press, 1974), Saul Brody begins by saying: "Since ancient times, leprosy has been considered an inclean diesase, and its victims have long been linked with moral impurity" (p. 51). He also notes that "the medieval link between leprosy and lechery still persists. There is no medical evidence to show that lepers are extraordinarily lustful, but a venerable tradition insists that they are." He quotes a twentieth-century medical opinion: "Leprosy in its early stages stirs the venereal appetite in a marked fashion. A strange, unbridled desire for pleasure flows in the veins of an incipient leper. . . . [T]he most phlegmatic temperaments become curiously sensitive and subject to the appeal of sex when the disease sets in" (p. 12).

26. Eileen Power, "The Position of Women," in *The Legacy of the Middle Ages,* ed. C. G. Crump and E. F. Jacob (Oxford: Oxford University Press, 1938), p. 403.

27. I am calling this invocation of miracle status an "interpretative stance," and this is clearly what it would be in a twentieth-century writer; the situation is more problematical in the case of a medieval writer. Was it in fact possible for a

medieval hagiographer to see a woman's public teaching role as anything but a miracle? Could he view a woman's active vocation and care for souls in the same way that he would view, for instance, a priestly vocation in a man? And if he were personally capable of making such a distinction, could he express it verbally, without recourse to the rhetoric of miracles? The language of saints' lives suggests that he could not.

28. 1 Corinthians 14:34–35.

29. 1 Timothy 2:12–15.

30. Quoted in Julia O'Faolain and Lauro Martines, eds., *Not in God's Image: Women from the Greeks to the Victorians* (New York: Harper & Row, 1973), p. 130.

31. These details of her life are strikingly parallel to the lives of beguines in northern Europe in the same time period.

32. "Facta est aliquando contentiosa disputatio inter Monachos S. Michaelis de Orticaria, qui eorum deberent ad imminens festum S. Jacobi de Podio destinari, ita quod usque ad dicti festi Vigiliam nullus ibat. Nolens autem B. Bona eorum discordiam in scandalum populi publicari, et ecclesiam Sancti sui Jacobi, in ejus festo praecipue, ministres necessario non habere; ad S. Michaelem in ipsa Vigilia festivitatis accessit, et in ecclesia in medio eorum stetit. Et ut illud, cuius causa venerat, adimpleret, dixit ad eos: Est aliquis vestrum, qui ad S. Jacobum velit ire? Quibus se excusantibus de eundo, ne de ipsis homines loquerentur, quia hora erat jam tarda, et quia strata multitudine illuc euntium erat plena; dixit eis iterum S. Bona: Et si a nullo videremini veniretis? Quo audito sperantes aliquod videre miraculum, illico sufficientes cum ipsa aggressi sunt iter. Et pergentes, per totam viam, a nullo ex tanta pariter euntium multitudine videbantur. Cum autem sic invisibiliter ambulantes, ad quadam largam planiciem pervenissent; ut miraculum miraculo cresceret, et Sanctae in omnibus obedirent, dicit eis illa: Vultis videre quomodo ad S. Jacobum ambulo, quando volo. Qui responderunt hoc se plurimum affectare. Et statim videntibus illis elevata est a terra, et perjactum arcus in aere, quasi sagitta transivit. Cumque ipsam cernerent sic euntem, currendo insequebantur eamdem, nullum impedimentum ab euntium multitudine sentientes. . . . Sic ista discordes Monachos per exhibitionem miraculi ad concordiam revocavit" (*Vita de S. Bona Virgine Pisana per supparis aevi scriptorem, ab ore testium oculatorum accepta,* chap. III, par. 32, in *Acta Sanctorum,* May 29). [My translation]

33. Actually the Latin text does not specify time: "ad S. Michaelem *in ipsa Vigilia* festivitis accessit," says her biographer. "Vigilia" could mean any time during the day before the feast, but the context suggests that evening must be intended, since Bona has been waiting to see if the monks would make their appearance and they have failed to do so. The ambiguity as to time is no doubt intentional.

34. *Vita de S. Bona Virgine,* chap. III, par. 32, in *Acta Sanctorum,* May 29.

35. "[S]olatiose ut aestimo injunxerunt [eam]. Illa vero caput flexit, et ut obediret librum sumpsit: quem ad locum aptum accedens aperuit, ea voce incipiens, Nolite despicere opera Dei, quia omnia vera justa sunt: super quo tam ardua, in coelum erectis semper luminibus, dixit quod totum Conventum currentem ad spectaculum . . . admirationem mirabilem excitavit: et dum sibi signum terminationis factum fuit, dicendo, Tu autem, uti decuit, Spiritu sancto edocta optime terminavit. Quae autem legit, nullus umquam in praefato codice prius vel post penitus adinvenit: et ex tunc Conventus, data sibi doctrice, ipsam litteras, quas et didicit, discere procuravit" (*Vita de Sanctae Humilitate Abbatissa,* chap. I, par. 6, in *Acta Sanctorum,* May 22).

36. "Qui considerans murorum altitudinem, portae ac Fratrum ejus extero-

rumque custodiam, phantastice fore quasi dictum existimans, ipsius verbis velut impossibilis non attendit. Superveniente vero nocte praedicta, vox quaedam insonuit: Soror Humilitas, surge: meque sequere, dixit. Paritura, ad lectum cujusdam Sororis valde pauperis prius accessit, tunicam suam consemptam pene totam subripuit, meliorem quam habebat eidem reliquit; et manu Psalterium tenens, signo Crucis se muniens, super muram in instanti posita ipsa fuit. Dum vero sic esset, et de descensu anxie cogitaret; quidam eam invisibiliter, ut prius, arripuit, et super muro libro praedicto dimisso, firmatis portis, clavibus Fratrum, illas ea praesente aperuit; forisque extra totum locum incolumem ipsam suaviter collocavit" (ibid., chap. i, par. 8).

37. "Fuit res omnino admirabilis, videre B. Humilitatem, quae numquam litteras didicerat, non solum legentem super mensa, uti dicitur in Vita; sed etiam discurrentem loquentemque Latina lingua, quasi multum in ea studii posuisset; dictando sermones et tractatus pulcherrimos de rebus spiritualibus, in quibus apparet profunda doctrina, aptissimis expressa verbis, etiam circa sublimiora sacrae Theologiae mysteria. . . . Ponderandum autem his imprimis est, quod verba ejus, non tam ab ipsa profecta fuerunt, quam coelitus a Spiritu sancto dictata" (*Analecta*, chap. i, par. 1, in *Acta Sanctorum*, May 22).

38. "Miror et timeo atque erubesco de iis rebus, quas audeo scribere et dictare: quia eas non legi in aliis libris, neque humanae scientiae addiscendae unquam me applicavi; sed solus Dei spiritus in me loquitur, qui implet os meum iis verbis quae debeo dicere" (ibid.).

39. "[V]erba divina quae loquor, non esse mea, sed venire a Patre et altissimo Deo, qui dat unicuique sicut magis ei placet. Ipse me docet interrogare et respondere, et mecum interim loquitur in abscondito: ego autem vobis exterius in publico loquor. Ipse me docet in silentio spiritus, et eo clara voce pronuntio vobis divina illa verba quae audio. Cavete igitur ne in vacuum recipiatis, quae mea lingua effert, mota a Spiritu sancto. . . . Ego vado ad Dominum, ut me jubeat hoc opus facere; et statim spiritus mei Jesu docet me. Ex tunc et semper de re omni secura sum, quod not loquor velut ignorans: sed intelligo quidquid video, plenaque instructa sum de eo quod cogito" (ibid.).

40. *Vita de B. Villanae Bottiae,* par. 5, in *Acta Sanctorum,* August 26.

41. Villana goes to her parish church to confess; the date must be 1349 or shortly thereafter. Santa Maria Novella is the church in which the storytellers of Boccaccio's *Decameron* meet and plan to flee Florence and the Black Death raging there in the spring of 1348.

42. "[S]icque novam omnino volens inchoare vitam, prioribus tenebris depulsis, ferrea pridem zona ad mamillas super nuda se praecinxit, quae tanta illius corpusculo tenacitate adhaesit, ut emortuo tandem vix sine carnibus posset avelli. Dein mordenti cilicio, et vestibus asperrimis atque vilibus contenta" (*Vita de B. Villanae Bottiae,* par. 6, in *Acta Sanctorum,* August 26).

43. Most of the texts she is said to have read were available at this time in Italian translations, except for the Pauline epistles, and these, I would venture, she read in Latin. It strikes me as rather unusual for a woman who was never admitted to a religious order to have had access to canonical biblical texts at this time.

10

Gender, Knowledge, and Power in Hadewijch's *Strophische Gedichten*

Hadewijch's *Strophische Gedichten*[1] is a collection of poems on the theme of *Minne,* or Lady Love. In these sophisticated and confident lyrics, the great Dutch mystic and poet re-creates some of the themes, images, and metrical forms of the Provençal love lyric to explore the experience of *Minne.* She is a very great poet:

> [T]he gift for poetry she displays in the *Poems in Stanzas* can only be termed lyrical genius. . . . Her poems themselves are proof that she had mastered the troubadours' art. It has been said that just as Bernard of Clairvaux used the Song of Songs to express his own intimate and personal experience of God, Hadewijch used the poetry of courtly love to express the emotional tensions of the longing for God, showing an unfailing mastery of all its techniques: stanza structure, the tornada, meter, rhyme, assonance, concatenation, and figures of speech.[2]

Hadewijch wrote in Dutch and is thought to have lived in Antwerp, where she participated in a rich culture based on both Romance and Germanic roots.[3] She had read widely in Latin, Old French, and Provençal, as well as Dutch, and she was obviously sensitive to poetic technique in all those literatures, since her own technique now suggests the forms of the Latin sequence, now the *chansons de geste,* and again, the Provençal lyric. She was a beguine, a member of a new spiritual movement for women, and this quite possibly allowed her to reach her full potential both as a writer and as a spiritual leader. She wrote for other beguines, often as their spiritual director. The beguines strove to live in the world without being of it, and Hadewijch's poetry demonstrates the same intention. She was a mystic, writing to illuminate her own experience of the deepest reality in order to share it with others. To this love in which she sought the fullest fruition, she gave the name of *Minne.*

The *Strophische Gedichten* form only one part of her collected works; she also wrote *Mengeldichten (Poems in Couplets),*[4] a collection of prose letters ("Letters to a Young Beguine"),[5] and *Visions.*[6] Each of these collections exhibits its own particular way of viewing the experience of love. Although courtly elements may be seen in all her works, it is in the *Strophische Gedichten* that she especially highlights the rhetoric of the courtly tradition as a framework for exploring and presenting her experience.

> Hadewijch wrote with the mentality of a knight. The qualities which she praised and aspired to—courage, loyalty, honour, and also cheerfulness, generosity, self-control—fit into the pattern of the courtly chivalric atmosphere. Although they were transplanted by her into a mystic-religious context, they are still recognizable as the old worldly ideals. The descriptions of the effect *minne* has on her are often couched in remarkably sensual terms.[7]

Like that in troubadour poetry, Hadewijch's rhetoric valorizes desire, her *orewoet* (literally, "stormy longing," but often translated as "madness") for *Minne.* (According to Jozef van Mierlo, the Dutch *orewoet* translates into the Latin *aestus, insania amoris,* or *furor amoris.*)[8] Like troubadour lyric, her poems depict a lover's role in relation to a distant and powerful beloved; in this depiction, her use of the first person creates a poetic self with a sublimely personal voice, often heard uttering complaints about the lack of attention from the beloved and claiming a right to better treatment. This personal voice also embodies meditations on the nature of love and on the inevitability and the meaningfulness of suffering and longing in the total experience of love. In these poems we nowhere find the poet taking refuge in the modesty topos or apologizing for being a woman and daring to write.[9]

Her affinities with Provençal lyric, with the *stil novisti,* and even with Dante, are not only formal ones:

> Hadewijch ranks with the earlier Dante and the other poets of the dolce stil nuovo as one of the great masters who, towards the close of the era of courtly chivalry, transformed the troubadour lyric with its rigidly circumscribed conventions into a form capable of expressing the highest aspirations of the human soul. Already in the finest songs of Jaufre Rudel and Bernart de Ventadorn one feels the breath of a passion too great for its terrestrial object. . . . Hadewijch freed her soul and immeasurably widened the scope of her song by directing an inborn genius for love trained and ennobled by the troubadours towards the Love which was embodied in Christ and is the sovereign power which controls God himself and hence all creation. . . . [Her works] convey with amazing clarity the image of a powerful, dominant personality, in fact of a woman of regal stature.[10]

It is in her representation of the lived experience of *Minne* that Hade-wijch explodes the boundaries of the troubadour tradition. *Minne,* for Hadewijch, is a Being, Lady Love, not the personification of an abstract idea and not the forbidden wife of the vassal's lord. At the same time, *Minne* is love, the total experience of love. As such, she is all-powerful and all-knowing. She is not God; she may contain God.[11] She is A-mor, "deliv-ered from death" (Hare[n] name amor es: vander doot [2.5.4]). *Minne* stands in the position of the Beloved, the *midons* or *dompna,* of the Proven-çal tradition, as the object of the poet's desire, and only she can satisfy that desire. Like the troubadour's lady, she may at times seem capricious, arbi-trary, fickle, but for Hadewijch her capriciousness is merely the way she appears when seen from the limited human point of view. Capriciousness is not in her character; although the lover may perceive her as capricious, this is his failure of fidelity, not hers. She is free, and she grants her lovers freedom if they will surrender to her. In addressing her and speaking about her, the lover-poet finds his or her own voice and nature and points the reader in the direction of that same nature.

At the same time, Hadewijch is a mystic who believes that "the soul, created by God after his own image, strives to be reunited with God, through ascetic concentration and complete surrender to divine love."[12] As a mystic, writing to illuminate her own experience of the divine and draw from it lessons for others, she was breaking new ground, just as she was breaking new ground as a Dutch poet in her use of the courtly tradition and the poetic forms of the troubadours. All mystics are seeking union with the divine; for Hadewijch particularly the divine was love, both as process and as goal:

> This love . . . and the desire with which it is sought, take up a central posi-tion in her work. *Minne* escapes sharp definition: sometimes it seems to mean love of God, in other cases God himself, or the Holy Ghost, or even the soul. The fact that *minne* has so many connotations is not a symptom of unclear thinking, but evidence that to Hadewijch these connotations were all aspects of the same thing: the relation between God and man.[13]

Mother Columba Hart observes of Hadewijch that "[h]er descriptions of experiencing the in-being in God belong to the most convincing and daring that mystical literature has to offer. God is such that he allows himself to be possessed in an incredibly intimate manner."[14] But Hade-wijch's *Minne* (for it is *Minne* that Hart refers to as God or as the Beloved) is completely Other, and in relation with this unfathomable Other, the mystic becomes more and more deeply her own being. Both partners in this relationship mirror each other, and both are infinite:

> When the soul preserves its excellence, it is an abyss in which God is sufficient to Himself, in which always he tastes the joy which He has in himself and which the soul has in Him. "Soul" is the road on which God travels from His depths into His freedom, and God is the road that the soul travels into its freedom, that is, into its depths, which cannot be attained except by sinking

down deep. And so long as God does not belong in His totality to the soul, He cannot be enough to it.[15]

The abyss of the soul is not a non-knowing, although a deliberate un-knowing will help one to reach these depths. Intelligence is discovered in this depth, for "in the union with the Beloved, his incomparable being-Other must now be known. Reason therefore is going to play a part in the highest mystical experience. . . . Through its intervention the mystic learns to love him in his independence and wholly being-Other."[16]

It is desire that exposes the abyss of the soul, revealing to her the abyss of the Other, the Beloved. In the *Strophische Gedichten* the desire for Love [orewoet van minnen] is rhetorically constituted by paradox, for *Minne* is beyond all systems of binary opposition and contains all opposites. The language of paradox forces the poet to abandon ordinary truth, to move mentally into a new space where real truth dwells. In Poem 28, Hadewijch provides a number of metaphors to display the paradox inherent in this passion for Minne:

> Orewoet van minnen
> Dats een rike leen . . .
>
> . . .
>
> Die tiersten waren twee
> Die doetse wesen een.
> Dies ic die waerheit toghe:
> Si maect dat soete es soer.
>
> (28.4.1–2, 4–8)

[The madness [passion] of love
Is a rich fief . . .

. . .

Those who at first were two
She can make into one:
Which truth I do attest.
She makes bitter what was sweet . . .]

> Si maect den onbekinder
> Die wide weghe cont
> Daer menich in moet dolen . . .
> In hogher minnen scolen
> Leert men orewoet,
> Want si brenghet dien in dolen
> Die hem wel verstoet.
>
> (28.5.5–7; 6.1–4)

[To those who know them not
She shows great broad roads
Where many go astray . . .
In the school of noble love
One learns the passion for her.
For she brings him in confusion
Who once had understood.]

Love or *Minne* as a country, a land [die lant minnen], is a recurring trope in Hadewijch's poetry, and in Poem 28 passion or desire [orewoet] is a rich fief in that land; here *Minne* has the power to defeat the laws of mathematics by making two into one. Personified as a guide, she leads men astray, and as a teacher she confounds those who thought they were wise.

In Poem 17, stanza 3, a spatialized Love is seen to be both confining and immense, as are its griefs:

> Wat mach hem bliscap ommevaen,
> Die minne in hachten heeft inghe ghedaen
> Ende die de wijdde van minnen woude ommegaen
> Ende vri ghebruken in trouwen.
>
> (17.3.1–6)

> [What joy can surround
> Him whom Love has thrown into close confinement,
> When he wishes to journey through Love's immensity
> And enjoy it as a free man in all security?]

The paradox of confinement that is expansive is suggested again in Poem 26, stanza 6: Love, Hadewijch says,

> Dats ene die aire scoenste hacht
> Ende ene onverwonne nuwe macht.
>
> (26.6.4–5)

> [is one of the most beautiful imprisonments
> And an unconquered new power.]

In Dutch, the rhyme "hacht" [imprisonment] / "macht" [power] supports the paradoxical equation between captivity and power. Another paradox is expressed in a martial metaphor, the hand-to-hand struggle of two champions:

> Want die minne nie en vervacht,
> Hine leefde nie vrie daghe.   (21.5.8–9)

> [For he who has never fought against Love
> Has never lived a free day.]

> Die minne verwint dat hise verwinne.   (40.5.1)

> [Love conquers him so that he may conquer her.]

> Die ghenoech der minnen rike wijet,
> Ic segge dat hi bi wike rijet.   (23.4.1–2)

> [If someone submits enough to the power of Love
> I say that he is empowered by submission.]

The fact that in Dutch the verbs, and the nouns associated with them, rhyme— "rike wijet, . . . bi wike rijet"—supports the grammatical parallelism that in turn reinforces the equation between submission and empowerment. Love is unknowable, yet can be experienced:

> En heeft forme, sake noch figuere;
> > Doch eest inden smake alse createure;
> > > Hets materie miere bliscape . . .

> > > > (22.3.3–5)

> [The thing has no form, no manner, no outward appearance.
> > It can only be tasted as something actual:
> > > It is the substance of my joy . . .]

Scholars know nothing of this force that strengthens and annihilates:

> So segghic dat en merke clerc
> > Hoe scone het den ghenen stoede
> Die in minnen wrachte sterc werc;

> > . . .

> > Hi soude in minnen oerewoede
> > Verbernen in hare diepste vloede
> > Ende versmelten alse caden . . .

> > > (23.11.2–4, 7–9)

> [I say no scholar is able to consider
> > How fortunate will be the state
> Of him who has wrought deeds of strength in Love;

> > . . .

> > Then, in the madness of Love,
> > He will burn in her deepest flood
> > And melt away like tallow.]

The expression "burning in the madness of love" [in minnen oerewoede . . . Verbernen] may seem to be a convention of love poetry, but when Hadewijch links that prepositional phrase to another, "in her deepest flood" [in hare diepste vloede], she brings her audience to an unthinkable yet experiential realm where opposites are united; there the lover's nature is consumed like tallow. But consciousness is not lost in this consuming; in fact, consciousness is ever greater, and the self that is lost is also found:

> Mijns selves en es mi bleven niet . . .

> > . . .

> > Ere ende raste hebbic begheven,
> > Omdat ic wille leven
> > Vri ende in minnen ontfaen . . .

> > . . .

> > Ic en machs niet ontberen,
> Ic en hebbe el niet: ic moet op minne teren.

> > > (24.5.8; 24.6.4–6, 9–10)

[Nothing of myself remains to me:

.   .   .

    I have given up honor and repose,
    Because I wish to live
    Free, and receive in love
Great riches and knowledge.

.   .   .

    I cannot do without this gift.
I have nothing else: I must live on Love.]

    Although no one poem can illustrate all of Hadewijch's skill, Poem 6 illustrates many of Hadewijch's techniques. Like the majority of the poems in the *Strophische Gedichten,* the poem opens with a seasonal description; just as all life quickens in March, so the lover's longing is intensified, and he wishes to conquer Love so that *"she* will give herself wholly in love" [Dat sie hare al in minnen gheve] and *he* will "live wholly as Love with love" [Ende minne met minnen leve]. A relationship is being defined here, one that at first seems to be a matter of domination and conquest but that in fact is characterized by specularity, to use Luce Irigaray's term for a kind of mirroring that leads to a full acceptance and merging of difference, of the other.[17] The terms, the rules, for this relationship are known to the poet and spelled out. If "he" (the representative lover) maintains his zeal and hope,

    Minne sainew wel ghessterken:
    Hi sal sijn lief ghewinnen;
        Want minne niene can
        Hare selve ontsegghen nieman,
    Sine gheve hem dat si hem an
    Ende meer dan daer sine selve toe spane.

                        (6.2.7–12)

    [Love will indeed strengthen him:
    He shall conquer his Beloved;
        For Love can never
        Refuse herself to anyone;
    Rather she gives him what she is willing he possess,
    And more than she herself promised him.]

    But March can be a cold month, too, and doubt, if it arises, will blight the lover's growth, as frost blights the leaves of trees. Only the sun (equated with *Minne*) can "call forth / flowers and fruit from the mind" [Die bloyen doet die sinne]. Love's promises are reiterated: if the lover demonstrates submission, strength, and understanding,

    Hi sal al vri ontfaen
    Dier onghehoerde macht: . . .

He sal noch die minne dwingen
Ende wesen al hare voghet.

(6.4.7–12)

([He] shall receive in full freedom
Love's unheard-of power. . . .
He shall yet subdue Love
And be her lord and master.)

Now suddenly, surprisingly, in the fifth stanza of a seven stanza poem, Hadewijch speaks in the first person, revealing the differences between her experience and what she has just described as the law of love. Perhaps, she thinks, the situation she has just described is not universally applicable. "Love makes me wander outside myself" [Waeer vindic der minnen iet], she says.

Mijn wederstoet die es te groet,
Ende mi es darven der minnen een doet
Want ic en macher ghebruken niet.

(6.5.10–12)

[My misfortune is too great,
And for me, to do without Love is a death,
Since I cannot have fruition of her.]

"Why," she asks, if she ought to "love totally . . . did she not give me total love?" [Sint ic al minnen soude, / Wan gave si mi al minne?] She has nothing of herself left:

Want ic hebbe so dat mine verlevet,
Ic en hebbe el niet sine ghevet
Ende al gave si iet, hongher blevet:
Want ict gheheel al woude.

(6.6.9–12)

[I have so spent what is mine,
I have nothing to live on. . . .
But even if she gave me something, hunger would remain,
For I want the whole.]

Hadewijch's personal assertions (we will call them that for simplicity's sake, although we know that the historical person Hadewijch is not to be equated with only this voice) greatly enrich and problematize the reader's appreciation of *Minne* the being and *minne* as experience. At the same time, this presentation of two optics, two voices, allows the poetic "I" to remember that she is not alone in this isolation. Many of Love's lovers have denied themselves for her sake, and

> Nu sijn si in swaren bande
> Ende vreemde in haers selfs lande.
> Daer dolen si in de hande
> Der vremder avonturen.
>
>   (6.tornada)

> ([Are] now . . . in heavy chains,
> Exiled in their own land.
> There they wander, subject
> To alien adventures.)

Literally, this reads "they are exiled in their own land, in the hands of alien adventures." The repetition of "vreemde" [exiled] and "vremder" [alien] in the poem's tornada underscores the dimension of alienation. At the same time, the language implicitly compares Love's lovers with the outcast protagonists of a *chanson de geste* or a Germanic heroic legend like *Beowulf*. Consequently, this ending to the poem surprises, as it moves us from a lyric to an epic context. Yet this conclusion is not, ultimately, discouraging. Why is this so?

We have moved, in the course of the poem, from a springtime landscape apparently in harmony with human desire, to the promised relationship with Love if the lover will do his part, to a personal assertion of the pain of waiting for Love to do her part, and, finally, to the fusion of "I" and "he" in the experience of alienation, a disjunction between man and his world. But thanks to the cyclical nature of the seasons and the episodic nature of the *chansons de geste*, we are led to think of love as an entire cycle (of seasons, of adventures) and of the events of this poem as just one moment in that greater cycle. Although the lover no longer dwells in the ordinary world because of his fidelity to love, his alienation from that world is the *sign*, the visible mark, of his relationship to Love and to other lovers who share his experience. In that relationship, gender and person are only the beginning of our experience, our life cycle. Ultimately gender and person have no fixed referent, for "I" and "he" have the same experience, and in seeking to lose themselves in Love, they abdicate any distinction between "her" (*Minne*) and "him" or "me" (the lovers). Even the metaphors of personal combat lose their original gender specificity, for we learn that all the persons of the poem, "I," "he," and "she" (*Minne*) seek to conquer in being conquered.

Yet in the language of the poem, it is initially very important that *Minne* is female and "anyone" seems to be male. In the courtly tradition, especially in the lyric, role reversal is an essential aspect of the new love experience being articulated. The (male) poet is placed in an unusual relation vis-à-vis his lady; he is powerless to gain her love unless she grants it freely. She has the upper hand. Yet in the course of many romance lyrics, the poetic "I" manages to turn the tables on the figure of the lady, who is seen to derive her very power from the poet's creation of her. Difference usually implies hierarchy, and in the proper order of things, males dominate. In Hadewijch's treatment of the love relationship, we also begin with what seems to be a role reversal, but it soon becomes clear that in their mutual conquest and surrender, Love and the lover are in not a hierarchical relationship, but one characterized by specularity. Each mirrors the difference and the sameness of the other. If power and knowledge are located anywhere in the poem, it is in Love, *Minne*—but the lover is located in her, and she in him. In this world that Hadewijch is creating in the *Strofische Gedichten* (a world that she claims to have experienced and is now bearing witness to in these poems), gender would seem to be irrelevant. Can this be true?

Gender and Body

It may be objected that we cannot generalize about gender identification on the basis of an analysis of just one poem. Gender may show up more strongly in those poems that depict the bodily experience of desire, particularly since the desire is felt for a being characterized as feminine, who also experiences desire. Hadewijch uses a number of image clusters to present the experience of love; some seem to have as their referent the physical body, whereas others speak more metaphorically of the soul's experience. Love may be seen in martial terms such as imprisonment, conquest, battle and its accoutrements, siege, and so on. It may also be presented in terms of physical sensation, primarily images of hunger and thirst and their opposites, devouring and swallowing. Veins, channels, and floods are the locus of sensation and anxiety. Images of madness and dissolution—whether of the body or the consciousness—appear often, especially in the later poems in the sequence. These image clusters often overlap within any one poem, resulting in a feeling of confusion, synaesthesia, in the reader, a state that corresponds to the totality of the state being depicted.

In the first poem, Love has the power to "strike" [slaen] the lover-narrator, to "scourge or pardon" [soenen ende slaen]. Love can "set us free or chain us fast" [. . . die minne fijn / Vri maken ende benden]. In Poem 2, the poet's "singing" [nuwe sanghe] is "hushed" [Ic mach wel vander]. The "I" of the poem suffers "pain and heartache" [Daer ic nu doghe pine / Ende van herten seer] and "wither[s] like an old man and waste[s] away" [Dies oudic ende dwine]. Love herself is "fertile" [drachtich], "mother of the virtues" [moedeer van alre doghet], and epitomizes the fidelity [die trouwe] that grants power. She is "so sweet in her nature / That she conquers every other power" [Soe suete es minne in hare natuere, / Dat si alle andere cracht verwint], yet to the immature lover she "taste[s] . . . bitter and sour" [Soe smaect hi bettere ende suere]. He who loves properly is "As the beautiful rose / Appears to us in the dew between the thorns" [Ghelijc dat ons die scone rose / Metten dauwe comt uten dorne gheghaen]. In Poem 3, the lover-narrator carries a shield that "has warded off so many stabs / There's no room left on it for a new gash" [Want mi es die scilt so sere dorehouwen / Hine can intoe niet meer slaghe ontfaen].

Love sometimes gives "consolations, then again wounds" [Alse nu den troest, alse nu die wonde], and "her pleasure gives / The sweet kisses of her mouth" [Den enen gheeft si, dien sijs an, / Die suete cussenne van haren monde]. In Poem 4, the male lover is "always new and afire with longing [Hi es altoes nuwe ende van niede heet]; he "has experienced silence amid great noise" [Ende in hoech gheruchte scilentie ontfaen].

Gender, as these verses indicate, is not fixed. At times, when martial images characterize the relationship between the lover and beloved, male gender seems implied for both beings. At other times, the lover is male (an old man), while *Minne* is female, a fertile mother. Some images are without gender and speak of sensation (*Minne* is sweet but tastes bitter to the immature lover) or beauty (the enlightened lover is like a "rose . . . in the dew between the thorns"). In the same poem, *Minne* may seem first male and aggressive, dealing wounds to the lover, and then a yielding female, giving sweet kisses to her lover.

Images of wounding and healing are central to the presentation of desire and body. In Poem 7, the madness of love is imaged as dissolution of the soul, and this in turn is imaged as an abyss into which the lover is hurled. The abyss is connected to wounding, and this means no more health [gesunde]. This would seem an impossible concatenation of metaphors, but look at what Hadewijch has done with it:

> Mi smelten mine sinne
> In minnen oerwoede;
> Die afgront daer si mi in sende
> Die es dieper dan die zee;
> Want hare nuwe diepe afgronde
> Die vernuwet mi die wonde:
> Ic en sjoeke meer ghesonde,
> Eer icse mi nuwe al kinne.

> (7.4.5–12)

> [My soul melts away
> In the madness of Love;
> The abyss into which she hurls me
> Is deeper than the sea;
> For Love's new deep abyss
> Renews my wound:
> I look for no more health,
> Until I experience Love as all new to me.]

The final line directs us to a fuller and truer experience of *Minne,* in which the lover will find health, not madness—but this experience requires a complete renewal of the concept and experience of Love. Another way of looking at this madness is found in Poem 12, where the frenzy of love is described in bold sexual images, underscored by the emphatic repetition of the word "minne":

Si selen met minnen ane minne een cleven,
Ende selen met minnen al minne doresien,
Ende met haren verhoelnen aderen al tien
In[t] conduut daer minne[n] haer minne al scincket.
Ende met minnen hare vriende al dronken drinket,
   In wondre vore haren woeden.

(12.6.3–8)

[With Love they shall cleave in oneness to Love,
And with love they shall contemplate all Love—
Drawing, through her secret veins,
On the channel where Love gives all love,
And inebriates all her drunken friends with love
   In amazement before her violence.]

In the real world, the madness of love is both physical and emotional, and here this higher love implies bodies with veins and channels for release, but it is a release that inebriates, goes to one's head, a release and an intoxication that stun by their violence. Body cannot be separated from body, nor can soul and body be distinguished, in this violent becoming one in love. Even a cliché like the proverbial arrow of love is depicted graphically and physically in Poem 14 so that we really feel the pain of penetration and the resulting infection.

    Alsenne der minnen strale ruren,
       So gruwelt hem dat hi levet.

    In allen tiden als ruert die strale
    Meerret hi die wonde ende brenghet quale.

. . .

    Die nied houdse open ende onghebonden.

(14.2.5–6; 14.3.1–2; 14.12.3)

[As Love's arrows strike it,
   It shudders that it lives.

At all times when the arrow strikes,
It increases the wound and brings torment.

. . .

Longing keeps the wounds open and undressed.]

("It" in this translation is the soul, and soul can be understood only with the language of the body.) If penetration is associated with the male gender, and yearning and openness with the female, then *Minne* is male and the lover female, but we know this is not so, for male pronouns are used for the lover and female ones for *Minne*.

    In Poem 17, Hadewijch describes her experience as being "again under the lash" [onder den slach]. She comforts herself with the observation that "Before the All unites itself to the all, / Sour bitterness must be tasted" [Eertt al met al wert vereent, / Smaect men bitteren suere]. In Poem 19, she describes Love's ways with "someone": "Although she forces him with violence, / She contents him and sweetens his chains" [Aldoet si hem cracht ende gheweldichede, / Si doet hem ghenoech ende suet den bant]. In the succeeding poem, Poem 20, she sums up her experience: "No living man under the sun / Can content Love" [Hine levet onder der sonnen / Die der minnen g[he]noech vermoghe]. Nor can the human be contented by love, for "Love is always possessed in violent longing: / Here one cannot find repose" [Altoes in woede hoemen minne ommeva: / Hier en doech gheseten]. In the twelfth and final stanza of Poem 20, the narrator speaks directly to Love:

> Sal mi minne bescarmen
>   Ende segghen: "dijns rouwen si keer.
>   Ic sal di warmen;
>   Ic ben dat ic was wilen eer;
>   Nu valle in minen armen
>   Ende ghesmake mijn[s] rike gheleer."
>
> (20.12. 5–10)

> ([When will you] reach out to me
>   And say: "Let your grief cease.
> I will cherish you;
> I am what I was in times past;
> Now fall into my arms,
> And taste my rich teaching!")

Sadly, this consolation is only a fantasy, albeit a very specific one that tells us of one dimension of Hadewijch's needs, to be cherished by a loving mother and teacher. The learning she offers is not easily grasped, as in Poem 22 we see that Love may command "in storm or in stillness" [Daeer sijt ghebiedet lude ende stillekine], for "She impels us to long desiringly for her / And to taste her without knowing her being" [Want si doet met begheerten na hare haken / Ende sonder kinnen hare wesen smaken]. The only knowledge the soul can possess is the knowledge that love cannot be gained without renouncing the self, and this is a burden that "weighs me down" [mi swaert]. Yet this poem is ultimately affirming, for in it we see an increase in Hadewijch's knowledge of herself and of Love's attraction, even if *Minne*'s being is unfathomable. Such self-knowledge is reflected in the use of first-person pronouns in each line of her conclusion:

> Al soude mi noch begherte therte tewriven
> Ende cracht van minnen node, mi en soude ontbliven,
>   Ic sal noch weten wat mi trect,
>   Ende dicke so onsachte wect
> Als ic mi selven in rasten soude gheriven.
>
> (22.7.3–7)

> [Even if desire crushes my heart,
> Even if strength slips away from me through Love's coercion,
>   I shall yet know what draws me

And awakens me so mercilessly
If for a moment I seek pleasure in repose.]

It has often been noted that in the later poems of this sequence of forty-five poems, Hadewijch complains more and more bitterly of what she has not received from Love. What has not been noted is how, from Poem 25 on, the descriptions of Love and the experience of love are cast in more explicit bodily terms. At the same time, the paradoxes of love are explored, and Reason is called on to help resolve them. To bring this home to the reader, the descriptions of Love and union are more extended and more erotic and involve all of the bodily senses. In Poem 25, the experience of Love is characterized by synesthesia, as when Hadewijch tells us that "That great noise, that loud gift / Of soft stillness makes me deaf" [Dat gherochte, dat hoghe prosent / Der neder[r]e stillen, doet mi verdoven]. The poem continues, moving from the first person narration of stanza 3 into the more impersonal narrative of stanza 4 and fusing the two points of view into one experience:

Hare nedere stille es onghehoert
Hoe hoghe gheruchte dat si maect,
En si allene dies hevet becoert
Ende dien minne in hare al hevet ghesaaect,
Dat hi hem al ghevoele in minne.
Alse sine met wondre also doresmaect,
Cessert een ure tgheruchte daerinne;
Ay, saen wect begherte die waect
Met nuwen storme die inneghe sinne.

(25.4.1–10)

[Love's soft stillness is unheard of,
However loud the noise she makes,
Except by him who has experienced it,
And whom she has wholly allured to herself,
And has so stirred with her deep touch
That he feels himself wholly in Love.
When she also fills him with the wondrous taste of Love,
The great noise ceases for a time;
Alas! Soon awakens Desire, who wakes
With heavy storm the mind that has turned inward.]

But the poem does not end here. Hart has entitled this poem "Reason, Pleasure, and Desire,"[18] and with good reason, for the fifth stanza sets out the difficulty:

Ghenuechte loke wel die oghen
Ende plaghe gherne dies si hevet,
Mocht die verwoede begherte ghedogen
Die altoes in woede levet.
Want si [haer] alle uren daertoe ghevet
Te roepenne: "ay, minne, wes al mine!"

Oec wec[t] se redenne, die hare dat seghet:
"Sich hier, dit steet di noch te volsine."
Ay, daer redenne ghenuechte ontseghet,
Dat quetst meest boven alle pine.

(25.5.1–10)

[Pleasure would certainly close her eyes
And gladly enjoy what she possesses
If fierce Desire, who always
Lives in fury, would tolerate it.
For every hour Desire begins anew
To cry: "Alas, Love! Be all mine!"
Thus she awakens Reason, who says to Pleasure:
"Behold, you must first reach maturity!"
Alas! That Reason should refuse Pleasure
Cuts more than all other pains.]

It is Reason who urges the soul to grow if she wishes to experience Love more deeply: "Behold! Take possession of the highest glory!" The next three poems urge the lover to greater and greater desire and reveal the paradoxes of *Minne* that force the reader toward the *aporia* that may catapult into a higher level of thought. (The constitution of *Minne* through paradox in Poem 28 is discussed at the beginning of this essay.) Poem 29 reveals the secret the soul needs to grow—the incarnation, with the transcendent paradox of the God Man. It would seem that Hadewijch deliberately structured her collection of poems to lead irrevocably to this point.

Hart notes that, according to J. Bosch, Hadewijch "structured this entire book according to the principles of medieval numerology, and that in the scheme she evolved (without giving the reader any hint of it) Stanzaic Poem 29, on the subject of the Virgin Mary, is the central poem of the entire series of forty-five."[19] In this poem, the Virgin Mary's willing acceptance of the incarnation initiates the possibility of the full experience of *Minne*. In the first stanza, the poet explains that "He for whom I languish / . . . /Has given me to understand / That by High Love" [Mijn swaere draghen / sonder claghen / . . . /Hi hevet mi doen verstaen/dat ic met hogher minnen sal ontgaen] she can go beyond the pain of love that she is experiencing at this stage of her spiritual growth. The Virgin Mary is the model of the humility that is necessary for this going beyond in high love:

En wardt nieman, die conste
Gherechte minne verstaen,
Eer dat marie, die goede,
Met diepen oetmoede,
Die minne hadde ghevaen.

(29.4.2–6)

[There was no one who could
Understand veritable Love
Until Mary, in her flawlessness,

> With deep humility,
> Had received Love.]

It is Mary who began to unlock the paradoxes of love by showing the potency of humility:

> Die vader van anebeghinne
> Hadde sinen sone, die minne,
> Verborghen in sinen scoet,
> Eerne one marie,
> Met diepen oetmoede ja,
> Verholentlike ontsloet.
> Doen vloeide die berch ten diepen dale,
> Dat dal vloyde even hoghe verwommen,
> Daer langhe strijt was an begonnen.
>
> (29.5.1–10)

> [The Father in the beginning
> Kept his Son, Love,
> Hidden in his bosom,
> Until Mary,
> With deep humility indeed,
> In a mysterious way disclosed him to us.
> Then the mountain flowed down into the deep valley,
> And that valley flowed aloft to the height of the palace.
> Then was the castle conquered
> Over which long combat had taken place.]

This humility affects the very course of nature by reversing high and low, life and death. Such a reversal, although prophesied in the Old Testament, could come about only by Mary's experience of *Minne,* and only through her could it be passed on to us:

> Dat was bi diepen niede
> Dat hare dat grote ghesciede,
> Dat die edel minne uut wert ghelaten
> Dien edelen wive
> van hoghen prise
> Met overvloedegher maten;
> Want si el ne woude, noch haerre el ne was,
> So hadse al daer elc af las.
> Dus heeftse dat conduut gheleit,
> Dat elker oetmoedegher herten es ghereit.
>
> (29.99.1–10)

> [It was by deep longing
> That this mystery happened to her,
> That this noble Love was released
> To this noble woman
> Of high praise
> In overflowing measure;

Because she wished nothing else and owned nothing else,
She wholly possessed him of whom every Jewish woman had read.
Thus she became the conduit
Open to every humble heart.]

Here the language of courtly and romance literature fuses with the language of Scripture to make of the Virgin Mary the model for the mystic's longing. As the Virgin Mary, in the incarnation of the God Man, brings the body into history, so the poet brings the body to transcendence in the experience of Minne. Thus it is that in Poem 31, Love has transformed Hadewijch's very body so that she can give birth to Love herself. Up to this point, the vocabulary devoted to the assaults of love on the lover have not been gender-specific, but now Hadewijch's physical being seems definitely feminine. As this new life is enclosed within her, so is she contained by that powerful female, Love.

> Want sie mii met harer groter crachte
> Mine nature maect so wijt,
> Dat ic mijn wesen al verpachte
> In die hoghe gheboert van haren gheslachte.
> Als ic wil nemen vri delijt,
> So werpt si mi in hare hachte.

(30.1.3–8)

> ([Love] . . . with her infinite strength
> So enlarges my heart
> That I have given myself over to her completely,
> To obtain within me the birth of her high being.
> But if I wish to take free delights,
> She casts me into her prison.)

In Poem 36, although the subject is apparently not Hadewijch but "someone," we see both genders implied in Love's actions of penetration and engulfment. The "Judgement of Love, / Pierces deep within / Through the inward senses," so that "By the fury of Love / He is all devoured / In Love" (Vonnesse van minnen / Gheet diepe binnen / Met inneghen sinnen. . . . Bider minnen woet / Wert hi al gheten / In die minne [36.5.1–3; 36.10.9–11]). Penetration is the reference again in Poem 37:

> Waer soudi nemen vremden nijt,
> Daer ghi den ghenen met doresnijt
> Die u gheeft cussen in alle tijt?

> [Where would you have come by the strange hatred
> With which you transpierced him
> Who gives you his kiss at all times?]

In Poem 38, more feminine associations characterize Love as she both devours and nourishes like an ancient Mother Goddess.

> Den selken besitti in uwe woet,
> Dat hi van binnen al wordt gheten;

Die selke sijn sachte van u ghevoedt
Ende sijn van u doch onbeseten!

. . .

Te niete werden al in minnen,
Dat es dat beste dat ic weet . . .

(38.5.5–8; 38.7.1–2)

[One you possess in your madness
So that, from within, he is utterly devoured;
Others you nourish tenderly—
Without making them yours for an instant!

. . .

To be reduced to nothingness in Love
Is the most desirable thing I know . . .]

Nevertheless, this accumulation of more specifically sexual images to describe the love experience does not mean that the old images of struggle and hand-to-hand combat have been abandoned. The difference is that now these images of battle are more suggestive of the sexual encounter. In this, Hadewijch is simply utilizing a view of sexuality that has long been found in European erotic poetry. What is unusual is that she has excluded this reading earlier, where images of combat suggested instead the male-bonded world of medieval heroic and chivalric poetry. Now the weapon employed by both Love and the lover is longing:

Ende die de minne met niede dan besteet,
Al sonder herte ende sonder sinne,
Ende minne dan nied met niede versleett:
Dats cracht daer men bi minne ghewinne.

. . .

Sine can verweren die storme heet,
Hine wone ghelijc met hare daer binnen.

(38.7.5–8; 8.3–4)

[And if anyone then dares to fight Love with longing,
Wholly without heart and without mind,
And Love counters this longing with her longing:
This is the force by which we conquer Love.

. . .

Love cannot resist the violence of the assault:
But he shall abide firm in the storm, conformed to Love.]

The combat motif is taken up again in Poem 40, where the lover's wound implies penetration, but this is followed by a more nurturing image, the image of the lover drinking from Love's veins:

Dien minne verwint dat hise verwinne

. . .

Als hi ghevjoelt die soete minne,
Wort hi met haren wonden ghewont.

Soe werdet utermaten goet:
Begherte scept, ghenluechte drincket,
Die fiere die dat sine in minne verdoet
Ende met woede in hare ghebruken sincket.

. . .

Endee so wert die minne al minne volvoet.

(40.5.1, 3–4; 40.6.1–4, 7)

[Love conquers him so that he may conquer her.

. . .

When he experiences this sweet Love,
He is wounded with her wounds;

. . .

He imbibes eagerly from Love's deep veins,
With continual thirst for a new beginning,
Until he enjoys sweet Love.

So for the soul things go marvelously;
While desire pours out and pleasure drinks,
The soul consumes what belongs to it in love
And sinks with frenzy in Love's fruition.

. . .

Thus is the loving soul well fed by Love alone.]

In Poem 42, we get another extended description, one of the most sensual in Hadewijch's collection. This description is unusual not because it is based on the imagery of the Song of Songs, for Hadewijch quotes more from this book of the Bible than from any other (Job is a close second), or in the borrowing of a female speaking voice, but because it reproduces the gender roles of that text, where the Beloved is male and the eager lovers are female. In the usual allegorical reading of the Song of Songs, Christ is the Beloved, and the Shulamite, the love-stricken young girl, represents the Church. Thus, as one would find in Hadewijch's *Visions* and "Letters," *Minne* can be—but is not always—identified with the figure of Christ. Yet Christ is never named (except in Poem 29, where the Son is *Minne*); the Beloved is always *Minne*. It is possible that the imagery in this poem is intended, at least unconsciously, to suggest differences between male and female experiences of union.

Het es ghelijc uwe hoghe name
Als olye ute gheghoten, minne,

. . .

Dies, minne, u name es uutgheghoten,
Ende met wonders vloede al avergaet,
So sijn die opwassende dorevloten
Ende minnen in woede boven raet.

(42.4.1–2; 42.5.1–4)

[It is your lofty name,
Like oil poured out, Love,

. . .

> Since, Love, your name is poured out,
> And since it overflows with a flood of wonder,
> The young maidens are melted away in you
> And love with violent longing, above counsel.]

What I have tried to demonstrate is that through her experience of desire for *Minne* [orewoet van minnen], Hadewijch acquires knowledge of Love's ways and knowledge of the divine, as well as self-knowledge. The acquisition of this knowledge comes through self-abandonment to a descent, an abyss of humility, where she discovers God and herself. *Minne,* the bearer of God to her, is Other, utterly unlike the poet's humanity, and yet this Other needs the human and finds itself in the abyss of love, just as the human lover does. It is this knowledge that empowers her as a poet and as a spiritual teacher. From her connection with *Minne,* and *Minne*'s physical birth in the Virgin Mary, I believe Hadewijch learns that her female nature does not have to be transcended, for it is already transcendent in its ability to seek love. Such transcendence, however, does not imply any denigration of the male gender; Love reconciles all contradictions and differences, including gender, and proves that ultimately being is profoundly androgynous, capable of experiencing all extremes of existence without being torn apart by them. *Orewoet,* the stormy longing that characterizes the soul seeking Minne, is, from one point of view, the storm of old dualities, of difference within the mind, warring for domination, and unable to do anything but find reconciliation in *Minne.*

Notes

1. The standard text is *Hadewijch: Strophische Gedichten,* ed. Jozef van Mierlo, 2 vols. (Antwerp: Standaard, 1942). See also the translation by Mother Columba Hart, *Poems in Stanzas,* in *Hadewijch: The Complete Works* (New York: Paulist Press, 1980), pp. 123–258.

2. Hart, in *Hadewijch,* p. 19.

3. Although little is known of Hadewijch's external life, most scholars date these poems to the second quarter of the thirteenth century. This makes Hadewijch a younger contemporary of Jacques de Vitry and the *mulieres sanctae* in the area of Liège, of St. Frances and St. Clare in Italy, and of the *trobairitz* (women troubadours) in Provence. She is only one generation removed from the Provençal troubadours, from Marie de France and Chretien de Troyes; seventy-five years later, Dante, another great religious poet who wrote in the vernacular, would compose his *Divina Commedia.* If it is true that Hadewijch was composing her works between 1221 and 1240, she would have been a contemporary of Mechthild of Magdeburg and Beatrijs of Nazareth. For more on Hadewijch's life, see Chapters 1 and 3.

4. *Hadewijch: Mengeldichten,* ed. Jozef van Mierlo (Antwerp: Standaard, 1952); *Poems in Couplets,* in *Hadewijch,* trans. Hart, pp. 307–358. Of the thirty-one poems included in this collection, the final thirteen are not by her, but by another Hadewijch, called Hadewijch II or Pseudo-Hadewijch.

5. *Hadewijch: Brieven,* 2 vols., ed. Jozef van Mierlo (Antwerp: Standaard, 1947); "Letters to a Young Beguine," in *Hadewijch,* trans. Hart, pp. 43–121.

6. *Hadewijch: Visioenen,* 2 vols., ed. Jozef van Mierlo (Louvain: Vlaamsch Boekenhall, 1924, 1925); *Visions,* in *Hadewijch,* trans. Hart, pp. 259–305.

7. Reinder P. Meijer, *Literature of the Low Countries* (Cheltenham: Thornes, 1978), p. 17.

8. *Hadewijch: Strophische Gedichten,* p. 178.

9. I recall only two occasions in the *Strophische Gedichten* where she refers to herself as a woman: "What must I, a poor woman, do?" (15.3.9) and "I expected to be a lady of her court" (21.5.3). In the first, she is a poor woman because she is deprived of love, not because she is a woman; in the second, she is saying that she thought she knew how Love's court worked, and now she is confused.

10. Theodoor Weevers, ed., *Poetry of the Netherlands in Its European Context, 1170–1930* (London: Athlone Press, 1960), p. 27.

11. According to Tanis Guest, "So for Hadewijch there is a confusion, on the conscious level, between her relationship—minne—with her Beloved and the Beloved—Minne—himself. In different contexts in the trofische Gedichten the word is used in now the one sense, now the other, and again—sometimes deliberately, sometimes perhaps unknowingly—with ambiguity, in either meaning or both together" ("Hadewijch and Minne," in *Poetry of the Netherlands,* ed. Weevers, p. 15).

"Minne is not, in many if not the majority of cases, to be simply identified with God or His Son. If we consider those relatively few cases where Hadewijch uses the word 'God,' we find for the most part stereotyped phrases such as 'God weet,' 'God gheve,' from which nothing can be deduced; but of the others there are only two which contain a positive identification, in XX, 25–6:

God, die ghemaecte alle dinghe,
End boven al es minne sonderlinghe,

and XXIX, 41–2:

Die vader van anegeghinne
Hadde sine sone, die minne:

of which the first is somewhat ambiguous, since the same stanza contains:

Hem [God] biddic dat hi ghehinghe
Na sijn ghenoeghen
Dat minne nu minne Also na noch dwinghe
Alsi can voeghen.

There are, on the other hand, a number of cases which seem to suggest that there is no exact equivalent of God and Minne" (p. 17).

12. Meijer, *Literature of the Low Countries,* p. 17.

13. Ibid.

14. Hart, in *Hadewijch,* pp. xiv–xv.

15. Hadewijch, "Letter 18," in *Mediaeval Netherlands Religious Literature,* ed. and trans. Eric Colledge (New York: London House and Maxwell, 1965), p. 79. Hart's translation is slightly different: "If it maintains its worthy state, the soul is a bottomless abyss in which God suffices to himself; and his own self-sufficiency ever finds fruition in this soul to the full, as the soul, for its part, ever does in him. Soul is

a way for the passage of God from his depths into his liberty; and God is a way for the passage of the soul into its liberty, that is, into his inmost depths, which cannot be touched except by the soul's abyss. And as long as God does not belong to the soul in his totality, he does not truly satisfy it" (Hadewijch, "Letter 18," in *Hadewijch,* trans. Hart, p. xv).

16. Hart, in *Hadewijch,* p. xvii.

17. Luce Irigaray, *Speculum of the Other Woman,* trans. Gillian C. Gill (Ithaca, N.Y.: Cornell University Press, 1985).

18. Hart says that Hadewijch did not title any of her poems, but van Mierlo provided titles for all the poems included in his 1950 Hadewijch *Anthology,* and modern editors of the "Letters" have done the same (*Hadewijch,* p. 41).

19. Ibid., pp. 19–20. Hart is referring to J. Bosch, "Vale milies: De structuur van Hadewijch's bundel 'Strofische Gedichten,'" *Tijdschrift voor Nederlandse taal-en letterkunde* 90 (1974): 173–175.

11

Writing the Body: Male and Female in the Writings of Marguerite D'Oingt, Angela of Foligno, and Umiltà of Faenza

Bodies—the visionary's own body and the body of Christ—are very important in women's visionary writings. Recent work by Caroline Bynum has focused attention on the meaning of body, especially for women, in the late Middle Ages.[1] Current literary theory, especially feminist theory, also pays a great deal of attention to bodies, particularly gendered bodies, and to the cultural messages inscribed on and in them. What do these portrayals of women's bodies—the ecstatic Christian tradition, on the one hand, and the theoretical models posited in feminist theory, on the other—have in common? How might these two areas illuminate each other? My purpose in this essay is to examine closely the writings of three medieval women to see what their texts really, literally, say about bodies and to compare these texts with ideas about future texts imagined by feminist theorists, with the *parler femme* called for by writers like Hélène Cixous and Luce Irigaray.[2]

In reading these medieval women's texts, I am guided by the concept of *l'écriture féminine,* or *writing the body:* the notion that in putting body into writing, by the use of bodily imagery along with the rhythms and cadences of speech, a writer allows repressed contents to emerge from the unconscious into the light of the text. In other words, in using the language of the body the medieval writer may be able to say unsayable or unthinkable things.[3] But to find out what those unsayable things might be, we have to be alert to a number of signals: how does the writer image body? Is body gendered; that is, is it portrayed as male or female? If it is gendered, how is the notion of gender communicated? Is body conceived of as being in opposition to something else—soul, for instance, or immortality? Is body associated with other concepts? Is it dark or light, good or bad? What about the style with which these notions are communicated? Are there discernible rhythms or cadences that are associated with body words or images or that express the relation between body and something else?[4] For the texts we will be looking at, we have to add another very basic question: Where does God fit into this experience of the body? And, since we are here dealing with Christian texts, we must ask how theology, in particular the doctrine of the incarnation, may be related to the notion of the body that is revealed in women's mystical writings.

Christianity has not been particularly interested in women's experience of the divine, except perhaps to control it, and the medieval world often used Christianity to justify its misogyny. But this should not be a surprise. In an article introducing the work of the major French feminists to the American audience, Ann R. Jones observes that these thinkers believe that "Western thought has been based on a systematic repression of women's experience." But, she continues, this is not to say that women have not resisted such repression: "resistance does take place in the form of *jouissance,* that is, in the direct reexperience of the physical pleasures of infancy and of later sexuality, repressed but not obliterated by the Law of the Father."[5] In spite of cultural repression, in spite of the fact that there was no place for the woman writer in the medieval scheme of things, some women did succeed in becoming writers, and many of those women were visionaries. It is my belief that feminist theory can help us understand why this was so.

Medieval women mystics were public figures. Yet medieval society put women away: in their homes, in convents, even in brothels. In medieval thought, women were bodies (men were characterized as mind or spirit), and bodies were dangerous—dangerous to men and, therefore, to society as a whole. The physical austerities undergone by women mystics, and that young women often imposed on themselves, underscored society's need to control and purify the female body—a "grotesque" as opposed to a "classical" body, to borrow Bakhtin's terminology.[6] But in the case of women who were put away in the religious life, something unexpected happened. The very techniques of prayer and meditation that were supposed to reinforce the withdrawal of a religious woman, to "contain and suppress [her] . . . body,"[7] turned into a powerful force that made women potent visionaries. As Laurie Finke observes, "the discourse of the female mystic was constructed out of disciplines designed to regulate the female body, and it is, paradoxically, through these disciplines that the mystic consolidated her power . . . [and] fashioned . . . the means of transcending [her] . . . own secondariness."[8] In other words, women mystics were extremely active in their enforced passivity, and they used the language of passivity to create a new discourse. Their visions were the source of their power, for they gave women a public language to use "not just within a 'woman's culture,' but in a 'man's world' as well."[9] The process undergone by the mystic was both empowering and dangerous. Cixous tells us:

> As for passivity, in excess, it is partly bound up with death. But there is a nonenclosure that is not submission but confidence and comprehension; that is not an opportunity for destruction but for wonderful expansion.
>
> Through the same opening that is her danger, she comes out of herself to go to the other, a traveller in unexplored places; she does not refuse, she approaches, not to do away with the space between but to see it, to experience what she is not, what she is, what she can be.[10]

In the texts I present in this essay, the "other" to whom the woman travels is divine, usually but not always Christ, and out of this experience of alterity, both parties in the dialogue are transformed, transcended. Each of the passages to be analyzed constitutes a dialogue between voices and between bodies, where language mediates difference. Difference here has meaning, not in reference to a masculine norm, but, as Josette Feral explains,

> difference is to be thought of as other, not bounded by any system or any structure. Difference becomes the negation of phallologocentrism, but in the name of its own inner diversity. . . . It means choosing marginality (with an emphasis on the *margins*) in order to designate one's difference, a difference no longer conceived of as an inverted image or a double, but as alterity, multiplicity, heterogeneity. It means laying claim to an absolute difference, posited not within the norms but against and *outside* the norms.[11]

I have chosen to study three medieval women who were contemporaries, although they knew nothing about one another. All three were mystics and writers of visionary literature; one was French, and the other two were Italian. Two lived under the Benedictine Rule: one Cistercian, the other Vallombrosan. The third was a Franciscan tertiary. Two had been married and had borne children before entering the religious life; the other was a virgin who probably became a nun while still quite young. This last writer was the only one of the three who was educated and had read fairly widely; the other two were illiterate when they began their religious careers. Of these two, one became literate in Latin and encouraged her nuns to learn to read and write, and the other probably never learned to write and dictated her works in Italian, although her followers read most of her works in Latin.

The three women are St. Umiltà of Faenza, Blessed Angela of Foligno, and Marguerite d'Oingt. You may have heard of Angela, for her book *Liber de vere fidelium experientia* (*The Book of the Experience of the Truly Faithful Soul, or The Divine Consolations*), is a classic of medieval spirituality. Marguerite d'Oingt apparently was well known in her own time, but now her writings are read only by scholars of female mysticism. The third woman in this group, St. Umiltà of Faenza, is the least recognized of the three, but a collection of her Latin sermons has survived.[12]

Umiltà of Faenza

Umiltà (1226–1310) was the earliest chronologically of these three women. Born Rosanese Negusanti in Faenza, she became a Benedictine nun after her infant children died and her husband contracted what was apparently a sexually transmitted disease. Shortly after entering the convent, she miraculously acquired literacy and began a remarkable career that saw her escape from her convent to become a recluse, and then leave her hermitage to found new houses for women in Faenza and in Florence. Some of her Latin sermons date from her period as a recluse, while others were written while she was supervising the building of a new convent in Florence. We will look at two passages from one of the later sermons.

Umiltà felt herself guided by a number of divine figures, the most important of whom were her two guardian angels, Emmanuel and Sapiel, and the two saints closest to Jesus, St. John the Evangelist and the Virgin Mary. In her sermons, she devotes a good part of her attention to describing these beings and her relationship to them, especially in times of trouble. In Sermon 8, "In Honor of Jesus Christ,"[13] she enlists the protection of her guardian angels. As she prays to them, she invokes their weapons against her enemies. This invocation constitutes an anatomy of her sense organs, for her whole body is involved in the transformation she desires. (Umiltà's text is transcribed clause by clause, so that the parallel structure will be apparent, since this rhythmic construction is also constitutive of body.)

> Et vos Angeli mei robusti, frequentate omnes vias meas;
> soliciteque custodiatis,
>   ita quod inimici mei non possint propinquare ad januas meas
> et vestrum mihi ante deponatis ensem,
>   quoniam in principio vos mihi dati fuistis:
> opportune me semper custodiatis ab inimicis meis.
> Ponatis autem ensem in prima porta manu vestra dextera
> et tenete ita clausam a verbos novis et a verbis otiosis,
>   quando volent inde exire, ut non possint esse egressa.
> Et meam linguam acuatis ut rasorium, ad incidendum vitia:
> et plantate virtutes,
>   ad laudem et gloriam summi Imperatoris et suae Matris divinae.
> Et juxta meos oculos duo ponatis sigilla amoris,
>   digitos vestros sanctos, propter correctionem,
>   ut non possint cernere ad delectationem rem istius mundi.
> Et continuo eos teneatis apertos et solicitos ad vigilandum,
>   ut ne per somnolentiam possint turbare divinam Officium,
>   et mentem gravare ad Dei laudes, suaeque Matris,
>   et Angelorum mei specialis coeli, et totius divinae Curiae.
> Et aures meas teneatis ita firmatas in nomine Jesu

>   cum vestris sanctis manibus,
>   quod nullum malum verbum possit in illas unquam ingredi,
>   quod portet venenum ad animam meam.
>   Et meos pedes mittatis in quamdam catenam amoris,
>   ut non possint transire in aliquam viam erroris,
>   et omnes mei passus sint Christi honor suaeque Matris.[14]

The tropes of the first six lines create an allegorical context that defines the relationship between her angels and herself. "Angeli mei robusti": these hardy beings belong to her. She calls on them to accompany her on all her paths, and keep watch most carefully ["frequentate omnes vias meas; soliciteque custodiatis"] so that her enemies cannot come near her door. She asks them to put down their sword before her, for the angels were given to her from the beginning, and they always protect her ["custodiatis"] from her enemies. So far the tropes are what one might expect as appropriate to guardian angels—they are to guard her on a path.

The lines that follow seem to continue the allegory and explicate it: the angels are to take up the sword in their right hand at the first gate and in that way keep it closed to vain and lazy words so that, when the words want to come out, they will be able to. The trope of the gate, which seemed to be associated with the paths of the beginning lines, is instead a bodily image, for *janua* and *porta* refer to bodily openings. Bahktin's distinction between the classical and the grotesque body is operative here, for there are two registers of body imagery being invoked: the angels are depicted as having impenetrable bodies that take up space and act on other bodies, whereas the speaker's body has doors and gates, body parts that need reinforcements. The mouth, the *prima porta,* must remain closed, not against something that might penetrate from the outside, as the siege metaphors might lead us to believe, but against what might emerge from the speaker.

Umiltà's role as speaker is further developed by a new trope as she asks her angels to sharpen her tongue like a hoe in order to cut off vices and to plant virtues. For her to speak in this new way, as a persuasive teacher, the hands of the angels are needed to protect other body openings. Now the threat of penetration comes from outside her: her eyes must be prevented from seeing and delighting in the things of this world, yet they must be kept open during vigils, so that her mind remains alert. Her ears are to be guarded by the angels' putting their hands over them to prevent any evil word from entering them and carrying poison to her soul. Her feet are to be shackled in a chain of love so that they cannot walk in the way of error and so that all her steps are in honor of Christ and his mother. Her senses have the capacity for good or for evil; it is the angels' task to ensure that they are devoted only to good. Her body is to become a classical, closed body, a body like that possessed by the angels.

The entire passage defines a speaking self—the person who gives these sermons. Composing a discourse to be given to a congregation of male and female religious, she utilizes a number of body tropes to speak about the responsibility and the danger of speaking. She must not say wrong things, or see or hear them. At the same time, she must speak to encourage virtue and uproot vice, and her eyes must remain open for her mind to function. We can hear how Umiltà composed orally, as the repetition of imperative and subjunctive clauses accumulates intensity over twenty lines.[15] This speaking self, in constructing these rhythmical clauses, affirms by means of language the rhythm and the continuity of her lived experience, the cooperation between "vos" and "me." Although she needs protection, she is utterly confident that it will be given to her as she directs; her standard of reference is completely within her own bodily experience. The verbs of the first few lines, "frequentate," "custodiatis," "Ponatis . . . ensem," suggest embodied beings, armed and ready to defend the gate. The use of the second person forms of address and the frequent imperatives suggest immediacy and reciprocity in the desired relationship. In the later lines, the bodies she suggests by metonymy are fragmented—her eyes, ears, tongue, feet; her angel's fingers and hands—but unified by her syntax: "Do this, to effect this, so that I don't do this." There is body everywhere, and sense experience, overlapping bodies, but no gender difference. Her body needs protection because it is human, not because it is female; her angels can protect her, not because they are male, but because they are angels. If a male gender role is implied by the martial imagery used throughout, the sword symbolizing that role has already, in times long past, been given to Umiltà. The use of a great many possessive pronouns and adjectives—your hands, my eyes—contributes to the sense of intimacy and cooperation between two orders of beings.

Many of these techniques are also apparent in another more erotic passage in the same sermon. Here she addresses St. John the Evangelist,[16] and here, in the nuptial metaphor she invokes, gender and difference are marked. St. John is responsible for Umiltà's current dilemma; it was he who told her to leave her hermitage and go to Florence to found a new female community. She obeyed willingly, taking with her a small band of women disciples, even though it meant crossing Italy from Faenza to Florence on foot and in wartime. Once in Florence, she was obliged to live in secular surroundings until the convent could be built, which took a very long time. Although many women wished to join her order, Umiltà was publicly criticized for her atypical female behavior. She now fears abandonment: What if her beloved John has sent her on a wild-goose chase and is now about to leave her to her own devices, in a strange land and in a very exposed position? She composes this prayer to induce him to take the desired action toward her:

> O Evangelista, dulcis amoris lator,
>> tu transmittis pulchra exenia magno amore
>> in ista die tuis te diligentibus,
>> quae ad tui honorem est celebrata.
> Memor esto mei, quae sum nuda,
>> si mi vidisti, aut me cognoscis.

> Et quando dives eram si mei habebas curam,
>   non me derelinquas in egestate.
> Quia si venissem, ut pro te veni,
>   pro Soldano Saracenorum Imperatore,
>   solicitudinem ferret de me sua curialitate.
> O Joannes benedicite, cogites,
>   quod veni sub nomine et securitate tua,
>   et a vulnerantibus fui vulnerata
>   sub spe adjutorii tui,
>   et tui causa intravi istud mare. . . .
> Nunc reminiscare doni continui,
>   et illarum pulchrarum rerum magnae pulcheritudinis,
>   et ambasseriarum magnae dulcedinis,
>   quas mihi transmisisti ad plus diligendum.
> Et si ego corde te amo, o Johannes,
>   quamvis sim folium modici valoris,
>   et tu es lilium olentis candoris,
>   non me contemnes.
> Et recorderis de illo gladio,
>   quem tu fabricasti tam pulcherrimum;
>   amore, et non flagello in corde meo eum infixisti,
>   et bene clavasti,
> et non potest unquam dissipari amor tuus, dulcis Johannes;
>   qui ligasti me catena,
>   et annulo me desponsasti,
>   et sub tua custodia recommendata sum.
> Amor dilectus, non me derelinquas.[17]

The invocation calls on the saint as the bearer ("lator") of sweet love, to bring lovely gifts on this, his feast day. She begs St. John to remember her ("Memor esto mei"), not to abandon her in poverty ("non me derelinquas in egestate") or to spurn her ("non me contemnes"). At present she is "nuda," "in egestate," "vulnerata," but when she was rich he took care of her. He is more discourteous than the Saracen emperor,[18] who out of his courtliness would have cared for her if she had come for him. St. John initiated their relationship, courted her with gifts and love messages to increase her desire. In fact, he transfixed her heart with his sword, bound her in chains, and married her with a ring—she is entrusted to his guardianship.

Umiltà employs the language of romance and love lyric to re-create the story of her relationship with her beloved St. John, and, as she tells the story, he doesn't look too good. The technique is reminiscent of some of the women troubadours, and I am reminded of what Peter Dronke says of a poem by the Countess of Dia:

> The song is, above all, a meditation: on her own character and qualities, on the seemingly contradictory qualities of her lover, so admirable in himself and yet having become so arrogantly indifferent towards her. It is a series of questions, to discover what has gone wrong in the affair, an attempt by the woman who

speaks to justify herself and remove any possible blame from herself. And finally, as becomes more and more clear, it is an attempt to persuade the lover, so that he will think of her lovingly again.[19]

For a poem that treats of love, particularized body words are infrequent. Yet a suffering, and a sexual, body is implied. The speaker is naked and wounded; both adjectives are used to describe her state in the present, when she finds herself at the mercy of her enemies; "naked" and "wounded" do not refer to her erotic relationship with St. John, but describe her present vulnerability and exposure. Objects that image an erotic relationship belong to the past, when her heart was transfixed by the sword—not in punishment but in love—and she was bound in chains and married with a ring, all thanks to St. John. It is this past relationship that she insists on bringing into the present by reminding St. John of his part in it. In the course of this passage, the female subject moves from being victim to being a bride and from being one who pleads to being one who commands. She uses a humility topos when she compares herself with her lover: he is a fragrant white lily, and she is just a leaf—but they belong to the same plant.

As these passages indicate, Umiltà structures her sermons rhetorically by the use of familiar tropes, which she turns to new uses. Parallel clauses depict the powers of the being whose aid she is soliciting and the powers she needs herself; just as the grammatical parallels underscore the shared qualities of both parties, the content of her prayer urges a union between the beseecher and the beseeched. When the oppositions she creates are real as well as grammatical, the polarities are rarely what one might expect and rarely congruent with gender stereotypes. In the first passage, the speaker is constituted by images that seem to imply that women ought neither to speak nor to move from their assigned path, yet the speaker's voice is that of a teacher and a corrector of others.[20] In the second passage, cast in the language of love lyric and romance, it is Umiltà who has journeyed actively to meet her beloved, who in the present is disappointingly slow to act.

Angela of Foligno

I turn now to a visionary with a very different speaking voice. Blessed Angela of Foligno (1248–1309) was an unlettered Franciscan tertiary, a widow, who dictated her spiritual autobiography to a male relative (probably her uncle), Fra Arnaldo.[21] After her conversion experience in middle age, she became an important Franciscan leader. Her *Liber de vere fidelium experientia* begins with her detailing thirty steps (*gradus*) or transformations in her journey to Christ. She likes to characterize her experience in steps and views her relationship to Christ in terms of parallels and symmetries rather than antitheses. Her guiding metaphors and her style stress continuity and progression. In the eighth step, she contemplates the crucifixion (actually she is contemplating a physical object, a crucifix) and understands that it is our sins, her sins, that are crucifying Christ: "[I]n ista cognitione crucis dabatur michi tantus ignis, quod stando juxta crucem ex[s]poliavi me omnia vestimenta mea [p. 8] et totam me optuli ei . . . promisi . . . non offendere eum cum aliquo membrorum, accusando singillatim omnia membra singulariter."[22]

If we imagine this little drama played out in the Franciscan church of Foligno, with Angela standing at the foot of a life-size crucifix such as hung in most Italian churches, we are witness to an intimate transformation in which the saint publicly bares her body and ritualistically points to each of her "members," promising for them not to sin. She writes her body by speaking her body's gestures. In this, she is truly the daughter of St. Francis; Francis too dramatized his religious life by publicly stripping himself, in his case in the cathedral square in Assisi.

For Angela, soul is truly embodied; there is hardly a paragraph in her spiritual *Liber* in which body metaphors or bodily gestures and movements are not invoked, yet, like Umiltà, the performing or speaking body often is not gender-specific. When she speaks of the thirty "steps" on the "path" to penitence, we feel the weight of the body: "Et intelligas quod in omnibus istis passibus est mora. Unde magna pietas et magnum cordolium est de anima quod tam graviter potest se movere, et cum dolore, et cum tam magno pondere versus Deum. Et valde parvum passum facit. Et scio de me quod in quolibet passu morabar et plangebam."[23]

She wants to counter this heaviness and slowness by its opposite: "quia inspiratum est michi quod si ego volebam ire ad crucem ex[s]poliarem me et essem magis levis et nuda irem ad crucem" [I was inspired with the thought that if I wanted to go to the cross I should strip myself so I would be lighter and naked I should go to the cross]. Although she offers an allegorical explanation, typically Franciscan in origin, of what she means: "[S]cilicet quod parcerem omnibus qui me offendissent et ex[s]poliarem me de omnibus terrenis et de omnibus hominibus et feminis, et de omnibus amicis et parentibus et de omnibus aliis, et de possessione mea et de meipsa" (I should forgive all who had offended me and strip myself of all earthly goods and of [attachments to] all men and women, of all friends and relatives and everyone else, and of my possessions and of my very self), the actions she takes are very physical ones, actions that identify her culturally as a woman: "Et tunc incepi dimittere pannos meliores, et de cibariis, et de pannis capitis" [I began to put aside my better clothes, and food, and my headcoverings]. Unlike Umiltà, Angela uses bodily imagery not just to describe the soul; there is also a physical body that may be either naked or clothed.

The other body in this text is that of Christ, and it is bruised and bleeding, as he shows it to her. As she had identified each of her sinning "members" and promised chastity, so he enumerates his wounds endured for her: "[O]stendo a pedibus usque ad caput penas. Etiam ostendebat pilos barbe sibi evulsos, et superciliorum et capitis, et numerabat omnes flagellationes, scilicet assignando singulas flagellationes."[24]

At this, Angela cried "tam ardenter quod lacryme coquebant carnem.

Unde opportebat me postea ponere aquam ad refrigerandum" [so ardently that my tears burned my flesh, and I had to put water on it afterward to cool it]. Here her bodily description tells of a real body that cried real tears and also reveals metaphorical tears of the soul. Fire and water are not in opposition; the flame that consumes her makes her tears like fire, too.

When Angela thinks of total renunciation, she fears the danger and the shame of begging, the risk of rape because she is still young and beautiful, and the possibility of dying "fame et frigore et nuditate" [of hunger and cold and nakedness]. Yet she can finally affirm that she will renounce all, even "si opportebat me, mori fame vel nuditate vel verecundia" [if it were necessary for me to die of hunger or nakedness or shame]. She makes the leap into the unknown, toward the Other. Once she can freely make this commitment, she is rewarded by Christ: "[V]ocavit me et dixit michi quod ego ponerem os meum in plagam lateris sui. Et videbatur michi quod ego viderem et biberem sanguinem ejus fluentem recenter ex latere suo. Et dabat michi intelligere quod in isto mundaret me."[25]

No more hunger or nakedness or shame. She desires a kind of symmetry in her imitation of Christ. After drinking his blood, she prays to be allowed "totum sanguinem meum propter amorem suum, sicut fecerat ipse pro me, spargere" [to shed all my blood for his love, just as he had done for me]. But the symmetry is not complete: "volebam quod omnia membra mea paterentur mortem aliam passione sua, scilicet magis vilem" [I wished that all my limbs might suffer a death unlike his passion, . . . a more vile death]. In this reversed competitiveness, she wants her death to be more vile than that of any of the saints as well, but her imagination fails her: "inmo multum dolebam quod non poteram invenire vilem mortem . . . quia eram omnino indigna" [I grieved deeply that I could not find a vile death . . . for I was totally unworthy].

It is not just her negative experiences that are cast in bodily form. She "tastes" the divine sweetness; she "thirsts" to see a word written in a missal when she is on retreat. The understanding of the Gospel is "delectable." And not surprisingly, after she has tasted the understanding of the gospel, she is unwilling to eat.

The culmination of this part of her spiritual journey comes on a pilgrimage to the church of St. Francis in Assisi. She invokes real physical space, walking along "between Spello and the steep path that comes after Spello and climbs up towards Assisi, there at the crossroads." She hears the voice of the Holy Spirit, saying he will give her a consolation that she has never "tasted." She is his daughter, his beloved, his temple: "Ego diligo te multum. Et postquam ego colcavi me in te; modo colca te tu in me" [I cherish you very much. I have rested within you, and now you may rest yourself on me].

God, like Angela, seeks symmetry in their relationship. She is worried that this is inappropriate language for the Holy Spirit to use; she might become vainglorious. He challenges her to think of something else, and she looks at the vineyards and tries to think of something but cannot, for "[e]t ubicumque respiciebam, dicebat michi, 'Ista est mea creatura'" [wherever I looked, he said to me, "This is my creature"]. He reminds her of his body: "Ego sum qui fui crucifixus pro te et habui famem et sitim pro te, et sparse sanguinem meum pro te, tantum te dilexi" [I am he who was crucified for you, and I had hunger and thirst for you, and I shed my blood for you, so much have I loved you]; "eo in omni verbo recipiebam magnam dulcedinem, et noluissem pervenire et quod finiretur via illa omni tempore mundi" [At every word I received the greatest sweetness, and I did not want ever to arrive at Assisi or that the road should ever end].

As her joy reaches its apex, she piles up words for joy and pleasure in her attempt to express the inexpressible: "Et quanta esset letitia et dulcedo Dei quam ego sentiebam non possem existimare, maxime quando dixit: 'Ego sum Spiritus Sanctus, qui intro intus in te'" [And I could not estimate how much . . . joy and sweetness . . . I felt, especially when he said, "I am the Holy Spirit, who enter into you."]. When she reaches the church of St. Francis and looks at the stained-glass depiction of Francis in Christ's bosom, this image becomes a mirror of her experience, and God explains:

> [D]ixit mihi: "Ita te astrictam tenebo, et multo plus quam possit considerari oculis corporis." . . . Et multa verba dulcedinis dixit michi quando discessit, et cum immensa suavitate et plane discessit cum mora. Et tunc post discessum cepi stridere alta voce vel vociferari. Et sine aliqua verecundia stridebam clamando, et dicebam istud verbum, scilicet: "Amor, non cognitus! Et quare scilicet me dimittis? . . . Quare? Quare?" Tamen verbum predictum ita intercludebatur a voce, quod non intelligebatur verbum. . . . Et ego clamabam volens mori. . . . Et tunc omnes compages mee disjungebantur.[26]

Her focus on physicality seems to be reinforced by God himself when she joyfully recalls on her way home: "Et dixerat michi per viam eundo A[s]sisium ita: 'Tota vita tua, comedere et bibere, dormire et omne tuum vivere michi placet.'" [And he had said to me on the road going to Assisi: "All your life, your eating and drinking, sleeping and all your living is pleasing to me"].

What I see in these passages is the writing of body and of speech, of two bodies and two speaking voices, whose manifestations are symmetrical, mirroring each other. Angela is seeking to imitate Christ; in her mimesis of his nakedness and his suffering, she mimes nakedness and suffering for us as readers. For her, Christ is not a text to be read, but a role to be acted, and so she acts out her understanding of his experience, acts out of her understanding. He speaks words of love, she screams them, but her voice is incomprehensible, while his is soothing and communicates absolutely.

Angela's confessor and amanuensis, Fra Arnaldo, was horrified at this display and ashamed to be related to her. Many critics have been just as appalled by Angela's acting out, by the violence of her exhibition of her self. Laurie Finke notes that Angela "measures her 'fire of love' exclusively by the bodily injuries she wishes to endure."[27] She continues,

Piety, for Angela, as for virtually all the female mystics, is palpably physical, as palpable as Angela, like a nursing baby, drinking the blood of Christ from the wound in his side. Their writings feature representations of grotesque bodies that open up and spill forth their contents—blood, milk, excrement—bodies that endure wounding and mutilation. The mystic's own body becomes the site of contested discourses about the body—and about culture.[28]

Dronke notes that Angela removed herself more and more from accepted norms of behavior:

> For Angela this distancing took a form that was akin to the rhetoricians' "topoi of outdoing"—yet hers was an existential outdoing even more than a rhetorical one. Thus the love-mysticism based on the Song of Songs, in which the loving soul becomes Christ's beloved bride, is invested by Angela with graphic physical detail of a kind not previously known. Many holy women had meditated on the loving surrender of the bride; but Angela acts it out [before the crucifix].[29]

Dronke sees Angela's drinking the blood of Christ's side as Angela playing the role of "a Bacchante: both ardent devourer and humiliated victim."[30] The body being written by Angela is clearly a female body, a doubled body, hers and Christ's, both naked, both marked by suffering, both "grotesque" bodies, in Finke's terminology. Both bodies are anatomized: Angela points to each sinful member and promises chastity; Christ enumerates each wound. The only gendered detail of Christ's body is his beard, which also shows signs of violence. Both bodies are penetrated and humiliated, until the scene in Assisi, where Angela's spiritual body is exalted and comforted, a blissful body experiencing *jouissance,* while her physical body is torn by pain and sobbing.

Marguerite d'Oingt

The third writer we discuss is Marguerite d'Oingt, the prioress of the Carthusian convent of Pelotens (now Poleteins), who was probably born about 1260 and who died in 1310. She wrote three books, in three different languages. Her first book, *Pagina Meditationum,* was written in Latin between 1286 and 1288. Her second book, *Speculum (Mirror),* was written in French and completed by 1294. The third book, written in Franco-Provençal, is the biography of another mystic, a younger contemporary whom she probably taught as a novice. This volume, the *Life of Beatrice of Ornacieux,* must have been written between Beatrice's death in 1303 and Marguerite's own death in 1310.[31]

Marguerite brings two new perspectives to mystical writing by women. The first is the idea that the visionary is not a vessel but a text, a body in whom or on whom a text is inscribed. The second point is her emphasis on the act of writing; the text written within her is physically transferred by her to the pages of a book: "et aussi tot come illi avoyt mis les mot ou livre et ce li sallioyt du cuer" [as soon as she put a word in that book, it left her heart].[32] The context in which she says this is a good example of the release of bodily repression through writing. While meditating during Mass, she had a profound vision of the love of God. In response, she asked him to give her whatever he knew was necessary for her. After this, she felt "suam dulcem consolationem" [such sweet consolation from him] and "tam magnam voluntatem bene faciendi" [so strong a will for doing good] that to her "videbatur quod essem tota mutata et renovata" [it seemed that I was totally altered and renewed]. "His cogitationibus fuit ita plenum cor meum quod perdidi comedere et dormire," she says [My heart was so filled with these thoughts and meditations that I failed to eat and sleep].

> Et cogitavi quod opportebat me aut mori aut languere nisi removerem cogitationes istas a corde meo, nec inveniebam in corde meo quod eas removerem quia tantum solatium in eis inveniebam quod mihi afferret omnia instrumenta et omnes res que possunt letificari cor hominis in hoc mundo, nichil esset mihi respectu illius quod sentiebam in corde meo de meo dulcissimo Creatore. Ego cogitavi quod cor hominis et mulieris est ita mobile quod potest vix esse in uno statu, et ideo ponebam in scriptis cogitationes quas Deus ordinaverat in corde meo ne perderem eas cum removissem illas a corde meo, et ut possem eas cogitare paulatim quando mihi Deus quam gratiam daret.[33]

The crisis was evidently more severe than is apparent in this passage, for in a letter (probably to her confessor, and written in the third person) she says:

> [I]lli les ot totes escriptes en son cuer en tel maneri que illi n'avoyt pueir de penser en autres choses. . . . Ainsi com Nostri Sires li mit au cuer, elle se pensa que s'ela metoyt en escrit ces choses que sos cuers en seroyt plus alegiez. Se comenca a escrire tot co qui est ou livro . . . et aussi tot come illi avoyt mis les mot ou livre et ce li sallioyt du cuer. Et quant illi ot tot escrit, illi fu tote garie. Je croy fermament se illi ne l'eust mis en escrit, que illi fut morta ou forsonet.[34]

The key words here are "heart" [cuer], "thoughts" [cogitationes], "thinking" ["penser" and its inflected forms], "writing" ["escrire" and its inflected forms], and "removal" or "erasure" [sallioyt]. The obsessiveness of the experience is reflected in the obsessive reiteration of the same words and clauses. Clauses and sentences are not subordinated, but flow into one another in pulsing rhythms. The implied body behind this experience is reduced metonymically to a thinking heart and a writing hand. The only reference to gender mentions both sexes: there is not a man or a woman whose heart is stable. The visionary is literally all heart, and she will die of it if she cannot write what is within her to write. (This sense of the visionary as text is reflected in her *Speculum,* in which Christ is also a text; his wounds are inscribed on his body, and she is the reader of his passion.)

Christ's body is not only a text, but also a female body. Near the close of the first section of the *Pagina Meditationum,* she speaks of Christ as her mother:

Nonne tu es mater mea et plus quam mater; mater que me portavit, in partu mei laboravit per unam diem forte vel per unam noctem, et tu, pulcher Domine dulcis, propter me fuisti vexatus non una nocte vel uno die solum modo, immo laborasti plus quam xxx annis. Ha! pulcher Domine dulcis, quam amare laborati pro me tota vita tua! Sed quando tempus appropinquabat quo parere debebas, labor fuit tantus quod sudor tuus sanctus fuit ut gutte sanguinis que per corpus tuum decurrebant usque as terram. . . . Sed cum venit hora parus tu fuisti positus in duro lecto crucis . . . et nervi et omnes vene tue rupte fuerunt. Et certe non erat mirum si vene tue rumpebantur quando totum mundum pariebas pariter una sola die.[35]

Conclusion: Defining the Speaking Self

I promised in the beginning of this essay that I would return to the image of Christ as Other (what feminist theory terms alterity) and save my discussion of similarities between these women for my conclusion. Before I do that, would like to quote from Laurie Finke again: "Any visionary experience made public is always, *ipso facto,* a revisioning of that experience, an attempt to represent the unrepresentable. These women claimed the power to shape the meaning and form of their experiences. Their words, and even their bodies when necessary, became the sites of a struggle to redefine the meaning of female silence and powerlessness."[36]

I would add that women's bodies were involved in a struggle to redefine God and the experience of God. In all these writers, we can distinguish grotesque bodies, but not as part of a binary opposition: classic–grotesque. If Umiltà's angels may be thought of as classic bodies and her own body with its various openings as grotesque, the text describes the making of her body into a classic body thanks to the protection of her angels. Angela's grotesque body is no more grotesque than Christ's, which she is imitating. For Marguerite, too, Christ's body is tormented and permeable, open; he, in fact, is she, her mother. As Bakhtin observes of Rabelais, "This is the ever unfinished, ever creating body, the link in the chain of genetic development, or more correctly speaking, two links shown at the point where they enter into each other."[37]

If the parameters of grotesque and classic may be used to describe a dialectics of body imagery through which the speaking female's body is constituted in these works, the redefinition of the female speaking self comes about through the rhythms of alterity, of the symmetries and differences in the love relationship between Christ and the visionary. All three of the women we have read use bodily imagery not to reinforce gender stereotypes but to undercut and subvert them, to show what is human in bodies and divine in souls. The syntax of their sentences and paragraphs reinforces this experience of alterity. Umiltà employs antitheses that turn out to be pairs, that, rather than creating a discourse on the basis of binary oppositions, actually circumscribe continuity. Angela, in her use of symmetry in her "topoi of out-doing," as Dronke puts it, in detailing her competitiveness in the imitation of Christ, presents two bodies, or, more accurately, a double body, that mirrors both extremes of experience and thus unifies them, brings the ends around to meet in a circle. Marguerite, by her obsessive repetitions of words and phrases, locates her struggle in the pulsing of the forward movement of her prose, the incremental changes that she imposes on the same words and phrases. The total effect, in all these women, is to see the pair God/visionary as a single whole, just as all the extremes of experience turn out to be not antitheses, not oppositions forever separated by the law of binary opposition, but unities, a whole seen from many different angles, the sum of its parts. Nevertheless, difference is as essential to these texts as sameness; God is and is not human, and the woman saint is and is not divine.

All three women are the subjects of their own narratives; all three succeed in writing their *jouissance,* their pleasure as whole beings in God, as they write their bodies and the body of Christ. They know who they are, thanks to their union with the Other who is Christ; each woman is an infinite body-soul, a beloved other to Christ, who is himself infinite. They write their own speech and God's speech, and through this colloquy they come to see themselves ever more clearly. Angela writes her *jouissance* through her amorous dialogue with Christ in Assisi, a dialogue that reaffirms the bliss of her bodily existence: "All your life, your eating and drinking, sleeping and all your living is pleasing to me." She expresses it in God's dalliance with her: "'Thus embraced shall I hold you, and much closer than you can imagine with the eyes of the body,' and many words of sweetness he said to me when he departed, and with immense gentleness and with gentle delays he departed." Umiltà's pleasure appears in the confidence with which she addresses her robust angels and entrusts her body to their protection. Even when she is complaining of St. John's neglect of her, she reaffirms his espousal of her and reminds him of what he owes her. Marguerite centers her experience of *jouissance* in her heart in the passage we have examined, and she affirms the sexual function in her depiction of Christ as mother and the crucifixion as childbirth.

I am reminded of a passage in Cixous's *The Newly Born Woman:*

> I look for . . . a kind of desire that wouldn't be in collusion with the old story of death. This desire would invent Love, it alone would not use the word love to cover up its opposite: one would not lead right back in a dialectical destiny, still unsatisfied by the debasement of one by the other. On the contrary, there would have to be a recognition of each other, and this grateful acknowledgement would come about thanks to the intense and passionate work of knowing. Finally, each would take the risk of *other,* of difference, without feeling threatened by the existence of an otherness, rather, delighting to increase through the unknown that is there to discover, to respect, to favor, to cherish.[38]

What Cixous seeks in the future was written once in the past, by three almost unknown women of the early fourteenth century. And I am now sure that if we examine more works by more medieval women we will find more variations on this same theme, "becoming God in God," as Hadewijch put it a generation earlier. For these medieval women mystics, writing the body is representing the self as subject and as other, both infinite, in the joy of going out to an unknown, infinite, and loving consciousness.

Notes

1. I am thinking particularly of Caroline Bynum, "Bodily Miracles in the High Middle Ages," in *Belief in History: Innovative Approaches to European and American Religion,* ed. Thomas Kselman (Notre Dame, Ind.: University of Notre Dame Press, 1991). The definition of body she provides is the one that will be followed in this paper: "the sexual and gendered body, not a raw biological fact but a cultural construct" (p. 68). Bynum's *Holy Feast and Holy Fast: The Religious Significance of Food to Medieval Women* (Berkeley: University of California Press, 1987) gives a sensitive reading of medieval women's attitudes toward the body and food and is indispensable for anyone who wishes to study these issues. Her "Introduction: The Complexity of Symbols," in *Gender and Religion: On the Complexity of Symbols,* ed. Caroline Walker Bynum, Stevan Harrell, and Paula Richman (Boston: Beacon Press, 1986), pp. 1–20, summarizes much recent theory, especially feminist theory, on gender in symbolic thought.

2. The texts that have influenced my thinking are Hélène Cixous and Catherine Clément, *The Newly Born Woman,* trans. Betsy Wing (Minneapolis: University of Minnesota Press 1986); Luce Irigaray, *Speculum of the Other Woman,* trans. Gillian C. Gill (Ithaca, N.Y.: Cornell University Press, 1985), and *This Sex Which Is Not One,* trans. Catherine Porter (Ithaca, N.Y.: Cornell University Press, 1985); and Elaine Marks and Isabelle de Courtivron, eds., *New French Feminisms: An Anthology* (Amherst: University of Massachusetts Press, 1980).

3. I do not intend to apply the theories of any particular writer to the medieval texts under discussion. Instead, I am going to take the advice of Ann Rosalind Jones: "Franco-feminist theory is most effective as a basis for interpretation to the extent that it is used *differentially*—to the extent that its diverse strands are put to different uses" ("Inscribing Femininity: French Theories of the Feminine," in *Making a Difference: Feminist Literary Criticism,* ed. Gayle Green and Coppélia Kahn [New York: Routledge, 1985], p. 96).

4. Irigaray is particularly interested in these issues, and I'm going to try to follow the example Carolyn Burke sets in her readings of Irigaray ("Irigaray Through the Looking Glass," *Feminist Studies* 7 [1981]: 288–306) and explore the connections between the patterns of grammar, rhetoric (tropes, images), and structure and the underlying ideas about gendered body.

5. Ann Rosalind Jones, "Writing the Body: Toward an Understanding of *l'Écriture féminine,*" in *The New Feminist Criticism,* ed. Elaine Showalter (New York: Pantheon, 1985), p. 362.

6. M. M. Bakhtin, *Rabelais and His World,* trans. H. Iswolsky (Cambridge, Mass.: MIT Press, 1968), pp. 19–54. As Bakhtin points out, the term derives from the name for the Roman frescoes first discovered in the late fifteenth century (pp. 31–33). Certain aspects of this grotesque body as Bakhtin describes it are relevant to the bodies depicted by medieval mystics: "Contrary to modern canons, the grotesque body is not separated from the rest of the world. It is not a closed, completed unit; it is unfinished, outgrows itself, transgresses its own limits. The stress is laid on those parts of the body that are open to the outside world, that is,

the parts through which the world enters the body or emerges from it, or through which the body itself goes out to meet the world. This means that the emphasis is on the apertures or the convexities, or on various ramifications and offshoots: the open mouth, the genital organs, the breasts, the phallus, the potbelly, the nose. The body discloses its essence as a principle of growth which exceeds its own limits only in copulation, pregnancy, childbirth, the throes of death, eating, drinking, or defecation. This is the ever unfinished, ever creating body, the link in the chain of genetic development, or more correctly speaking, two links shown at the point where they enter into each other" (p. 26).

7. I am indebted to an article by Laurie Finke, "Mystical Bodies and the Dialogics of Vision," in *Maps of Flesh and Light: New Perspectives on the Religious Experience of Medieval Women Mystics,* ed. Ulrike Wiethaus (Syracuse, N.Y.: Syracuse University Press, 1992), pp. 28–41. Following up on an observation I made in *Medieval Women's Visionary Literature* (New York: Oxford University Press, 1986), she "asks *how* the female mystic's identification as a 'genuine religious figure' freed her from 'conventional female roles' that mandated docility, passivity, subservience and reticence and how her public activities came to be 'socially sanctioned' by a Church anxiously guarding its spiritual and temporal power ("Mystical Bodies," p. 33). She believes that "these questions can only be answered by examining the relation of mystical discourse to institutional structures and ideology, by taking into account not only the subversiveness of mystical discourse, but also its cooptation by the institutional church" (ibid.).

8. Ibid., p. 29.

9. Ibid., p. 33.

10. Hélène Cixous, "Sorties," in Cixous and Clément, *Newly Born Woman,* p. 86.

11. Josette Feral, "The Powers of Difference," in *The Future of Difference,* ed. Hester Eisenstein and Alice Jardine (New Brunswick, N.J.: Rutgers University Press, 1987), p. 91.

12. See St. Umiltà of Faenza, "Sermons," trans. Richard J. Pioli, pp. 247–253; Blessed Angela of Foligno, "From the *Liber de Vere Fidelium Experientia* (*The Book of the Experience of the Truly Faithful*), pp. 254–263; and Marguerite d'Oingt, "The Mirror of St. Marguerite d'Oingt," trans. Richard J. Pioli, pp. 290–294, all in *Medieval Women's Visionary Literature,* ed. Petroff. Paul Lachance has translated Angela of Foligno: *Angela of Foligno: The Complete Works* (Mahwah, N.J.: Paulist Press, 1993). He is also the author of *The Spiritual Journey of the Blessed Angela of Foligno According to the Memorial of Frater A.* (Rome: Pontificium Athenaeum Antonianum, 1984). The Latin texts of Angela with modern French translations are *Le Livre de la Bienheureuse Soeur Angéle de Foligno,* ed. and trans. Paul Doncoeur (Paris: Librairie de l'Art Catholique, 1926), and *Le Livre de l'expérience des vrais fidèles par Sainte Angele de Foligno,* ed. M.-J. Ferre, trans. M.-J. Ferre and L. Baudry (Paris: Editions Droz, 1927).

The French edition of the writings of Marguerite d'Oingt gives her texts in Latin, French, and Franco-Provençal, with modern French translations by A. Duraffour, P. Durdilly, and P. Gardette, *Marguerite d'Oingt: Edition critique des ses oeuvres* (Paris: Les Belles Lettres, 1965). A complete English translation is Renate Blumenfeld-Kosinski, *The Writings of Marguerite d'Oingt: Medieval Prioress and Mystic* (Newburyport, Mass.: Focus Library of Medieval Women, 1990).

Italian translations of the sermons of Umiltà of Faenza are in Pietro Zama, *Santa Umiltà: La vita e i "sermones"* (Faenza: Fratelli Lega Editori, 1974). The

Latin text was edited by T. Sala, *Sanctae Humilitatis de Faventia. Sermones* (Florence, 1884); I have not been able to locate it in the United States. The Latin text I have used is from the *Acta Sanctorum,* vol. 7, Appendix ad diem XXII Maii, "Sermo de S. Humilitate Abbatissa," pp. 815–826. A complete English translation of the sermons is by Cathy Mooney: *Umiltà of Faenza Sermons* (Newburyport, Mass.: Focus Library of Medieval Women, 1992). An English translation of the *Life of St. Umiltà of Faenza* is found in Elizabeth A. Petroff, *Consolation of the Blessed: Women Saints in Medieval Tuscany* (Millerton, N.Y.: Alta Gaia, 1979); see also "The Analects of St. Umiltà," *Vox Benedictina* 7 (1990) 31–52, and "Women's Bodies and the Experience of God in the Middle Ages," *Vox Benedictina* 8 (1991): 91–115 [a preliminary version of this essay, utilizing several other sermons by Umiltà].

13. In the Italian translation by Zama, this is Sermon 6, not 8 (*Santa Umiltà,* pp. 151–159). He bases his numbering on the edition of T. Sala, which was not available to me. I have utilized the texts given in the *Acta Sanctorum,* Appendix ad diem XXII Maii, pp. 815–826.

14. "And you, my hardy Angels, be present on all my pathways, and keep watch most carefully, so that my enemies cannot come near the door. Put down your sword near me, for you were given to me from the beginning; rightly protect me always from my enemies. Put your sword in your right hand at the first gate, and keep it closed to vain and lazy words, when they want to come out, so they can't exit. Sharpen my tongue like a hoe, so that it may cut away vices, and plant virtues, to the praise and glory of the highest Emperor and his divine Mother. And with your holy fingers, put two seals of love on my eyes, for their improvement, so that they may not perceive for enjoyment the things of this world. Unceasingly hold them open and alert for keeping vigil, so that out of sleepiness they may not disturb the divine office, and so my mind does not tire in the praise of God, and his Mother, and the Angels in their particular heavens, and the whole of the divine court. And with your holy hands hold my ears sealed in the name of Jesus, so that no evil word may enter into them which may carry poison to my soul." [My translation]

15. She dictated her sermons to Sister Donnina, one of her disciples, who had accompanied her from Faenza to Florence. There are numerous references to her dictation in her biography and in the biography of her most intimate disciple, Blessed Margherita of Faenza. For translations of these texts, see Petroff, *Consolation of the Blessed.*

16. St. John the Evangelist, believed to be the author of the book of Revelation and the most beloved of Christ's disciples, may have recommended himself to women mystics because he was a mystic himself and because he was particularly intimate with Christ and his mother. Illuminated texts of Revelation (or the Apocalypse, as it is sometimes known) with commentaries were very important for developing new ideas about visions and often established connections between contemporary visionary ideas and the neo-Platonic current of thought associated with the Victorine school (Barbara Nolan, *The Gothic Visionary Perspective* [Princeton, N.J.: Princeton University Press, 1977]). Nolan is particularly interested in tracing how Dante, in his *Vita Nuova,* borrowed from biblical and visionary literature a prophetic voice and the idea of a progressive series of visions to shape his personal love story into a book of revelation. Umiltà would have been writing her sermons in Florence at about the same time Dante was composing the *Vita Nuova,* and they may have shared a similar cultural outlook, even though the woman saint was much less educated. A passage illustrating Nolan's argument suggests affinities with Um-

iltà's understanding of the body: "Unlike conventional conversions, this young boy's imaginative initiation into spiritual understanding—his transforming apparition—comes not from poring over the pages of sacred scripture nor from prayer and penance. Nor does grace enter the stream of memory as it did for St. Augustine, from an unknown, unimagined source. On the contrary, it enters through senses open to experience. An image, realized as extraordinary in a moment of wonder and then shaped by reason, baptizes the soul into the new life of grace. By properly responding to a given, personal, sensible event, the narrator moves toward transcendence. Experience radically human and immediate is to be the source of blessedness" (p. 95).

17. "O Evangelist, bearer of sweet love, you bring lovely gifts in great love on this day which is celebrated in your honor by those who love you. Be mindful of me who is naked, if you have seen me, if you still recognize me. If you were concerned for me when I was rich, don't abandon me in this poverty. If I had come here, as I have come, not for you, but for the Sultan Emperor of the Saracens, he would have brought me aid out of his courtliness. O blessed John, think how I have come here in your name and under your guarantee, and I have been wounded by wounders while hoping for your aid, and for your sake I entered this sea. . . . Remember now your continuous gift of those lovely things, lovely with the highest loveliness, and remember those messages of the greatest sweetness that you sent me to increase my desire. If I love you, O John, although I am a leaf of no value and you are of lily of sweet-smelling whiteness, do not despise me. Recall that lovely sword which you fashioned out of love not chastisement, which you fixed in my heart, and held tightly; may your love never dissipate, with which you have bound me [as] with a chain, and married me with a ring, which entrusted me to your protection. Beloved love, do not abandon me." [My translation]

18. This is ironic; in popular tales, Saladin, the sultan of Babylon, is the quintessence of chivalry, often at the expense of Christian knights striving for a reputation for courtesy. See, for instance, the ninth tale of the tenth day in Boccaccio's *Decameron,* the story of Saladin and Messer Torello, told as an exemplum of magnanimity.

19. Peter Dronke, *Women Writers of the Middle Ages: A Critical Study of Texts from Perpetua to Marguerite Porete* (Cambridge: Cambridge University Press, 1984), p. 104. Dronke's section on the women troubadours (pp. 98–106) bears rereading in the light of Umiltà's creation of a speaking voice. More work needs to be done on the rhetorical and poetic strategies shared by secular and religious writers in the twelfth and thirteenth centuries. Many of the essays in William D. Paden, ed., *The Voice of the Trobairitz: New Perspectives on the Women Troubadours* (Philadelphia: University of Pennsylvania Press, 1989), suggest approaches that would be valuable for a study of women mystics in the same period: Joan Ferrante, "Notes Toward the Study of a Female Rhetoric in the Trobairitz," pp. 63–72; Amelia Van Vleck," 'Tost me trobaretz fenida': Reciprocating Composition in the Songs of Castelloza," pp. 95–112; H. Jay Siskin and Julie A. Storme, "Suffering Love: The Reversed Order in the Poetry of Na Castelloza," pp. 113–128. On Na Castelloza, see also Peter Dronke, "The Provençal *Trobairitz:* Castelloza," in *Medieval Women Writers,* ed. Katharina M. Wilson (Athens: University of Georgia Press, 1984), pp. 131–152.

20. In two articles on women poets of the Renaissance, Ann Rosalind Jones outlines the strategies writers might use to circumvent rigid strictures on public movement and public speech: "Surprising Fame: Renaissance Gender Ideologies

and Women's Lyric," in *The Poetics of Gender,* ed. Nancy K. Miller (New York: Columbia University Press, 1986), pp. 74–95, and "City Women and Their Audiences: Louise Labé and Veronica Franco," in *Rewriting the Renaissance: The Discourses of Sexual Difference in Early Modern Europe,* ed. Margaret Ferguson, Maureen Quilligan, and Nancy Vickers (Chicago: University of Chicago Press, 1986), pp. 299–316.

21. There are obvious problems of authorship here, since Angela was dictating her memories to a scribe, Frater A., who is usually but not always identified with her relative Fra Arnaldo. She dictated in the Umbrian dialect of Italian; Frater A. took notes in Latin (and perhaps in Italian as well), which he later expanded into a full Latin text; he then read this text back to her in Italian for her correction. Umiltà also dictated her works, but in the same language, and she was capable of reviewing them in written form. For more on this dilemma, see Lachance, *Spiritual Journey of Angela of Foligno,* pp. 112–115.

22. "[I]n this understanding of the cross there was given to me such a great fire, that standing next to the cross I stripped myself of all my clothing, and I offered myself to him completely. . . . I promised . . . not to offend him with any of my members, accusing all my members one by one." [My translation]

23. "And you should understand that at each of these steps there is a pause. For this reason it is a great pity and heart-break for the soul that it can only move so slowly, and experience so much pain, and it moves toward God so ponderously. It takes such tiny steps. And I know that for myself I stopped and wept at every step."

24. "[S]howing me his pains from his feet up to his head. He even showed me the hairs plucked from his beard and his eyebrows and his head, and he enumerated all his flagellations . . . pointing out each individual welt."

25. "[H]e called me and said I should put my mouth to the wound in his side. And it seemed to me that I saw and drank his blood flowing freely from his side. And I was given to understand that by this he would cleanse me."

26. "[H]e said to me, 'Thus embraced shall I hold you, and much closer than you can imagine with the eyes of the body.' . . . [A]nd many words of sweetness he said to me when he departed, and with immense gentleness and with gentle delays he departed. And then after his departure I began to scream or shriek loudly, without any shame I screamed, crying, and I said these words, 'Unknown love! Why have you left me? Why? Why?' . . . These words so suffocated in my throat that the words could not be understood. . . . And I wanted to die while I was crying out. . . . And then all my joints were loosened."

27. Finke, "Mystical Bodies," p. 37.

28. Ibid., p. 38.

29. Dronke, *Women Writers of the Middle Ages,* p. 215.

30. Ibid., pp. 215–216.

31. See *Writings of Margaret of Oingt.* The translations are from the original Latin and Franco-Provençal.

32. *Marguerite d'Oingt,* p. 143. [My translation]

33. Ibid., p. 72. "And I thought that I would have to either die or waste away, unless I could remove these thoughts from my heart, but I could not find in my heart any way to remove them, because I found so much solace in them [that everything] which might make happy the heart of man was nothing to me in comparison with what I felt in my heart concerning my beloved Creator. I thought that the heart of a man or a woman is so unstable that it can scarcely remain in one state, and so I put down in writing the thoughts that God had arranged in my

heart, so that I wouldn't lose them when I removed them from my heart, and so that I might meditate on them occasionally when God should give me his grace [to do so]."

34. Ibid., p. 142. "[Her visions] . . . were all written in her heart in such a way that she could not think about anything else. . . . She thought that if she were to put these things in writing, as Our Lord had sent them to her in her heart, her heart would be more relieved for it. She began to write down everything [that is] in this book, . . . and as soon as she put a word in the book, it left her heart. . . . I firmly believe that if she had not put it in writing she would have died or become crazy."

35. "For are you not my mother and more than my mother? The mother who bore me labored in delivering me for one day or one night but you, my sweet and lovely Lord, labored for me for more than thirty years. Ah, . . . how painfully you labored for me and bore me through your whole life. . . . But when the time came for you to be delivered, your labor pains were so great that your holy sweat was like great drops of blood that came out from your body and fell on the earth. . . . [W]hen the hour of your delivery came you were placed on the hard bed of the cross . . . and your nerves and all your veins were broken. And truly it is no surprise that your veins burst when in one day you gave birth to the whole world."

36. Finke, "Mystical Bodies," p. 44.

37. Bakhtin, *Rabelais,* p. 26.

38. Cixous and Clément, *Newly Born Woman,* p. 78.

Suggestions for Further Reading

Angela of Foligno. *Angela of Foligno: The Complete Works*. Translated and edited by
  Paul Lachance. Classics of Western Spirituality Series. Mahwah, N.J.: Paulist
  Press, 1993.
Attwater, Donald. *The Penguin Dictionary of Saints*. Baltimore: Penguin, 1965.
Baker, Derek, ed. *Medieval Women*. Oxford: Basil Blackwell, 1978.
Bell, Rudolph. *Holy Anorexia*. Chicago: University of Chicago Press, 1985.
Berman, Constance H., Charles W. Connell, and Judith Rice Rothschild, eds. *The
  Worlds of Medieval Women: Creativity, Influence, Imagination*. Morgantown:
  West Virginia University Press, 1985.
Boulding, Elise. *The Underside of History*. Boulder, Colo.: Westview Press, 1976.
Bowie, Fiona, ed., and Oliver Davies, trans. *Beguine Spirituality: Mystical Writings
  of Mechthild of Magdeburg, Beatrijs of Nazareth, and Hadewijch of Brabant*.
  Crossroad Spiritual Classics Series. New York: Crossroad Books, 1989.
Bridenthal, Renate, and Claudia Koonz, eds. *Becoming Visible: Women in European
  History*. Boston: Houghton Mifflin, 1977.
Brown, Peter R. L. *The Body and Society: Men, Women, and Sexual Renunciation in
  Early Christianity*. New York: Columbia University Press, 1988.
———. *The Cult of the Saints: Its Rise and Function in Latin Christianity*. Chicago:
  University of Chicago Press, 1980.
Bynum, Caroline Walker. *Fragmentation and Redemption: Essays on Gender and the
  Human Body in Medieval Religion*. New York: Zone Books, 1991.
———. *Holy Feast and Holy Fast: The Religious Significance of Food to Medieval
  Women*. Berkeley: University of California Press, 1987.
———. *Jesus as Mother: Studies in Spirituality of the High Middle Ages*. Berkeley:
  University of California Press, 1982.
St. Catherine of Siena. *St. Catherine of Siena Dialogue*. Translated and edited by

Suzanne Noffke. Classics of Western Spirituality Series. New York: Paulist Press, 1987.

Cazelles, Brigitte. *The Lady as Saint: A Collection of French Hagiographic Romances of the Thirteenth Century*. Philadelphia: University of Pennsylvania Press, 1991.

Charewatuk, Karen, and Ulrike Wiethaus, eds. *Dear Sister: Medieval Women and the Epistolary Genre*. Philadelphia: University of Pennsylvania Press, 1993.

St. Clare of Assisi. *Claire d'Assise Écrits*. Edited by Marie-France Becker, Jean-François Godet, and Thaddée Matura. Paris: Editions du Cerf, 1985.

———. *Legend and Writings of St. Clare of Assisi*. Edited and translated by Ignatius Brady. St. Bonaventure, N.Y.: Franciscan Institute, 1953.

Colledge, Eric, ed. and trans. *Mediaeval Netherlands Religious Literature*. New York: London House and Maxwell, 1965.

Dronke, Peter. *Women Writers of the Middle Ages: A Critical Study of Texts from Perpetua to Marguerite Porete*. Cambridge: Cambridge University Press, 1984.

Eckenstein, Lina. *Woman Under Monasticism*. Cambridge: Cambridge University Press, 1896.

Ferrante, Joan. *Woman as Image in Medieval Literature*. New York: Columbia University Press, 1974.

Flinders, Carol Lee. *Enduring Grace: Living Portraits of Seven Women Mystics*. San Francisco: HarperCollins, 1993.

Frantzen, Allen J., ed. *Speaking Two Languages*. Albany: State University of New York Press, 1991.

Gies, Frances, and Joseph Gies. *Women in the Middle Ages*. New York: Harper & Row, 1978.

Goodich, Michael. *Vita Perfecta: The Ideal of Sainthood in the 13th Century*. Stuttgart: Hiersmann, 1982.

Hadewijch. *Hadewijch: The Complete Works*. Translated and edited by Mother Columbia Hart. Classics of Western Spirituality Series. New York: Paulist Press, 1980.

Hamburger, Jeffrey. *The Rothschild Canticles: Art and Mysticism in Flanders and the Rhineland circa 1300*. New Haven, Conn.: Yale University Press, 1990.

Hildegard of Bingen. *Hildegard of Bingen Scivias*. Translated and edited by Mother Columbia Hart and Jane Bishop. Introduction by Barbara Newman. Classics of Western Spirituality Series. New York: Paulist Press, 1990.

Hrotsvit of Gandersheim. *The Dramas of Hrotsvit of Gandersheim*. Translated and edited by Katharina Wilson. Saskatoon: Peregrina Press, 1985.

Jacobus de Voragine. *The Golden Legend of Jacobus de Voragine*. Translated and edited by Granger Ryan and Helmut Ripperger. New York: Arno, 1969.

Jacques de Vitry. *The Life of Marie d'Oignies by Jacques de Vitry*. 2nd ed. Translated and edited by Margot King. Toronto: Peregrina Press, 1989.

Johnson, Penny. *Equal in Monastic Profession: Religious Women in Medieval France*. Chicago: University of Chicago Press, 1991.

Julian of Norwich. *Julian of Norwich Showings*. Translated and edited by Eric Colledge and James Walsh. Classics of Western Spirituality Series. New York: Paulist Press, 1978.

Kempe, Margery. *The Book of Margery Kempe*. Edited and translated by B. A. Windeatt. New York: Penguin, 1986.

Kieckhefer, Richard. *Unquiet Souls: Fourteenth-Century Saints and Their Religious Milieu*. Chicago: University of Chicago Press, 1984.

King, Margot. *The Desert Mothers*. Toronto: Peregrina Press, 1989.

Klapisch-Zuber, Christiane, ed. *Silences of the Middle Ages*. Vol. 2 of *A History of Women in the West*, edited by Georges Duby and Michelle Perrot. Cambridge, Mass.: Belknap Press of Harvard University Press, 1992.

Labalme, Patricia, ed. *Learned Women of the European Past*. New York: New York University Press, 1980.

Lerner, Gerda. *The Creation of a Feminist Consciousness: From the Middle Ages to Eighteen-seventy*. New York: Oxford University Press, 1993.

Lucas, Angela M. *Women in the Middle Ages: Religion, Marriage, and Letters*. Brighton: Harvester Press, 1983.

Lutgard of Aywières. *The Life of Lutgard of Aywières*. Translated and edited by Margot King. Toronto: Peregrina Press, 1985.

Margolis, Nadia. *Joan of Arc in History, Literature and Film: A Select Annotated Bibliography*. New York: Garland, 1990.

Marguerite d'Oingt. *The Writings of Marguerite d'Oingt: Medieval Prioress and Mystic*. Edited and translated by Renate Blumenfeld-Kosinski. Newburyport, Mass.: Focus Library of Medieval Women, 1990.

McDonnell, Ernest W. *The Beguines and Beghards in Medieval Culture*. New Brunswick, N.J.: Rutgers University Press, 1953; New York: Octagon, 1969.

Monson, Craig, ed. *The Crannied Wall: Women, Religion, and the Arts in Early Modern Europe*. Ann Arbor: University of Michigan Press, 1992.

Moorman, John. *A History of the Franciscan Order from Its Origins to the Year 1519*. Oxford: Clarendon Press, 1968.

Newman, Barbara. *Sister of Wisdom: St. Hildegarde's Theology of the Feminine*. Berkeley: University of California Press, 1987.

Nichols, John A., and Lillian Thomas Shank, eds. *Medieval Religious Women*. Vol. 1, *Distant Echoes*. Kalamazoo, Mich.: Cistercian Publications, 1984.

———. *Medieval Religious Women*. Vol. 2, *Peace Weavers*. Kalamazoo, Mich.: Cistercian Publications, 1987.

Paden, William D., ed. *The Voice of the Trobairitz: New Perspectives on the Women Troubadours*. Philadelphia: University of Pennsylvania Press, 1989.

Petroff, Elizabeth A., ed. *Medieval Women's Visionary Literature*. New York: Oxford University Press, 1986.

Phillips, Dayton. *The Beguines in Medieval Strasbourg: A Study of the Social Aspect of Beguine Life*. Ann Arbor: University of Michigan Press, 1941.

Power, Eileen Edna. *Medieval Women*. Edited by M. M. Postan. Cambridge: Cambridge University Press, 1975.

Radice, Betty, ed. and trans. *Letters of Abelard and Heloise*. Baltimore: Penguin, 1974.

Reuther, Rosemary, and Eleanor McLaughlin, eds. *Women of Spirit: Female Leadership in the Jewish and Christian Traditions*. New York: Simon and Schuster, 1979.

Rose, Mary Beth, ed. *Women in the Middle Ages and the Renaissance: Literary and Historical Perspectives*. Syracuse, N.Y.: Syracuse University Press, 1986.

Southern, Richard W. *Western Society and the Church in the Middle Ages*. Baltimore: Penguin, 1970.

Stanton, Domna C., and Jeanine F. Plottel, eds. *The Female Autograph: Theory and Practice of Autobiography from the Tenth to the Twentieth Century*. Chicago: University of Chicago Press, 1987.

Stuard, Susan Mosher, ed. *Women in Medieval Society*. Philadelphia: University of Pennsylvania Press, 1976.

Szarmach, Paul, ed. *An Introduction to the Medieval Mystics of Europe.* Albany: State University of New York Press, 1984.

Thomas of Cantimpré. *The Life of Christina of St. Trond, Called Christina Mirabilis, by Thomas of Cantimpré.* Translated and edited by Margot King. Saskatoon: Peregrina Press, 1980.

Umiltà of Faenza. *Umiltà of Faenza Sermons.* Translated and edited by Cathy Mooney. Newburyport, Mass.: Focus Library of Medieval Women, 1992.

Underhill, Evelyn. *Mysticism: A Study in the Nature and Development of Man's Spiritual Consciousness.* 1911. New York: Dutton, 1961.

———. *The Mystics of the Church.* London: James Clark, 1925.

Waddell, Helen, ed. and trans. *The Desert Fathers.* Ann Arbor: University of Michigan Press, 1971.

Waithe, Mary Ellen, ed. *A History of Women Philosophers: Medieval, Renaissance, and Enlightenment Women Philosophers, A.D. 500–1600.* Boston: Kluwer Academic Press, 1989.

Ward, Benedicta. *Harlots of the Desert: A Study of Repentance in Early Monastic Sources.* Kalamazoo, Mich.: Cistercian Publications, 1987.

Weinstein, Donald, and Rudolph M. Bell. *Saints and Society: The Two Worlds of Western Christendom, 1000–1700.* Chicago: University of Chicago Press, 1982.

Wiethaus, Ulrike, ed. *Maps of Flesh and Light: New Perspectives on the Religious Experience of Medieval Women Mystics.* Syracuse, N.Y.: Syracuse University Press, 1992.

Wilson, Katharina, ed. *Hrotsvit of Gandersheim: Rara Avis in Saxonia?* Ann Arbor: MARC, 1987.

———. *Medieval Women Writers.* Athens: University of Georgia Press, 1984.

Zum Brunn, Emilie, and Georgette Epiney-Burgard. *Women Mystics in Medieval Europe.* New York: Paragon, 1989.

Index

Visions, experience of, 19–20. *See also individual saints and mystics*
Vita B. Benevenutae, 108n.22, 177n.4
Vitae Patrum (Lives of the Fathers), viii, 110, 114, 116, 118, 129
Vito da Cortona, 104, 120, 122, 129
Vocation, female, 7

Waddell, Helen, 114
Walter (character in Chaucer's "Clerk's Tale"), 27
Ward, Benedicta, 179n.22
Wealtheow (character in *Beowulf*), 9
Weasel, 119–120, 133n.33

Weinstein, Donald, and Rudolph M. Bell: *Saints and Society,* 114, 116, 136n.56
Women
  as leaders, 6
  in population, 7
  spiritual practices of, 8. *See also* Asceticism
  as teachers, 156, 211
  as warriors, 38
Worms, 125
Wounding, as image, 192

Ziegler, Joanna E., 63n.19
Zum Brunn, Emilie, 11, 12